LIFE IS FOREVER
EVIDENCE FOR SURVIVAL AFTER DEATH

SUSY SMITH

LIFE IS FOREVER

EVIDENCE FOR SURVIVAL AFTER DEATH

G. P. Putnam's Sons

New York

*To Frank L. Bang, who spends all his time
helping others, this book is dedicated
with appreciation for his friendship*

CONTENTS

FOREWORD

DURING a visit to Hawaii in June, 1973, I first attended one of Miss Susy Smith's lectures. Fascinated by what I heard and previously having read several of her earlier volumes, I valued the time we were able to spend in discussion afterward at dinner.

As Miss Smith unfolded the nature of this, her latest work, I became more and more intrigued with what she had to say. At that time she was still searching for a suitable title. When I suggested *Life Is Forever*, she was delighted, and then she asked that I write the book's Foreword. In turn, I invited Miss Smith to speak at my church in Las Vegas, which she subsequently did twice. We have since become good friends.

What people do not understand they usually fear. Particularly is this true of that vast unknown which is so loosely referred to as "life after death." The realm of the human psyche is a vast mystery to most people, so we must be grateful to authors such as Susy Smith whose meticulous research unravels the marvels of the paranormal, making it possible for the average person to absorb in one volume account after account of the scientific evidence for human survival after death.

Such is the volume you are about to read. *Life Is Forever* is absorbing reading to those who wish to penetrate the "veil." The incidents related are not science-fiction fantasies that are the result of a vivid imagination but lucid accounts of the personal experiences of people from all walks of life and of varying religious, cultural, educational, ethnic, and national backgrounds.

Miss Smith does not offer a personal opinion in regard to her research findings. Instead, there is a straightforward presentation of case histories, tied together by her own delightful style of writing. The facts speak for themselves; the reader may form his own opinion and draw his own conclusions.

My own personal experiences have left no doubt in my mind that "life *is* forever." Miss Smith simply corroborates what I know to be true. It is a privilege to write this brief Foreword to what I feel to be a most fascinating and revealing book.

THE REVEREND DAVID HOWE, D.D., D.S.D.
Chancellor of the Ministerial Senate,
United Church of Religious Science

I

NOT ONE RETURNED

Strange, is it not? that of the myriad who
Before us pass'd the door of Darkness through,
Not one returned to tell us of the Road,
Which to discover we must travel too.
       —THE RUBÁIYÁT OF OMAR KHAYYÁM

POOR CYNICAL OMAR and his materialistic friends dominated the
thinking of generations of our society. Yet even as his philosophy
was being translated into English in the mid-nineteenth century,
certain individuals with hope in their hearts were working avidly to
try to prove that someone *had* returned to tell us of the Road . . .
and not just one someone but many.

It is so easy for us still to ignore all the documented material that
has been accumulated and just state categorically: "No one has returned to prove life after death." But a perusal of thousands of case
histories might give us an altogether different point of view. Even if
no one has yet actually *proved* by scientific standards that there is a
life after death, there is a surprising amount of evidence that is at
least suggestive of proof.

Much that has been written on this subject is in journals and proceedings of psychical research societies or in out-of-print books. Even
a lot of the new material is in specialized magazines not much read
by the general public. I have here made an effort to dig out some
of the old and obscure and to gather up some of the new, and to
present it in as condensed a form as possible for easy reading.
Surprisingly, I found that there are such vast quantities of interesting
material that it has been difficult to select from the many good ac-

9

counts. If anyone can say after having read this book, "But no one has returned," he will at least say it from the point of view of knowing what the literature of the field has to offer.

First we should discuss whether or not the survival of the human consciousness is scientifically improbable. There is a vast body of evidence in the fields of neurology, neurosurgery and biochemistry which would indicate that our memory, our intellect and even our personality are controlled by our neurological structure and body chemistry. "From this point of view," says Dr. Karlis Osis, Director of Research for the American Society for Psychical Research, "death is the ultimate destruction and end of a human personality."

Yet perhaps the pure behavioral psychologists like Harvard's B. F. Skinner are seriously misinterpreting human nature. As Stanislav Andreski, professor of sociology at England's Reading University, says in *Social Sciences as Sorcery:* "When the psychologists refuse to study anything but the most mechanical forms of behaviour—often so mechanical that even rats have no chance to show their higher faculties—and then present their most trivial findings as the true picture of the human mind, they prompt people to regard themselves as automata, devoid of responsibility or worth."

I am glad a creditable social scientist has come out with such a statement. I have been saying for years that because our behaviorists tell us we are nothing more than animals, many people believe them and act like animals.

Fraser Nicol said in "The Founders of the S.P.R.," "Nowadays, to many thousands of conventional psychologists, s**l and even m*nd are four-letter words unmentionable in polite psychological company." In bleeping out soul and mind, we have also bleeped from our thinking all ideas of the possibility of a life after death. A machine certainly isn't going anywhere.

Many people, however, feel a need, as I did, for an afterlife in order to be comfortable in this life, and certainly in order to accept any kind of a God at all.

At the same time that the philosophy of materialism was offering us a godless, mechanistic universe in which man has no more worth than an experimental hamster, there has been a small coterie of investigators endeavoring to prove just the opposite. Instead of concluding that we were mere machines or animals, early psychical researchers hoped to discover that man really does have a soul and that this soul survives death. If this were true, they believed, then there really is an overall Good Plan or God.

Dr. Karlis Osis says in *Deathbed Observations by Physicians and Nurses:*

> . . . researchers in parapsychology over a period of eighty years have unearthed information rather difficult to explain without assuming some modus of survival after death. Some studies of spontaneous psi occurrences provide enough challenging material to justify continued research efforts. These studies include collective hallucinations of the dead; mediumistic messages; and especially the so-called cross correspondences, *i.e.*, fragments of messages independently communicated through several participants which, like pieces of a puzzle, have no meaning by themselves but, fitted together, provide a complex idea. [Although some attempts in this direction] were extremely naïve. . . . Other studies have been quite sophisticated, including those of Columbia University philosopher Dr. J. H. Hyslop, University of Dublin physicist Sir William Barrett and others. Their conclusion was that the large collections of observations concerning hallucinations or visions of dying patients gave some evidence pointing to post-mortem existence.

Such researchers as these have either been ignored by scientists of other persuasions or have been the butt of their scorn. The pride and stupidity of respected classes fought Copernican astronomy, Newtonian physics, Darwinism, the existence of meteors, and hypnotism. Then, said Dr. Hyslop in *Science and a Future Life*, "When they were proved, they appropriated them as their own and made it the mark of intelligence to believe them."

Even today there is a contention in scientific circles that spontaneous psi (psychic) occurrences lack authenticity because they are not repeatable and thus are of scientific value only as providing suggestions for lines of experimental investigation. It is only barely permissible to disagree with this, but a few brave souls in the field have dared to do so. Professor C. J. Ducasse says in "Realities of Perception":

> Concerning this contention, one can only remark that if it were correct, then large portions of the sciences of astronomy, volcanology, geology, and meteorology would not exist at all —the portions, namely, that draw conclusions from observations of such spontaneous phenomena as eclipses, volcanic eruptions, earthquakes, and rains, hurricanes, and thunderstorms. These are not experimentally reproducible and therefore have to be studied as and when they happen. But repeated, careful, exact, and intelligent observations of them has yielded a considerable amount of truly scientific knowledge.

There is, indeed, a vast caseload of carefully documented evidence of spontaneous psi phenomena, but in the face of evidence there is still much disagreement. Since even parapsychologists argue among themselves about what is acceptable as evidence, why must we bother trying to make our case material as factual as possible? Perhaps it is only a matter of "belief" and we should agree with the late great medium Arthur Ford when he says in *The Life Beyond Death*:

> An ecologist friend of mine, much upset about the destruction of our natural environment, once said to me, "There is only one thing preventing clean air, pure drinking water, healthy streams, productive soil, and unpolluted food—a failure to believe that these things can be had. The moment we believe such a world to be obtainable, and worth attaining, we will quickly create it."
>
> I have often thought that something similar applies to our failure to abolish our fear of death by an open-minded consideration of the possibilities of a progression to an exciting and fulfilling life in another sphere. In the face of an almost palpable will-not-to-believe, evidence means nothing and is not even considered.

I almost never disagreed with Arthur. Our minds seem to have gone along on similar tracks. But I would like to point out that many persons who disregard philosophical and theological reasoning are impressed by facts. So facts are what I am going to present. I can't say this book will provide proof of life after death. But it is going to try from the evidence available . . . and there is actually a fantastic amount of it.

I have gathered together here some well-documented cases and others not so well-documented but so similar that they stand by comparison. Many researchers contend that a few well-documented cases are strong enough to support the authenticity of other similar cases which are not documentable. A few of those which do not have the verification of witnesses, or which are possibly suspect because of their age, are thus used here because of their similarity to those others which are stronger.

I believe, on the whole, the great number of cases reported here gives pretty sound evidence for survival of the human soul. Read them and see what you think.

II

ASTRAL
ADVENTURE

THERE IS AN event which occurs to a great many people in which their consciousnesses seem to leave their bodies while they are asleep, under anesthesia, in a coma, or even while awake and resting. This is termed an out-of-body experience (OOBE) or astral projection. They are as varied as the characters and personalities of the individuals who undergo them, but they are real. There is no doubt about that. And they frequently bring about a change in thinking about life after death.

An example of an extremely simple and uninvolved experience of this sort occurred to J. G. Bennett, Director of the Institute for the Comparative Study of History, Philosophy and the Sciences at Kingston-on-Thames, England. During the great German attack in Flanders on March 21, 1918, Bennett received shrapnel wounds in the head and for over one hundred hours afterward he was in a coma, completely unconscious and expected to die.

"During this time," he says in *Tomorrow* (Spring, 1958), "I had experiences that gave my life an entirely new direction.

"Although I could not see, hear or feel anything, I was clearly aware of my own existence, and of other people—not of their outward appearance, but of what was going on in their minds. I knew that one man was terrified of shells bursting near the casualty clearing station and that another was soon going to die but was not afraid, and so on."

It was clear to him that although his body might at any moment be destroyed, his consciousness would remain. He was not in any "place," and yet he was "somewhere." He had rich and varied experiences, but when he returned to ordinary consciousness five days later he could not remember a hundredth part of what had happened to him.

"These experiences forced me to search for the real meaning of my existence," he says, "and that search has continued for nearly forty years and will, I hope, continue until my last breath."

Usually there is more travel than this involved in an astral projection. The person knows himself actually to be out of his body, frequently seeing it on the bed while he soars off to have an adventure. The reason we know that such experiences are not just imagination or daydreaming is because frequently one who cavorts in this unconventional manner returns with information he had no normal way of knowing.

Onetime Harvard University Professor of Philosophy William Ernest Hocking wrote in *The Meaning of Immortality* that he had previously dismissed out-of-body experiences as insignificant. Then a friend related an experience she'd had with extraordinary detail and clarity. He says, "She, the wife of a colleague, had been at the crisis of pneumonia; her husband and the physician were at her bedside. She was presumed to be, if not in coma, at least unconscious of her surroundings. But she heard their conversation, which was not encouraging."

Shortly after the physician left the room, her husband also went out. She wanted to go with him and found herself free to move at will. Apparently leaving her body, she saw herself lying there on the bed; then she followed her husband. "He crossed the hall, closing the door, and went into his library. She saw him pace to and fro, then take down a book from a shelf, open it and gaze at the page without reading on. She saw the page. He put the book back, and returned to her bedside." Her body had not moved. She heard him plead with her, in the hope that his words might reach her consciousness, to try to come back to life.

She was aware that it was in her power to make this effort, and difficult and unwelcome as it was, she made it for his sake. When she had recovered, she tested her experience. When her husband was in the library, she took down the book from which she had seen him read, opened it to the same page, and asked him whether he had any recent memory of it. Much startled, he recounted the episode as she had seemed to see it.

Retired Army Colonel Frank Adams, who has made himself an authority on Edgar Cayce by his years of delving into records in the library of the Association for Research and Enlightenment in Virginia Beach, Virginia, has also done a great deal of study of all existing data about the Shroud of Turin. In his book *A Scientific Search for the Face of Jesus*, Colonel Adams reports a spectacular OOBE, of the type called traveling clairvoyance because of the supernormal information gained by the percipient. Adams describes his story as a "fairly typical out-of-the-body experience." However I find it very unusual and special because of the evidence it brought. It is an instance in the life of the late Peter Ballbusch, an acquaintance of Adams who at the time lived in an apartment in Hollywood, California. Once while Peter's wife was in Europe he had been out with a young couple on a Saturday night and in order to save them a long drive home in the early morning hours he offered them his bedroom, assuring them he would be very comfortable on the couch in the living room.

After he went to sleep he had an out-of-body experience and found himself standing beside his body. When he realized what was happening, he decided to make the most of it, so he willed himself to go to an apartment on the top of the old Hollywood Hotel which he had never seen and had always wanted to visit.

"Knowing as much as he did about psychic phenomena," Frank Adams writes, "he was amused at himself when he dodged some electric power lines as he started down the world-famous Hollywood Boulevard. Passing a popular and well-known nightspot he witnessed an altercation between two renowned movie personalities. When he entered the apartment it was empty. It had apparently been rented by a photographer as there were remnants of film packs, etc. in the yet uncleaned rooms."

Ballbusch next decided to visit the home of his boss, director Cecil B. De Mille, who he knew was out of town for the weekend. He had never been invited there, and so did not know what to expect, but he looked for something out of the ordinary for evidence. He found several large packing cases in one of the rooms, which reminded him that Mr. De Mille had told him he was expecting a shipment of paintings he had bought in Europe. Only one had been opened; it was the picture titled "A Lady Descending a Staircase."

At this point Peter felt a need to return to his own home, and he experienced a sharp shock as he reentered his flesh body. He was then immediately aware of loud argument between the young couple in his bedroom. It turned out that the wife wanted to call the doctor, because she'd found what she thought was Ballbusch's dead body when she went through the living room to go to the bathroom. Her husband was trying to quiet her, saying it was silly to call anybody at three in the morning. Peter was obviously dead and the delay wouldn't matter to him. Peter "rose from the dead" and assured them he'd only been having an astral projection. He then told them the details of his experience, determined to verify them as soon as possible. It was not difficult. The next morning's edition of the Los Angeles *Times* had flaming headlines about the fisticuffs between two prominent screen stars on the sidewalk outside a restaurant on the Boulevard. Then Ballbusch and his friends went to the hotel he had visited astrally and tipped the janitor generously to get him to show the apartment on Sunday. It was just as Peter had described it, with lots of debris from photographic activities. And, writes Frank, "to clinch the reality of the experience, on Monday morning my friend asked his boss if he had received the shipment of paintings. Mr. De Mille answered in the affirmative but stated that so far he had only uncrated 'A Lady Descending a Staircase.' "

This case is typical of most in that the people concerned were not aware of the importance of evidential testimony. If we had the statement of Ballbusch as to the date, time and details of his experience, as well as the signed independent witnessing of the young couple that he had told them the details exactly as they had later proved to be, this would be a fantastic case for the records of parapsychology. However, Colonel Adams is a man of such integrity that his report of the incident is the next best thing.

The reader may say, "Nobody I know has anything like that

happen to him." This, of course, may not be true. Persons who have undergone such weird adventures are extremely reluctant to speak of them unless absolutely sure they will not be rebuffed or laughed at.

A prominent psychical researcher of the early part of this century, Dr. Walter Franklin Prince, has pointed out that people will talk about their experiences, however, if conditions are just right. He says in *The Case for and Against Psychic Belief*, "If a small group of intelligent men, not supposed to be impressed by psychical research, get together and such matters are mentioned, and all feel that they are in safe and sane company, usually about half of them begin to relate . . . some incident which happened to him or to some member of his family, or to some friend whom he trusts, and which he thinks odd and extremely puzzling."

As I pointed out in *The Enigma of Out-of-Body Travel*, this is the experience I also have all the time. Now that those who meet me are aware that they will get a sympathetic hearing for any startling or curious supernormal problems they may wish to confide, my ear is bent with almost tedious inevitability by at least every third person I encounter. And a great many of the stories I hear are of astral journeying.

So actually, dear reader, your own sister, or the man next door, may be enjoying exciting out-of-body excursions night after night, but you will probably never hear of it until the mental climate of our civilization changes a bit more.

These people often bring back evidence, too. Cases of traveling clairvoyance are common among astral travelers. More rare are "reciprocal" cases, in which the person having the OOBE is seen while doing so, and bilocation, where he is seen in two places at once. As seldom as they occur, they have been documented on occasion.

But what we are looking for in this book is evidence for survival, and there are plenty of people who have gone through out-of-body experiences which have convinced them of life after death. Sylvan J. Muldoon, for instance, a man who had perhaps more of such events than anyone else in recorded history, said in *The Projection of the Astral Body*, "Had no one else in the world suspected 'life after death,' I should still believe implicitly that I am immortal—for I have experienced the projection of the astral body." And Cyril Butcher observed, "I don't mind dying because I have died once and *know* what it is like!"

An OOBE that came to a man named Bruce Belfrage caused him to say, "The experience proves to me, beyond doubt, as no formal religion could do, that the body and the Spirit are quite separate, that the Spirit, the Real Me, cannot be hurt and cannot die."

If such events are conclusive to any ordinary traveler, what must they be to one near death who receives their reassurance? Mrs. Olga Jalink is not afraid of dying anymore because she is certain she has had a glimpse of the world that follows after. As reported in a survey of cases recorded by doctors and psychiatrists at Central Middlesex Hospital, London, Mrs. Jalink had just given birth to her first child. There were complications and suddenly her heart stopped.

"There was no blackout," she said. "It was not like fainting or drifting into a coma. One moment I was lying in bed feeling very poorly, and the next I was looking down at myself."

She was absolutely aware of being detached from her body, as if she were suspended somewhere. She could see, but not hear. "It was strange to be looking down at oneself," she said. "I was no longer a part of my body. I was looking down and there was a nurse and sister running around me. There was no noise. I couldn't hear voices. Everything was peaceful."

As suddenly as she had found herself in the air, Mrs. Jalink found everything going black and then she returned to the world of the living. She said, "I have no fear of death now. The question of whether there is some form of existence after death was answered for me that day."

A much more involved incident of a similar nature occurred to Dr. A. S. Wiltse of Skiddy, Kansas, in the summer of 1889, when he had typhoid fever and went into a coma. Here is a shortened version of the account he gave of his experiences, as it was published in several medical periodicals of his day and eventually in the *Proceedings* of the Society for Psychical Research.

Dr. Wiltse told of how he felt himself sinking into unconsciousness. After that, he wrote:

I passed about four hours in all without pulse or perceptible heartbeat, as I am informed by Dr. S. H. Raynes, who was the only physician present. During a portion of this time several of the bystanders thought I was dead, and such a report being carried outside, the village church bell was tolled. Dr. Raynes informs me, however, that by bringing his eyes close to my face, he could perceive an occasional short gasp, so very light as to be barely perceptible, and that he was upon the point, several times, of saying, "He is dead," when a gasp would occur in time to check him. He thrust a needle deep into the flesh at different points from the feet to the hips, but got no response. Although I was pulseless about four hours, this state of apparent death lasted only about half-an-hour. [During this time he lost consciousness and when he became aware once again he realized his condition.] [I] reasoned calmly thus: "I have died, as men term death, and yet I am as much a man as ever. I am about to get out of the body." I watched the interesting process of the separation of soul and body. By some power, apparently not my own, the Ego was rocked to and fro. . . . [He recollects distinctly that he eventually seemed to be something like a jellyfish in color and form.] As I emerged from the head I floated up and down and laterally like a soap-bubble attached to the bowl of a pipe until I at last broke loose from the body and fell lightly to the floor, where I slowly rose and expanded into the full stature of a man. I seemed to be translucent, of a bluish cast and perfectly naked. . . . I turned and faced the company. As I turned, my left elbow came in contact with the arm of one of two gentlemen who were standing in the door. To my surprise, his arm passed through mine without apparent resistance, the severed parts closing again without pain, as air reunites. I looked quickly up at his face to see if he had noticed the contact, but he gave me no sign, only stood and gazed toward the couch I had just left. I directed my gaze in the direction of his, and saw my own dead body. . . . [He saw a number of persons sitting and standing about the body, and particularly noticed two women (his wife and sister) apparently kneeling by his left side, weeping. He tried to get their attention.] I bowed to them playfully and saluted with my right hand. I passed about among them also, but found that they gave me no heed. Then the situation struck me as humorous and I laughed outright.

> They certainly must have heard that, I thought, but it seemed otherwise, for not one lifted their eyes from my body.

He concluded the matter by saying to himself, "They see only with the eyes of the body. They cannot see spirits. They are watching what they think is I, but they are mistaken. That is not I. This is I. This is I and I am as much alive as ever." He turned and walked out the door and through the town. "How well I feel," he thought. "Only a few minutes ago I was horribly sick and distressed. Then came that change called death, which I have so much dreaded. It is past now, and here am I still a man, alive and thinking, yes, thinking as clearly as ever, and how well I feel! I shall never be sick again. I have no more to die." In sheer exuberance of spirits he danced a figure. A little later he found himself up in the air, upheld by what felt like a pair of hands. As he traveled along he could see a roadway beneath him and the sky above. After a while he came to three large rocks blocking his way. He received the impression that someone was telling him he would enter the eternal world if he passed between those rocks. He made the attempt, because of his strong curiosity to look into the unknown future. He writes:

> As I did so, a small, densely black cloud appeared in front of me and advanced toward my face. I knew that I was to be stopped. I felt the power to move or to think leaving me. My hands fell powerless at my side, my head dropped forward, the cloud touched my face and I knew no more.
>
> Without previous thought and without apparent effort on my part, my eyes opened. I looked at my hands and then at the little white cot upon which I was lying, and realizing that I was in the body, in astonishment and disappointment, I exclaimed: "What in the world has happened to me? Must I die again?"
>
> I was extremely weak, but strong enough to relate the above experience despite all injunctions to be quiet. . . .

Dr. Wiltse made a rapid recovery and wrote the paper about his experiences just eight weeks later. He received corroboration from those present at his bedside of all he had observed as far as the physical conditions surrounding "the day he died" were concerned. So he felt that since he had seen them factually, the rest of what he had experienced must also have been true.

Although all this seems very unusual, we accept it because it comes from a man supposed to be more than ordinarily critical because he was a physician. Dr. Wiltse got to what might be described as the Gates of Heaven and was sent back, perhaps so that he could write the report of his experiences. But there are apparently those who have actually "passed through the portals" during out-of-body experiences. Some of their accounts are rather farfetched and hard to take. But are we justified in saying that such and such a flight is authentic if it brings back clairvoyant data, and hallucinatory if it merely seems to romanticize about conditions after death?

III

BRINKMANSHIP

SOME WHO HAVE done the highest flying in what seems to be worlds of fantasy, have also produced authentic evidence on other occasions. Such things come to us on the recommendation of no less an authority than St. Paul, who writes in II Corinthians 12.2–4:

"I know a man in Christ, fourteen years ago (whether in the body, I know not; or whether out of the body, I know not; God knoweth), such a one caught up even to the third heaven. And I know such a man (whether in the body, or apart from the body, I know not; God knoweth), how that he was caught up into Paradise, and heard unspeakable words, which it is not lawful for a man to utter."

St. Paul believed that these were "visions and revelations of the Lord." But some persons with psychic powers have similar visions and revelations—whether from On High or not, who knoweth? And some who do out-of-body traveling run into similar situations.

One of the best instances of this sort comes from Dr. George C. Ritchie, an M.D. who is now associated with the University of Virginia at Charlottesville. Ritchie had just completed basic training at Camp Barkeley, Texas, early in December, 1943, and was getting ready to take a train to Richmond to enter medical school as part of the Army's doctor-training program. In the original account of his experience written for *Guideposts*, he says, "It was an unheard-of break for a private, and I wasn't going to let a chest cold cheat me out of it." But he was suffering from more than a chest cold, and the night he was about to leave on the train for Richmond he became much worse. While being X-rayed, he fainted. Then, "when I opened my eyes, I was lying in a little room I had never seen before. . . . For a while I lay there, trying to recall where I was. All of a sudden I sat bolt upright. The train! Now I'd miss the train!

"Now I know that what I am about to describe will sound incredible," Ritchie goes on. "I do not understand it any more than I ask you to; all that I can do is relate the events as they occurred." He sprang out of bed and looked around the room for his uniform. As he glanced back, he stopped, staring. Someone was lying in the bed he had just left.

"I stepped closer in the dim light, then drew back," he writes. "He was dead. The slack jaw, the gray skin were awful. Then I saw the ring. On his left hand was the Phi Gamma Delta fraternity ring I had worn for two years."

Ritchie ran into the hall, eager to escape the mystery of that room. Outside were people, but no one could see him. He was unable to make contact with anything he touched. He was confused, but as his mind became clearer, he says, "I was beginning to know too that the body on that bed was mine, unaccountably separated from me, and that my job was to get back and rejoin it as fast as I could."

He had trouble finding the room with his body, and when he finally found it, a sheet had been drawn over the face. He recognized himself by the fraternity ring on the hand outside the blanket. He tried to draw back the sheet, but could not seize it, and then, "This is death," he thought. "This is what we human beings call death, this splitting up of one's self."

Then the room began to fill with light, with love. "That room was flooded, pierced, illuminated, by the most total compassion I have ever felt. It was a presence so comforting, so joyous and all-satisfying that I wanted to lose myself forever in the wonder of it." Simultaneously with this Christ presence something else was in that room—every single episode of his entire life, and each asked the question, "What did you do with your time on earth?"

Then Ritchie's consciousness expanded to take in wider vision. He writes: "I followed Christ through ordinary streets and countrysides

26

. . . thronged with people. People with the unhappiest faces I ever had seen. Each grief seemed different. I saw businessmen walking the corridors of the places where they had worked, trying vainly to get someone to listen to them. I saw a mother following a sixty-year-old man, her son I guessed, cautioning him, instructing him. He did not seem to be listening.

"Suddenly I was remembering myself, that very night, caring about nothing but getting to Richmond. Was it the same for these people; had their hearts and minds been all concerned with earthly things, and now, having lost earth, were they still fixed hopelessly here? I wondered if this was hell. To care most when you are most powerless; this would be hell indeed."

He was permitted to look at two more worlds, but they were too real, too solid to be called "spirit worlds," he felt. He saw a realm where the preoccupation was not with worldly things but with truth—sculptors and philosophers, composers and inventors, great universities and libraries and scientific laboratories that surpass the wildest inventions of science fiction. Then he saw a great city of light—it was blinding in its beauty.

Finally he woke up in his bed. Before he left the hospital cured he caught a glimpse of his chart. On it he read: "Pvt. George Ritchie, died December 20, 1943, double lobar pneumonia." He talked to his doctor later and was told the same thing, that he had been dead, but that a shot of adrenalin had brought him back to life. Ritchie says, "My return to life, he told me, without brain damage or other lasting effect, was the most baffling circumstance of his career."

Guideposts stated that it had in its possession affidavits from both the Army doctor and attending nurse on the case which attest to the fact that Dr. Ritchie had been pronounced dead.

Arthur Ford, in The Life Beyond Death, tells that one of the most vivid experiences of his life was a journey into the highest realms. The American medium wrote: "Some years ago I had an experience that forever lifted the whole matter of survival out of the realm of faith and brought it clearly down to the plane of realism, so far as I am concerned. . . . I was critically ill. The doctors said I could not live, but as the good doctors they were, they continued doing what they could." He was in a hospital and his friends had been told he would not live through the night. He was given an injection to make him more comfortable, and then he was floating in the air above his bed. He could see his body below and had no interest in it, for he had such a feeling of peace and well-being where he was. Then he was floating in space, without effort, without any sense of possessing a body, yet he was *himself*. A green valley appeared with mountains on all sides, illuminated everywhere by a brilliance of light and color impossible to describe. People he had known who had died all came to greet him. It was a joyous occasion.

"There was one surprise," he writes. "Some people I would have expected to see here were not present. I asked about them. In the instant of asking a thin transparent film seemed to fall over my eyes. The light grew dimmer, and colors lost their brilliance. I could no longer see those to whom I had been speaking, but through a haze I saw those for whom I had asked. They, too, were real, but as I looked at them, I felt my own body become heavy; earthly thoughts crowded into my mind."

It was evident to him that he was being shown a lower sphere. Then it was over. He was told, "Don't worry about them. They can come here whenever they want to if they desire it more than anything else."

Back in the happy place again he found everyone busy and contented. A group of people were deciding whether he must return or not. He began to take inventory of his life. "It did not make a pretty picture," he said. The judges were trying to make out the main trend of his life. They mentioned his having failed to accomplish what he knew he had to finish. The word "dissipation" occurred again and again—not in the usual sense of intemperance but a waste of energies, gifts and opportunities.

"When I was told I had to return to my body, I fought having to get back into that beaten, diseased hulk I had left behind in a Coral Gables hospital. . . . Like a spoiled child in a tantrum, I pushed my feet against the wall and fought. There was a sudden sense of hurtling through space. I opened my eyes and looked into the face of a nurse. I had been in a coma for more than two weeks."

Arthur, with his misbehaving heart, had many close calls with death after that, but he never was afraid.

Neither was Johnnie Duncan of Tulsa, Oklahoma, afraid after the experience she had in May, 1942. "The local doctors have said that I was nearer death without dying than anyone they had ever seen," she wrote in *Fate*, March, 1962. She had a serious operation in her late twenties, and the outcome was so in doubt that her family was told she didn't have much chance. However, use of the then new drug penicillin pulled her through, and after she was on the way to recovery her doctor told her how surprised and baffled he was at her survival. Then, she says, "I told him what I experienced during those eight long days when I hovered between life and death." She thought it might have been a dream. It could have been an out-of-body experience; it was certainly an example of Brinkmanship. "Call it what you will," she says; "it was as real to me as any experience of my life."

And she brought back evidence; that's the main thing. She "dreamed" that, with a group of other passengers, she was boarding a plane for the White City. Her Uncle Jake was there, but he was refused. An Assyrian whom she knew named Mr. Swyden had just managed to rush up the ramp and gain admittance, the last passenger to be allowed in before the doors closed.

The journey through beautiful white clouds had her almost ecstatic with joy. Then they stopped on the bank of a very small stream which was the River Jordan. She got off the plane, left her bag on the bank of the stream, and ran across a narrow wooden plank into the arms of her mother's sister, Aunt Dove, who had been dead ten years.

Aunt Dove cried, "Oh, honey! We've been waiting for you. Are you going to stay? And when is your mother coming?"

Johnnie assured her she was staying and that her mother would be coming soon. With her aunt were two small children she had never seen before. When asked who they were, Aunt Dove seemed surprised, but explained, "Why, these are my babies, Ima and Cameron." These were names Johnnie did not remember ever having heard before.

Next Aunt Dove pointed out Johnnie's grandmother, who had died years before she was born. She was wearing a long white dress with ruffles on the wrist-length sleeves and around the high collar, and an old-fashioned, white ruffled bonnet.

Then Johnnie saw a classmate of hers, Edith M. who had died eight years previously, and other deceased friends. When she then ran back to the stream for her bag she came back to the land of the living.

She writes: "My mother wept when I told her this strange experience. 'Ima and Cameron were Dove's babies,' she explained in astonishment. When I described the woman in white, Mom became even more surprised and excited. 'That is exactly how your grandmother was dressed for burial,' she gasped."

It was Johnnie's turn to be startled after she mentioned her Uncle Jake and the Assyrian Mr. Swyden. Those standing at her bedside told her Mr. Swyden, who had just made the plane for the White City in her dream, had died a few days before and that Uncle Jake was now recovering from a very serious illness.

"My mother's recent death," writes Johnnie Duncan, "has brought back this experience most vividly, for her last words were, 'Dove, Dove, I'm coming.'"

Even though Johnnie came back with information she had no normal way of knowing, her experience was still mostly subjective. What we need here is the kind of hard evidence which might in some way prove the ability of the spirit of the dying or the nearly dying to separate from the body and return. What we need is a witness, someone who was personally involved in the OOBE of another. We have just such a case, too. While old, occurring in the mid-nineteenth century, it is reported by a highly reputable man who assures us he had it from a very responsible person. And it brings us an instance which combines traveling clairvoyance, bilocation and death.

Robert Dale Owen was a distinguished personality of the last century who was the famous son of an even more famous father. The elder Robert Owen rose from mill hand in England to great industrialist and social reformer. A pre-Marxist socialist, he founded the utopian community of New Harmony, Indiana, after he immigrated to America.

Robert Dale Owen inherited his father's philanthropical leanings. He served in the Indiana legislature and then two terms in Congress, where he took a leading part in the settlement of the Oregon boundary dispute and the founding of the Smithsonian Institution.

He opposed slavery and championed social reform. He also strongly supported Spiritualism. During the time he was the American ambassador in the court of Naples, he had the opportunity to meet many outstanding people of his day and to study many interesting psychical cases. After he retired from public office he researched and wrote about such phenomena almost exclusively. And when he prepared his most successful book about the paranormal, *Footfalls on the Boundary of Another World*, he was extremely careful to get accurate facts and to ask for direct, written or oral verification from all the individuals concerned.

This particular case depends on the testimony of one woman alone, and she was thirteen years old when the event occurred. He knew her personally, however, and she was the wife of a learned London professor and the active and respected mother of a family. She had very little, he says, of the idle enthusiast or dreamy visionary about her, and so Owen had no compunction about believing her story.

While the young Miss H ____ was visiting Mr. and Mrs. E ____ at their countryseat in Cambridgeshire, England, in November, 1843, Mrs. E ____ was taken desperately ill. Her husband took her to London for medical advice, leaving their guest and their two children at home with the servants. Mrs. E ____ continued so ill that it was impossible for her to return.

In the meantime, the youngest child, little Fannie, who was only ten weeks old, sickened at home, and, after a brief illness, she died. Mr. E ____ came at once to make arrangements for the baby's funeral, but he did not tell his wife the reason for his trip. He then returned to London, where she was on her deathbed. The day before the baby's funeral, Miss H ____ received a letter from Mr. E ____ asking her for certain letters that were on his desk in his study . . . and it was in that room that the body of the infant lay in its coffin. As the girl proceeded into the study and picked up the papers, she saw a figure reclining on a sofa near the casket. It was Mrs. E ____, the mother of the baby, who was actually on her deathbed in London.

Now Miss H ____, Owen says, was one of those exceptional young people who had from infancy been accustomed to the occasional sight of spirits, so she was not alarmed. She approached the sofa to satisfy herself that it was indeed the apparition of her friend she saw. Standing within three or four feet of Mrs. E ____ for several minutes, she assured herself of her identity. The apparition didn't speak, but raised one arm, which first pointed to the body of the infant, and then signaled upward. Soon afterward, and before the apparition had disappeared, Miss H ____ left the room. She particularly noted the time, which was a few minutes after four o'clock.

The next day Miss H ____ received a letter from Mr. E ____ saying that his wife had died the previous afternoon at half-past four. When he arrived for the joint funeral of his wife and infant daughter, Mr. E ____ said that just before his wife died she had seemed to swoon for a few moments. When she recovered she had asked her husband why he had not told her that her baby was in heaven. When he replied evasively, still wishing to conceal from her the fact of the child's death, lest the shock might hasten her own, she said to him, "It is useless to deny it, Samuel; for I have just been home and have seen her in her little coffin. Except for your sake, I am glad she is gone to a better world, for I shall soon be there to meet her myself." Very shortly after this she died.

Owen added in a footnote, "In exemplification of the manner in which such phenomena are often kept hushed up, I may state that Miss H ____, though with an instinctive feeling of how it would be received, ventured, soon after she left the study, to say to a lady then residing in the house, that *she thought* she had just seen Mrs. E ____ and hoped there would be no bad news from London the next day. For this she was so sharply chidden, and so peremptorily bid not to nurse such ridiculous fancies, that, even when the confirmatory news arrived and Mr. E ____ returned home, she was deterred from stating the circumstance to him."

There is indeed a need for revolutionary changes in our philosophical way of thinking, but many of us have not allowed ourselves to face it. This, as much as anything, is because of our fear of being considered unsophisticated if we let our thoughts dwell on something so old-fashioned as the concept of a "soul," and if we are simple enough to wonder what actually becomes of us after death. Yet when we read of data conclusive to the fact that it is possible for the human mind to leave the body on occasion while the body is alive, it is implied that the mind might also leave at the moment of death and survive when the physical body is destroyed. Even though we are quite alert to opposing arguments, we can't help but think that this at least "indicates" that survival of the consciousness is possible. That is not an unhappy speculation for any of us in this ridiculous, frightening, seemingly purposeless world in which we live.

IV

GHOSTS, APPARITIONS, PHANTOMS

HERE IS ONE thing we should bear in mind. If even one apparition is ever definitely authenticated to be the actual conscious surviving revenant of the deceased person he purports to be . . . then the survival of some aspect of the human soul has been proved. As William James so cleverly said, and as has been quoted almost *ad nauseum* ever since, it takes only one white crow to prove that all crows are not black. The only trouble is that such an apparition would probably have to make its appearance before a group which included several rank materialists, a few prominent scientists, and probably even the President of the United States himself before its existence would be believed.

Psychical researcher Hereward Carrington defined a ghost as "a phantasmal being which is seen by sensitive individuals under certain conditions," and here he got to the crux of the matter. "Sensitive" people are those who are psychic—who have more sensitivity to supernormal phenomena than others. And such people are not as likely to become scientists or even President of the United States. This does not make their testimony any the less reliable, but because it usually concerns areas of experience that are difficult to accept by the majority of people in our materialistic culture, it may be considered by many to be less reliable.

And so in discussing the possibility of the existence of ghosts and apparitions, we have to make sure to use only such cases as bring evidence of some kind. This has to be the criterion by which we judge the validity of any report we use. Of course, we do not look for evidence to the chain-clanking haunts of old castles or the ordinary filmy fellows who appear for the purpose of scaring someone. We naturally discount them as mere hallucinations or trickery or fiction. In cases of haunting there is rarely any evidence worth the name to link the figure seen with any particular deceased person. In fact, as Frank Podmore, an early psychical researcher, once observed, "The vast majority of post-mortem apparitions do not suggest the operation of anything which could be called personality."

It is best, therefore, not to leap to the conclusion just because someone reports to have seen his grandfather's ghost, that it has to be the actual spirit of his grandfather who appeared. The Reverend W. Stainton Moses, one of the most respected natural mediums of the last century and a founder of the Society for Psychical Research, said in *Human Nature* that a sitter's "will to believe" in survival could easily be exploited by fraudulent operators. He was talking about those who go to materialization mediums, but the statement applies just as well to many of those who see ghosts. "Some people would recognize anything," Moses said. "A broom and a sheet are quite enough to make up a grandmother for some wild enthusiasts who go with the figure in their eye and see what they wish to see."

This is why it is seldom wise to accept the report of uncritical persons who may or may not have seen their apparitions "with the figure already in their eye." Cases in this book, therefore, have been chosen almost invariably because the experience brought evidence of one kind or another. Yet even where information comes from the alleged apparition—and these cannot readily be dismissed if the percipient is a person of integrity—it is simpler to suppose that telepathy is somehow involved. Or possibly clairvoyance can explain the perception of information not normally known. Researchers are always carefully on the alert to eliminate these if possible. However, if the report is sound, if the experience indicates the acquisition of knowledge that could not normally have been known, and if the case is similar to others which have been carefully documented, we might as well give it the benefit of the doubt and not quibble about it.

There are a great many instances in which the ghost has shown itself so distinctly as to reveal its identity to someone who had no previous knowledge of its existence, but who subsequently identified it from its picture. Sometimes the appearance of the ghost has brought the news of its death, or in some other way has given the percipient information unknown to him. It is to fact-laden phantoms such as these that we now turn for their contribution to our search for evidence of survival.

From *Proceedings* S.P.R., Vol. V, p. 416 we have a well-attested case of a postmortem apparition who was recognized from his picture. John E. Husbands' letter of testimony to the Society for Psychical Research follows:

September 15, 1886

Dear Sir,—The facts are simply these. I was sleeping in a hotel in Madeira in January 1885. It was a bright moonlight night. The windows were open and the blinds up. I felt someone was in my room. On opening my eyes, I saw a young fellow about twenty-five, dressed in flannels, standing at the side of my bed and pointing with the first finger of his right hand to the place I was lying. I lay for some seconds to convince myself of someone being really there. I then sat up and looked at him. I saw his features so plainly that I recognized them in a photograph which was shown me some days after. I asked him what he wanted; he did not speak, but his eyes and hand seemed to tell me I was in his place. As he did not answer, I struck out at him with my fist as I sat up, but did not reach him, and as I was going to spring out of bed he slowly vanished through the door, which was shut, keeping his eyes upon me all the time. . . .

(Signed) John E. Husbands.

A letter accompanied this from a Miss K. Falkner, who had been a resident of the hotel when the incident occurred. It states that the figure Mr. Husbands saw while in Madeira was that of a young man (Mr. D., she called him) who had died unexpectedly months previously in the room Mr. Husbands was occupying. Mr. Husbands had never been told about Mr. D. or his death. Husbands informed Miss Falkner of the apparition the morning after he saw it, and she recognized the young fellow from his description. "It impressed me very much," said Miss Falkner, "but I did not mention it to him or anyone." But she loitered about until she heard Mr. Husbands tell the same tale to her brother. When she and her brother left they said simultaneously, "He has seen Mr. D."

Miss Falkner deliberately said no more about the subject for days; then she abruptly showed Husbands a photograph of Mr. D. He said at once, "Why, that's the young fellow who appeared to me the other night, but he was dressed differently." He then described a cricket or tennis suit fastened at the neck with a sailor knot. This was an outfit Mr. D. had frequently worn. Miss Falkner concludes, "I must say that Mr. Husbands is a most practical man, and the very last one would expect 'a spirit' to visit." She enclosed the photograph of the young man in her letter to the S.P.R.

From Mrs. Jeanne Robert Foster, former literary editor of *Review of Reviews* magazine, comes this account of a personal experience of her mother's, by way of Dr. Walter Franklin Prince's *Human Experiences*. Her mother's confirmation was also included.

Mrs. Foster wrote that in about 1918 her mother, Mrs. Lucia N. Oliviere, often visited Mrs. Harry V.N. Philip at Mrs. Philip's home, an old mansion at 27 Washington Avenue, Schenectady, New York. On the occasion of her first visit she was shown by the maid into Mrs. Philip's sitting room, where she had some wait until her hostess arrived. As she sat there quietly, she saw, standing in the doorway, a little old lady with beautiful white hair and delicate features dressed in a long, full black dress with a fichu around her neck and a cap on her head. Mrs. Oliviere expected her to speak, but she did not. She walked slowly to a globe and, bending over it, remained in contemplation of its surface. She was as tangible, as visible as any living person, and it never occurred to Mrs. Oliviere that she was not some relative of her hostess.

After about ten minutes Mrs. Philip came into the room, apologizing for keeping her guest waiting. "Have you been lonely?" she asked.

"No," Mrs. Oliviere replied, "I have had a most charming little old lady to keep me company." She then looked, but her companion was gone.

"What little old lady?" asked her hostess.

"Someone with long full skirts, a cap and a lace fichu. She came into the room and spent several minutes looking at the globe."

Mrs. Philip asked for a more minute description, and she received it. Then she showed her several pictures, and Mrs. Oliviere picked out the right one. Mrs. Philip then acknowledged, "She was my mother. She dressed exactly like that, and her fondness for the ancient globe was well known to us all."

Now we have a simple instance of a ghost who appeared to tell of his death. This comes to us from *Fate*, a magazine most helpful to writers in the psychical field. In a period when high copy magazines would not dream of publishing anything of this nature and parapsychological publications give primarily clinical or statistical reports, there are few written sources of material. Fortunate is the author whose readers send him documented accounts of their experiences, such as many this book contains. We can only be grateful to the publishers of *Fate* for consistently requiring notarized affidavits of authenticity, plus corroborative documentation, from those whose stories they run in their columns.

In the issue of May, 1961, Louise W. Crahan of San Diego, California, writes: "In 1944 Walter J. Hill, son of James J. Hill, founder of the Great Northern Railroad, asked my mother, Marion C. Whitney, to marry him." Louise was delighted that late in life these two lonely people found happiness together.

The couple planned to wed when Mr. Hill returned to California from a business trip to Montana. He had been gone about a week when someone knocked on the door early one evening. Louise was dressing to go out and, thinking her date had arrived, asked her mother to answer the door. She did, and moments later returned to Louise's room.

"That was Walter," she said in a perplexed tone. "Something must be wrong. I didn't expect him back for at least another week. When I opened the door he just stood there looking at me, saying nothing. When I asked him to come in, he shook his head sadly, and turned away."

Louise ran to the door, but saw nothing of their strange visitor. She then went out on her date, and when she returned about midnight she found her mother pacing the floor in a nearly hysterical condition.

"After you left," Mrs. Whitney explained between sobs, "I received a long distance call from Walter's business manager in Montana. Walter dropped dead of a heart attack tonight in Livingston, Montana—at the same time he came to our door here."

Perhaps the best known case of a ghost who announced her death is the one involving David Belasco's mother, who walked into his room in the East early one morning, even though he knew her to be in San Francisco. He wrote the play *The Return of Peter Grimm* because of his conviction that it was his mother's ghost he had seen. In a booklet he issued in connection with the play's production he said:

> As I strove to speak and sit up, she smiled at me a loving, reassuring smile, spoke my name—the name she called me in my boyhood—"Davy, Davy, Davy," and then leaning down, seemed to kiss me; then drew away a little and said, "Do not grieve. All is well and I am happy," then moved towards the door and vanished.

The next morning Belasco told his family about this with the assurance his mother was dead, and a few hours later a telegram arrived with the sad news.

I have noticed that parapsychologists tend to laugh at such ardent believers in spooks and spirits as British minister Charles L. Tweedale, because he wrote several books about the phenomena which seemed constantly to be occurring in his home that sound almost naïve in their insistence on the reality of the happenings. But Tweedale had an amazing family. As he wrote in *News from the Next World*: "I have married a psychic and my wife is one of those wonderful persons through whom spiritual beings can and do manifest, and who forms a means of, or channel for, communication whereby those persons now alive in the spirit world—who have either been connected with the house in which we reside, or who desire to communicate with mankind—can and do so communicate." His daughters inherited this ability from their mother, and, for that matter, the Reverend Mr. Tweedale himself was no slouch as a ghost seer. So something supernormal was going on around their various parsonages all the time, and they were aware of it and enjoying it.

It will be noted when reading his books, however, that the good pastor was always careful to control each situation that occurred as carefully as possible under the circumstances. He always wrote down all the details of each event as soon as he could, giving time and conditions, and appended the testimony of whoever was involved, including the servants. If his accounts are read carefully and not just dismissed out of hand, there is a lot to be said for them.

In *Man's Survival After Death* Tweedale tells of his own first experience:

> On the night of January 10, 1879, I had retired early to rest. I awoke out of my first sleep to find the moon shining in my room. As I awoke my eyes were directed toward the panels of a cupboard or a wardrobe, built into the east wall of my room. . . . I watched the moonlight on the panels. As I gazed I suddenly saw a face form on the panels of the . . . wardrobe. Indistinct at first, it gradually became clearer until it was perfectly distinct as in life, when I saw the face of my grandmother. What particularly struck me at the moment and burnt itself into my recollection was the fact that the face wore an old-fashioned frilled or goffered cap.

During the few minutes he gazed on it, it was as plain as a living face. Then it gradually faded and was gone. He was not alarmed, thinking it was an illusion of the moonlight, and turned over and went to sleep again. At this time he had not seen his grandmother for many years.

At breakfast as he began to tell of the night's experience his father sprang from his seat and hurried from the room.

"What's the matter with father?" he asked. His mother replied, "Well, Charles, it is the strangest thing I ever heard of, for when I awoke this morning your father informed me that he was awakened in the night and saw his mother standing by his bedside and that when he raised himself to speak to her she glided away."

This conversation took place about 8:30 in the morning of January 11. Before noon the family received a telegram announcing the grandmother's death during the night. They later learned that Charles's father's sister, who lived twenty miles away, had also seen the grandmother's apparition standing at the foot of her bed.

So this remarkable old lady had manifested herself to three persons independently. Tweedale's father was dead by the time he published his account of the incident, but his mother wrote confirming his statement:

> June 22, 1906
>
> I have carefully read my son's account of the strange appearance to him and my late husband, Dr. Tweedale. I perfectly well remember the matter, my son telling us of what he had seen and my husband telling me of the apparition to him, also the telegram informing us of the death during the night.
>
> I distinctly remember my husband also being informed by his sister of the appearance to her.

The letter was signed "Mary Tweedale." The time of the occurrences was later noted: Mr. Tweedale's experience and that of his father were at about 2 A.M. The death took place at 12:15 A.M. It was learned that the frilled cap Charles saw her wearing was exactly like the one she had worn all the time she was ill and when she died.

There are many such cases of ghosts that appear for the purpose of announcing their deaths or their continued existence afterward. One of the oldest researched cases involves a young soldier. Robert Dale Owen published it in *Footfalls on the Boundary of Another World* in 1860, among several other quite old ghosts about whom he, with his wide acquaintance in England and Scotland, was able to dig up a good bit of verification. The Wynyard apparition dates from the year 1785, but there were still people living in Owen's day who had heard the story firsthand from the participants. It had also been reported in several publications.

Sir John Sherbroke and General Wynyard, prominent gentlemen in their time, were only young officers when the incident occurred. They were in the same regiment, stationed at that time in Canada.

On October 15, 1785, about 4 P.M. and therefore in daylight, they were studying in Wynyard's parlor. It was a room with two doors, one opening on an outer passage, the other into Wynyard's bedroom. From the bedroom there was no exit except back through the parlor. Owen writes:

> Sherbroke, happening to look up from his book, saw beside the door which opened on the passage the figure of a tall youth, apparently about twenty years of age, but pale and much emaciated. Astonished at the presence of a stranger, Sherbroke called the attention of his brother officer, sitting near him, to the visitor. "I have heard," he said in afterward relating the incident, "of a man's being as pale as death; but I never saw a living face assume the appearance of a corpse except Wynyard's at that moment."

The two men gazed silently at the figure as it passed slowly across the room and entered the bedchamber. It glanced at young Wynyard as it passed with a look, his friend thought, of melancholy affection. Wynyard, grasping Sherbroke's arm, exclaimed in scarcely articulate tones, "Great God! My brother!"

"Your brother! What can you mean?" replied the other officer, thinking there must be some deception. He instantly ran into the bedroom, followed by Wynyard. There was no one to be seen there! The two men searched everywhere, Wynyard persisting all the while in declaring that he had seen his brother's spirit.

The two men naturally waited with great anxiety for the next ship bringing letters from home. When they came they contained the news of the death of Wynyard's favorite brother, John Otway Wynyard, lieutenant in the 3rd Regiment of Life Guards, on October 15, the same day they had seen his ghost.

Owen adds:

> It remains to be stated that, some years afterward, Sir John Sherbroke, then returned to England, was walking in Piccadilly, London, when, on the opposite side of the street, he saw a gentleman whom he instantly recognized as the counterpart of the mysterious visitor. Crossing over, he accosted him, apolo-

gizing for his intrusion, and learned that he was a brother of Wynyard.

Owen felt this was a strong indication of the validity of Sherbroke's account of the apparition. The fact that his memory of the features of the apparition, after so many years, should cause him to accost a stranger, who proved to be a brother of the deceased was more than a coincidence. Also, it cannot be said that the close association he had with the general influenced him because apparently the general's features were not similar to those of the apparition and the stranger, who looked so much alike.

In order to indicate that ghosts appearing to tell of their passing are not necessarily from the long ago and the faraway, here is a case as recent as today.

Mrs. Linda Melville, a mother of two who lives in Fullerton, California, was thirteen years old when her mother died on the night of March 31, 1961. Linda's mother, suffering from cancer, had been in and out of the hospital for almost a year, but her children had never been told the truth about her problem. Linda says in a documented account in the *National Enquirer*, March 4, 1973:

> Father kept assuring us that mother would get better soon and come home to us. During her final three months in the hospital, none of us really knew how close she was to death. One evening about midnight, I suddenly felt very sad and started to cry. I sat up in bed in the dark.
>
> As I wiped away my tears, I glanced up toward my mirror. In its reflection, I was shocked to see the blurred image of my mother just behind me.
>
> She extended her hand as though to touch me—but then she pulled back and away, fading into the air until she was gone. She made no attempt to say anything. I knew she was dead.

Linda felt strangely calm and serene after that. "I was no longer sad," she said, "because mother had shown me that there is an afterlife."

Shortly afterward her father came home from the hospital, and before he could way a word, Linda blurted out, "Mother is dead, isn't she?" It was later revealed that she had died at just about the time Linda had seen her.

Kellogg Jung, Linda Melville's father, later said, "I don't know how she knew it, but Linda told me that night in 1961 that her mother had died—before I had a chance to tell anyone. I can't explain how she knew that." Linda can. She saw her mother, and received the information directly from her.

V

GHOSTS WITH A GOAL

CAN YOU IMAGINE that if someone had passed over yonder and found himself continuing to exist he would wish mightily to let those on earth know he was still around? But how could he be sure of indicating his identity? Perhaps if he were a great classical scholar like F. W. H. Myers, one of the founders of the Society for Psychical Research, he might feel that an indication of his continued knowledge of the classics would be convincing if he could bring it through several mediums. Or if he could find a strong medium, he might bring personal messages that he hoped would reveal his identity. Then again, if he could show himself as an apparition with some particular personal idiosyncrasy . . . would that be successful?

Here is an account of a young lady who apparently tried to use a scratch as such evidence of identity. And she succeeded in convincing her mother, whose imminent demise she was evidently attempting to make easier.

A letter dated January 11, 1888, from Mr. F. G. of Boston, published in the *Proceedings* of the Society for Psychical Research, is self-explanatory. He wrote:

Sir:
    Replying to the recently published request of your society for actual occurrences of psychical phenomena, I respectfully sub-

mit the following remarkable occurrence. . . . I have never mentioned it outside of my family and a few intimate friends, knowing well that few would believe it, or else ascribe it to some disordered state of my mind at the time, but I well know I never was in better health or possessed a clearer head and mind than at the time it occurred.

In 1867, my only sister, a young lady of eighteen years, died suddenly of cholera, in St. Louis, Missouri. My attachment for her was very strong, and the blow a severe one to me. A year or so after her death, the writer became a commercial traveler, and it was in 1876 while on one of my Western trips that the event occurred.

I had "drummed" the city of St. Joseph, Missouri, and had gone to my room at the Pacific House to send in my orders, which were unusually large ones, so that I was in a very happy frame of mind indeed. . . . I had not been thinking of my late sister, or in any manner reflecting on the past. The hour was high noon, and the sun was shining cheerfully into my room. While busily smoking a cigar, and writing out my orders, I suddenly became conscious that someone was sitting on my left, with one arm resting on the table. Quick as a flash I turned and distinctly saw the form of my dead sister, and for a brief second or so looked her squarely in the face; and so sure was I that it was she that I sprang forward in delight, calling her by name, and, as I did so, the apparition instantly vanished. Naturally I was startled and dumbfounded, almost doubting my senses; but by the cigar in my mouth and pen in hand, with the ink still moist on my letter, I satisfied myself I had not been dreaming and was wide awake. I was near enough to touch her, had it been a physical possibility, and noted her features, expression, and details of dress, etc. She appeared as if alive. Her eyes looked kindly and perfectly naturally into mine. Her skin was so lifelike that I could see the glow of moisture on its surface, and, on the whole, there was no change in her appearance, otherwise than when alive.

Now comes the most remarkable confirmation of my statement. . . . This visitation . . . so impressed me that I took the next train home, and in the presence of my parents and others I related what had occurred. . . . Later on I told them of a bright red line or *scratch* on the right-hand side of my sister's face, which I distinctly had seen. When I mentioned this, my mother rose trembling to her feet and nearly fainted away, and as soon as she sufficiently recovered her self-possession, with tears streaming down her face, she exclaimed that I had indeed seen my sister, as no living mortal but herself was aware of that scratch, which she had accidentally made while doing some little act of kindness after my sister's death. She said she well remembered how pained she was to think she should have, un-intentionally, marred the features of her dead daughter, and that unknown to all, how she had carefully obliterated all traces of the slight scratch with the aid of powder, etc., and that she had never mentioned it to a human being, from that day to this. In proof, neither my father nor any of our family had detected it, and positively were unaware of the incident, yet *I saw the scratch as bright as if just made*. So strangely impressed was my mother that even after she had retired to rest, she got up and dressed, came to me and told me *she knew* at least that I had seen my sister. A few weeks later my mother died, happy in her belief she would rejoin her favorite daughter in a better world.

Here is a modern account of an apparition who brought evidence of his identity while on a lifesaving mission. Elaine V. Worrel of Anaheim, California, wrote in *Fate* (April, 1972), that in the fall of 1949 she and her husband Hal lived on the top floor of a century-old house in Oskaloosa, Iowa. A tiny apartment on the same floor was rented by a young girl, Patricia Burns, who had recently lost her husband.

"We smiled at each other when passing in the hall but otherwise I respected her privacy," writes Mrs. Worrel.

One Saturday Elaine Worrel headed down the hall for a hot bath. As she was groping in the dark bathroom for the long cord that turned on the light, she unaccountably smelled pipe smoke. And then she plainly saw the figure of a tall young man with curly black hair and gray eyes. A faint white horseshoe-shaped scar shone on his left cheekbone. Cupped in one hand was a briar pipe from which the scent was very heavy.

A feeling of urgency swept through Elaine. As if compelled by the ghost's will she followed him up the hall toward Patricia's apart-

49

ment. She hesitated to enter, but the sliding door was unlocked, so she opened it and groped for the light. She writes: "As I entered her bedroom I nearly fainted. Patricia lay on her bed with bright red blood dripping from her wrists!" Hurriedly she made tourniquets, then called her husband at his office. Soon he arrived with a doctor, who stitched the girl's wrists. Later Patricia thanked Elaine for saving her life, saying she had been drinking and, overcome by her grief, had determined to join her husband. "Then she showed me a picture of her husband Raymond. He was the ghost I had seen! I never had seen a picture nor heard a description of him before that time."

In his presidential address to the Society for Psychical Research in 1964, Dr. D. J. West, disregarding such accounts as I have mentioned, made the statement, "The 'perfect' case seems unattainable but this may not be because none are genuine, but because hardly any occur in the specific circumstances in which unambiguous verification is possible."

A modern case which may suit Dr. West better because verification was available from several sources is that of Johnnie Minney, a poor sick little boy who made his mark in the world by becoming a ghost. This was published by the S.P.R. in December, 1966, but the names and locale were not then given. Andrew MacKenzie investigated it further while writing *Frontiers of the Unknown* and received permission to use the names of the people involved and the location, Vicarage Farm, a 500-year-old building in the little village of Waresley in Huntingdonshire, where it all happened. Mrs. Stella Herbert, a visitor from Kenthurst, New South Wales, who had been strongly psychic all her life, is the lady who saw the ghost. She had arrived in England three days before, and on Wednesday, July 7, 1965, had just come to the farm to stay with her fellow Australian, Mrs. Shirley Ross.

On her arrival Mrs. Herbert had been introduced briefly to Miss Margaret Minney, who had lived at the farm all her life. She occupied separate quarters there, for this was her family home. The two women had exchanged only a few words, none of a personal nature.

The following evening, between seven and eight o'clock, Mrs. Ross called on Miss Minney and asked her, "Has a little boy ever died in this house?"

"Yes," replied Miss Minney, "my brother Johnnie."

"Come to my room, then, and listen to Mrs. Herbert," Mrs. Ross said.

Now, this is Mrs. Herbert's story, as she related it to Miss Minney, and as she wrote it on July 10, 1965. It describes her first night at Vicarage Farm.

> I quickly fell asleep as I usually do, and I think I had been asleep for some time when I was awakened by a little boy kneeling at the side of my bed and looking at me with a pleading look. I can still see his face, so thin and drawn and he gave me the impression that had he stood up he would have been tall and bony. His hair was fair and straight and falling to one side.
>
> I sat up in bed, and although he did not speak, I could feel he was asking me to call his mummy, and I tried to call, "Mummy!" The strange thing was that I knew Mrs. Ross was sleeping in the next room, but I also knew that was where he wanted me to call his mother from. I could feel his hands clawing at my arm—almost hurting it. I can remember the sensation vividly. This seemed to go on for a long, long time, and I was very distressed but not afraid.
>
> Eventually I called "Mummy!" rather loudly, and at that moment he disappeared.
>
> He seemed to be dressed in night clothes. (I got the feeling he was wearing pajamas.)
>
> Soon after that I went back to sleep.
>
> I felt very distressed all the next day, and the experience was with me all day, although I went out, and my friend tried to keep me amused and help me to forget it.

When Miss Minney heard this story as it was related to her the day after it occurred, she was speechless until the end. Then she said, "But I know that was Johnnie, my brother, who died when he was five."

Forty-five years before, the dear little boy Johnnie had died of meningitis. He had fair hair which fell over his left eye as Mrs. Herbert described it, was tall for his age and had grown terribly thin. He had been sleeping in the room she was using when he was taken ill in February, 1921, and had been moved to another room, where he remained until his death. Miss Minney remembered the date because it had been Princess Margaret's brithday. He had been unable to speak in the later stage of his illness, but at first he would shout and cry out with pain and call constantly for "Mummy." He was loved by all his family and was a particularly good child. His old nurse was recalled to have said he was "too good to live."

Mr. G. W. Lambert of the S.P.R., who carried out the inquiries into this case, visited Vicarage Farm and interviewed Mrs. Ross and Miss Minney. He was given a statement from Mrs. Kitty Hampton, then aged ninety-five, the only surviving member of the family of eleven which included Miss Minney's mother. She said, "I am the aunt who was keeping house at the time of Johnnie's illness. I took him into my bed during the night before his parents returned. He was a very lovable child. Everyone loved him. At his death he was wasted to skin and bones."

Johnnie Minney's death certificate confirmed that he died on August 21, 1921, aged four years, of cerebro-spinal meningitis. This disease, if prolonged over some months—and it was from February to August in this case—usually leads to severe emaciation.

I am trying to keep this book to the narrative form and not append too much testimony from witnesses or anything else that would slow down the reading, but it seems important here to show Mrs. Ross's corroborating account, primarily because it was written just two days after the appearance of the ghost. She wrote on Saturday immediately after it happened that on Thursday morning when she took her a cup of tea Peg (Mrs. Herbert) had told her of the strange dream she had. Mrs. Ross's use of the word "dream" here was unfortunate, for it caused much controversy. But Mrs. Herbert afterward declared, "The boy was definitely there. It was no dream." And Mrs. Ross's further testimony confirmed this, for she spoke of Mrs. Herbert having told her she was awakened by a boy in distress. And then she continued with the almost identical information given by Mrs. Herbert in her testimony.

Mrs. Ross had come to live at Vicarage Farm in November, 1964. In Australia previously she had lived near Mrs. Herbert and their children were school friends. Mrs. Ross had little knowledge of the farm family's background and had never heard of Miss Minney's little brother who had died. The only picture of Johnnie, a snapshot taken when he was three, was kept in a drawer and Mrs. Ross had never seen it. Anyway, he was a chubby tot then, not the emaciated nearly five-year-old boy he had been at the time of his death.

When Andrew MacKenzie investigated the case, he visited with Miss Minney the grave of her little brother. On the cross above his grave is the inscription, "In loving memory of John Alex, son of Alex and Florry May Minney, who died 21 August 1921 aged four years. 'Until the day Break.'"

When his little body was buried, who would have dreamed that this child would go down in the history of psychical research as a ghost still seeking his "Mummy!"

For long gone entities who attempt to make themselves known, we have another of Robert Dale Owen's . . . and it is my favorite story of its kind because of the lady who walked through a ghost. How brave can one woman get? People in those days were most reluctant to have their names used in connection with such suspicious subject matter, and so Owen used only initials once again; but he assures us that he personally knew both women involved.

Mrs. R. was the wife of a field officer of high rank in the British Army, who resided for a time in 1857 at Ramhurst Manor House near Leigh, in Kent. During the entire time she lived there, there were disturbances in the night—knockings, footsteps, and, more especially, voices which seemed to be talking in loud tones and even sometimes screaming. The servants were much alarmed. Mrs. R.'s brother, a bold, lighthearted young officer, fond of field sports and "without the slightest faith in the reality of visitations from another world," was much disturbed and annoyed by these voices, which he declared must be those of his sister and a friend sitting up to chat all night. On two occasions, when the voices rose to a scream, he rushed from his room at two or three o'clock in the morning, gun in hand, into his sister's bedroom, there to find her sleeping quietly.

In October Miss S. came to visit Mrs. R. She was a young woman who had frequently seen apparitions from early childhood. When, on their return from the station at about four o'clock in the afternoon, they drove up to the entrance of the manor house, Miss S. observed on the threshold two figures, apparently an elderly couple, dressed in the costume of a former age. She did not hear any voices coming from them, so, realizing they were apparitions, she didn't mention them. She saw the same figures, in the same dress, several times within the next ten days, sometimes in one of the rooms of the house, sometimes in one of the passages . . . always by daylight.

On the third occasion they spoke to her, stating that they were husband and wife, that in former days they had owned and occupied the manor house, that their name was Children. The man's name was Richard and he had died in 1753. Since they appeared so sad and downcast Miss S. inquired why. They replied that they had idolized that property, and that their pride and pleasure had centered in its possession. Now they were troubled to see that it had passed away from their family and was in the hands of careless strangers.

Robert Owen later asked Miss S. how these apparitions spoke. She replied that the voice was as audible to her as that of any human being. She described their clothing as of the period of Queen Anne or one of the early Georges—the fashions being similar.

Miss S. finally told Mrs. R. what she had seen and heard. Up until that time, Mrs. R., although her rest had frequently been broken by the noises in the house, had seen nothing; nor did anything appear to her for a month afterward. Owen writes:

> One day, however, about the end of that time, when she had ceased to expect any apparition to herself, she was hurriedly dressing for a late dinner—her brother, who had just returned from a day's shooting, having called to her in impatient tones that dinner was served and that he was quite famished. At the moment of completing her toilet, and as she hastily turned to leave her bedchamber, not dreaming of anything spiritual, there in the doorway stood the same female figure Miss S. had described—identical in appearance and in costume, even to the old point-lace on her brocaded silk dress—while beside her, on the left, but less distinctly visible, was the figure of her husband. They uttered no sound; but above the figure of the lady, as if written in phosphoric light in the dusk atmosphere that surrounded her, were the words "Dame Children," together with

some other words intimating that, having never aspired beyond the joys and sorrows of this world, she had remained "earth bound." These last, however, Mrs. R. scarcely paused to decipher; for a renewed appeal from her brother, as to whether they were to have any dinner that day, urged her forward. The figure, filling up the doorway, remained stationary. There was no time for hesitation: she closed her eyes, rushed through the apparition and into the dining room, throwing up her hands and exclaiming to Miss S., "Oh, my dear, I've just walked through Mrs. Children!"

Don't you love that? At the apparent insistence of the ghosts to be identified, the ladies made inquiries among the servants and neighbors whether any family bearing that name had ever occupied the manor house. A nurse, Mrs. Sophy O., recollected that one of her sisters-in-law, who was now an old woman of seventy, had fifty years before been housemaid to a family then residing at Ramhurst. When Sophy O. went home for a holiday she inquired of this woman if she had ever heard anything of a family named Children. The sister-in-law recollected that an old man had once told her that in his boyhood he had assisted with keeping the hounds for a family named Children, who were then residing at the manor house.

When Robert Dale Owen received these particulars in December, 1858, from both ladies together, he started an intensive search for evidence. He began by calling on the nurse, Mrs. Sophy O. She told of having heard the strange noises in the house and the voices. Then she sent him to see her sister-in-law, who fully confirmed the information she had previously given.

Owen then visited neighboring churches. Sextons and tombstones having failed him, he eventually discovered a clergyman who owned a document containing the very details for which he searched. Owen writes:

> He kindly intrusted it to me; and I found in it . . . certain extracts from the "Hasted Papers," preserved in the British Museum; these being contained in a letter addressed by one of the members of the Children family to Mr. Hasted. Of this document, which may be consulted in the Museum library, I

here transcribe a portion, as follows: "The family of Children were settled for a great many generations at a house called, from their own name, Childrens. George Children of Lower Street, who was High-Sheriff of Kent in 1698, died without issue in 1718, and by will devised the bulk of his estate to *Richard* Children, eldest son of his late uncle, William Children of Hedcorn, and his heirs. This Richard Children, *who settled himself at Romhurst* . . . married Anne, daughter of John Saxby . . . by whom he had issue four sons and two daughters," etc.

Owen was happy, for he had thus ascertained that the first of the Children family who occupied Ramhurst was named Richard and that he settled there in the early part of the reign of George I. The year of his death, however, was not given. That was not found until months afterward, when a friend versed in antiquarian lore suggested that the same Hasted who had been his source for the previous material had also published in 1778 a history of Kent. In that work Owen discovered that Richard Children, Esq., who resided at Ramhurst, died possessed of it in 1753, aged eighty-three years. He also learned that circumstances compelled the descendants to sell the property and that the family mansion, passing into the hands of strangers, was degraded into an ordinary farm house, all this completely tallying with the communications given by the ghosts.

Sarah Evanston of Phoenix, Arizona, has always been psychic. She told me that once when she was four or five years old she had gone across the street to play with a little girl friend. As she was waiting for her outside her house, an elderly lady in a black dress came up to her.

"She asked me to take the spoon I had in my hand and go dig where she told me to," Sarah said. "Then I was to take what I found and give it to my mother, telling her that it was a gift from Agnes. I dug where she said and found a beautiful yellow rose pin surrounded by crystal beads. When I took this to my mother, she questioned me. I told her that Agnes wanted me to give it to her. Mother said that was impossible, for Agnes had been dead for years. But I saw that woman; and I found the pin where she told me to dig for it."

Now, unless Sarah is fibbing about this, and I don't believe she is because I know her personally and she is an honest person, and also her mother verified her story, how do we account for it? If it were the only case of such a nature, we would have to discount it. But it isn't. If we had only a single veridical ghost story to deal with, it would be difficult to conceive of the kind or amount of evidence which would be necessary to cause us to prefer the idea of a ghostly agency to all other possible explanations. But instead we have so many cases that merely selecting the most appropriate to use is a chore. And they involve a large mass of apparently strong testimony of facts which, as recounted, would seem to admit of no other satisfactory explanation. If we insist upon a counter-hypothesis, we can only attack the veracity of the tellers of the tales; and this would be a very unwarranted thing to do in most of our cases. While being very careful to give all the other arguments before we suggest that our accounts *must* involve the spirits of the dead, we can't close our minds to the possibility that they *might*.

Sir William Barrett discussed this point in his *Death-Bed Visions*. Sir William, professor of physics at the Royal College of Science, Dublin, for almost forty years, was one of the most prominent and most active founders of the Society for Psychical Research. He wrote:

> . . . every scientific society ought to have as its motto the opinion expressed by Sir John Herschel in his discourse on "Natural Philosophy" . . . , "that the perfect observer . . . will have his eyes as it were opened that they may be struck at once with any occurrence which, according to received theories, ought *not* to happen; for these are the facts which serve as clues to new discoveries." Unfortunately, as Goethe remarked in one of his conversations with Eckermann, "in the sciences . . . if anyone advances anything new . . . people resist with all their might; they speak of the new view with contempt, as if it were not worth the trouble of even so much as an investigation or a regard; and thus a new truth may wait a long time before it can win its way."

VI

DEATHBED VISIONS

UNTIL THE TIME Dr. Karlis Osis' pilot study entitled *Deathbed Observations by Physicians and Nurses*, was published in 1961, there had been only two other comprehensive treatments of the subject: Dr. James H. Hyslop's *Psychical Research and the Resurrection*, published in 1908, and Sir William Barrett's *Death-Bed Visions*, published in 1926. These were comprised mostly of factual accounts of the ghost-seeing experiences of the dying—or as it is more scientifically put, hallucinations or visions at the time of death. Dr. Osis' object was to collect as many statements on this subject as he could from doctors and nurses, and he queried 5,000 doctors and 5,000 nurses in order to discover the frequency and types of deathbed visions they had observed among patients.

His results were surprising, especially to him. In the first place, he received 640 questionnaires in reply, a number about three times larger than his medical advisers had led him to expect. And the respondents claimed to have made observations of 35,540 dying patients in all. Osis says, "Apparently, the survey gave us access to a surprisingly large body of empirical information."

Thus, from his questionnaires, Dr. Osis learned that a great many people hallucinate visions of other people, but that healthy persons hallucinate predominantly the living; terminal patients hallucinate predominantly the dead; and visions and hallucinations of religious figures are much more frequent in the sample of the dying than in the samples of healthy individuals. Perhaps, however, their religious beliefs influenced the patients to describe what they saw in religious terms. As Scott Rogo points out in "Deathbed Visions and Survival," (*Fate*, June, 1972), "A dying person might easily construe a white apparitional form as an angel of mercy."

"Of course," says Dr. Osis, "it would be extremely naïve, for example, to take at face value the anthropomorphic idea of one patient in our survey who 'shook hands with the Lord' (an ultra-Americanized bit of religious behavior!)."

Most surprising, to him, was the large number who are said to be elated at the hour of death. This mood is apparently quite frequent among terminal patients. "Naturally," he says, "there are some variations in our sample, but all three percentage groups indicate substantial proportions of patients elated . . . at the most dreaded time of life."

Of those patients seeing hallucinatory persons, 83.1 percent saw close relatives (a mother, father, spouse, sibling, offspring), 50 percent saw other dead relatives and 42.9 percent saw deceased persons who were not relatives. Although such observations are significant and interesting, Dr. Osis drew few conclusions from his study. His major endeavor was to verify the basic findings of Barrett and Hyslop—that predominant among the visions seen by the dying are the "dead." "Why do dying persons see apparitions of the dead so much more frequently than of living persons, when compared with the apparitions seen by the general population?" he asks. "I have not been able to think of explanations of the pattern under discussion which would be based upon a non-survival hypothesis and not be far-fetched except for the rather remote possibility of chance coincidences. It is very strange, indeed, that hallucinations of eight out of nine parents or siblings should represent dead persons."

Unless, as we've been suggesting here, the spirits of those dead persons are actually there and trying to make their presence known in order to give assurance to the dying patient.

We will begin our illustrative material with a case which, while heartbreaking and at the same time inspiring, is also the weakest of all. This is because its account was written by very emotionally involved observers, which makes it sound, as Osis says, "like a nursery tale." Dr. Hyslop published it first in the *Journal* of the A.S.P.R. just as he received it from the little girl's mother.

Daisy Irene Dryden was born in Marysville, Yuba County, California, on September 9, 1854, and died in San José, California, on October 8, 1864, aged ten years. She was the daughter of Reverend David Anderson Dryden, a Methodist missionary. While convalescing from a fever she seemed to be improving rapidly until one afternoon when, as her father sat by her bed, he noticed a strange expression on her face of both pleasure and amazement. Her eyes were directed to one place above the door.

"What do you see, Daisy?" asked her father. She replied softly, "It's a spirit. It is Jesus. He says I am going to be one of His little lambs." "Yes, dear," said her father, "I hope you are one of His lambs." "Oh, papa!" she exclaimed, "I'm going to heaven, to Him!"

That night she was taken with enteritis and lived only four days. She suffered much for the first twenty-four hours, being unable to retain food, water, or medicine, but from that time on she had very little pain; and her mind was very active and remarkably clear. Her faculties appeared sharpened. During this time she dwelt in both worlds, as she expressed it.

Her mother wrote of her that, "Although she was on the whole a good child, possessing ordinary good sense, yet in no way was she more remarkable than many other children. Her dying experience, therefore, was not the outgrowth of a life highly spiritual, nor was it one which had been educated in the least degree on the lines of mysticism or modern Spiritualism." Yet what she said while dying was so strange and interesting that her mother sat by her bed and took notes.

Daisy seemed to be able to see the spirit world surrounding her as well as the physical, and it wasn't always what she would have expected it to be. Two days before she died, the Sunday School superintendent came to see her. She talked very freely about going, and sent farewell messages by him to her classmates. When he was about to leave, he said, "Well, Daisy, you will soon be over the dark river." After he had gone, she asked her father what he meant by the "dark river." He tried to explain it, but she said, "It is all a mistake;

there is no river; there is no curtain; there is not even a line that separates this life from the other life." She stretched out her hands from the bed, and with a gesture said, "It is here and it is there; I know it is so, for I can see you all, and I see them there at the same time." They asked her to tell something of that other world and how it looked to her, but she replied, "I cannot describe it; it is so different I could not make you understand."

Mrs. B., a neighbor, was told about Daisy's inner sight being opened, but she did not believe in an afterlife. She was, however, in deep distress, having just lost her husband and a son who was about twelve years old named Batemen. She came to visit Daisy and began to ask questions. Daisy told her:

"Batemen is here, and says he is alive and well, and is in such a good place he would not come home for anything. He says he is learning how to be good. . . . He says to you, 'Mother, don't fret about me, it is better I did not grow up.'" This communication set the mother to thinking, says Mrs. Dryden, and she became a firm believer in a future state.

Once Daisy said, "Oh, papa, do you hear that? It's the singing of the angels. You ought to hear it, for the room is full of it. I can see them, there are so many. I can see them miles and miles away."

During her last days Daisy loved to listen to her sister Lulu sing to her, mostly from hymnals. Lulu sang one song which spoke of the angels and their "snowy wings." When she had finished, Daisy exclaimed, "Oh, Lulu, is it not strange? We always thought the angels had wings; but it's a mistake. They don't have any." Lulu replied, "But they must have wings, else how do they fly down from heaven?" "Oh, but they don't fly," she answered. "They just come. When I think of Allie, he's here."

Allie was her brother who had passed over seven months before at the age of six of scarlet fever. He seemed to be with her a great deal during those last days. Whenever they asked her questions she could not answer she would say, "Wait till Allie comes and I'll ask him."

Daisy's mother writes:

> I was sitting beside her bed, her hand clasped in mine. Looking up so wistfully at me, she said, "Dear Mamma, I do wish

you could see Allie; he's standing beside you." Involuntarily I looked around, but Daisy thereupon continued, "He says you cannot see him because your spirit eyes are closed, but that I can, because my body only holds my spirit, as it were, by a thread of life." I then inquired, "Does he say that now?" "Yes, just now," she answered. Then wondering how she could be conversing with her brother when I saw not the least sign of conversation, I said, "Daisy, how do you speak to Allie? I do not hear you or see your lips move." She smilingly replied, "We just talk with our think." I then asked her further, "Daisy, how does Allie appear to you? Does he seem to wear clothes?" She answered, "Oh, no, not clothes such as we wear. There seems to be about him a white, beautiful something, so fine and thin and glistening, and oh, so white, and yet there is not a fold, or a sign of a thread in it, so it cannot be cloth. But it makes him look so lovely." Her father then quoted from the Psalmist: "He is clothed with light as a garment." "Oh, yes, that's it," she replied.

The child often spoke of dying, and seemed to have such a vivid sense of her future life and happiness that the dread of death was all dispelled. To her it was only a continuation of life, a growing up from the conditions of earth life into the air and sunshine of heaven. Her mother wrote:

The morning of the day she died she asked me to let her have a small mirror. I hesitated, thinking the sight of her emaciated face would be a shock to her. But her father, sitting by her, remarked, "Let her look at her poor little face if she wants to." So I gave it to her. Taking the glass in her two hands, she looked at her image for a time, calmly and sadly. At length she said, "This body of mine is about worn out. It is like that old dress of Mamma's hanging there in the closet. She doesn't wear it any more, and I won't wear my body any more, because I have a new spiritual body which will take its place. Indeed, I have it now, for it is with my spiritual eyes I see the heavenly world while my body is still here. You will lay my body in the grave because I will not need it again. It was made for my life here, and now my life here is at an end, and this poor body will be laid away, and I shall have a beautiful body like Allie's." Then

63

she said to me, "Mamma, open the shutters and let me look out at the world for the last time. Before another morning I shall be gone." As I obeyed her loving request, she said to her father, "Raise me up, Papa." Then, supported by her father, she looked through the window whose shutters I had opened, and called out, "Goodbye sky, goodbye trees, goodbye flowers, goodbye white rose, goodbye red rose, goodbye beautiful world," and added, "how I love it, but I do not wish to stay."

That evening she remarked, "It's half past eight now; when it is half past eleven Allie will come for me." She was then reclining on her father's breast, with her head on his shoulder, a favorite position because it rested her. She said, "Papa, I want to die here. When the time comes, I will tell you."

At about a quarter past eleven she said, "Now, papa, take me up; Allie has come for me." Then she asked her parents to sing. When the hands of the clock pointed to half past eleven, she lifted up both arms and said, "Come, Allie," and breathed no more. Then tenderly laying her loved but lifeless form on the pillow, her father said, "The dear child has gone. She will suffer no more."

His wife adds, "There was a solemn stillness in the room. We could not weep, and why should we?"

Could a little girl have made all this up? Possibly. It was certainly nothing like what she had been taught in school and Sunday School, and it was unlike any of her preconceived ideas about how death would be. And yet it was remarkably like what others who have claimed to have glimpses of conditions in the spiritual world have described.

In our next case a patient was apparently saved from dying by the appearance of her brother's ghost, although what he was able to do to help is not stated.

Wilma S. Ashby in "My Personal Miracle," *Fate* (June, 1972), tells of a premonition she had of grave and imminent danger just before she, her husband Walter, and their two children left on a trip on Saturday, August 2, 1930. She writes that when they got into the car she insisted that two-year-old Billy be seated between his father and her rather than placed in his comfortable bed on the rear seat. Her husband gave her a quizzical look, but did as she requested. She held four-week-old Bobby on a pillow on her lap. When a car crashed into them just outside Henderson, Kentucky, and completely wrecked their vehicle, the children were not hurt; but the back seat, where Billy was to have slept, was a crumpled mess, littered with slivers of glass.

Wilma herself was so badly injured that she was not expected to live. Relatives had been notified of her impending death and were gathering around. She writes, "At eight that evening, fully conscious, I said a simple prayer of thanks that my family had been spared any great harm. Suddenly something compelled me to open my eyes. I was astonished to see the gray wall in front of me changing. In the middle of a beautiful purple mist stood my twin brother, robed in white."

Mrs. Ashby's twin, Willard, had died in 1926. Now, he was smiling the same kind of infectious grin he used to have when he teasingly called her his "sin-twister." His arms outstretched, he moved slowly forward. She reached out to embrace him. She says, "My brother had reached the foot of my bed and our fingers were about to touch when my husband entered the room. My twin instantly vanished. I began to cry, 'Willard was here but he left before I could touch him.' My husband looked amazed. 'When I opened the door,' he said, 'it was as if an electric shock passed through my body.'"

Two hours later the doctor returned expecting to find Wilma dying. Instead he led her husband outside the room and said, "A miracle has happened here tonight and I had nothing to do with it. Your wife will live."

Sometimes a vision seen by a child may bring more conviction because of his innocent lack of conditioning. From *Light*, London, April 7, 1888, comes a story reported by the Reverend William Stainton Moses as it was told to him by Miss H., the daughter of a clergyman of the Anglican Church.

Miss H. said she was sitting up with a poor woman in her father's parish whose baby was dying. There were two beds in the cottage chamber, one a crib in which a child of three or four, the baby's older brother, had been asleep for several hours. Miss H. and the mother stood beside the other, larger bed, on which the infant lay gasping its last breaths.

Suddenly an eager young voice called from the crib, and the little brother was sitting up, wide awake, and pointing, with a kind of rapture on his face. "Oh, mummy, mummy," he cried out, "beautiful ladies all around baby. Beautiful ladies. Oh, mummy, mummy, they are taking baby."

The watchers turned their eyes to the bed again. The infant had expired.

Stainton Moses made the following comment about this, a little bit sarcastic, but a point well taken: "In view of the style of criticism which it is the fashion to level against mediumship, it is of real importance to gather cases such as the preceding, where the 'babes and sucklings' can hardly be described as trained conjurors or accomplished rogues. . . ."

Yet in contrast, it is also nice to receive an account of an apparition seen by someone who is likely to be as critical and objective as a trained nurse. We have two nurse stories, one new and one from 1890 by way of *Proceedings* S.P.R., and both ghosts brought them information.

Mrs. Caroline Rogers, a seventy-two-year-old widow who had been twice married, was the patient in this latter case, and Mrs. Mary Wilson, a professional nurse, saw the ghost. She had remained with Mrs. Rogers almost constantly during her illness, but had not known her beforehand, nor did she know anything of her family or history. Mrs. Rogers spoke frequently to Mrs. Wilson, and also to others, of her second husband, Mr. Rogers, and children, expressing a desire to see them again.

On the afternoon of April 14, Mrs. Rogers became unconscious and remained so all the time until her death twenty-four hours later. In a thoroughly locked house, the other occupants of which were all asleep, Mrs. Wilson kept watch. Between two and three A.M., while she was wide awake, she happened to look toward the door into the adjoining chamber and saw a man standing in the open doorway. He was middle-sized, broad-shouldered, with shoulders thrown back. He had a florid complexion, reddish brown hair and beard, and wore a brown sack overcoat, which was unbuttoned. His expression was grave, neither stern nor pleasant, and he seemed to look straight at Mrs. Wilson, and then at Mrs. Rogers, without moving. Mrs. Wilson supposed, of course, that it was a real man, and tried to think how he could have got into the house. Then, as he remained quite motionless, she began to realize that it was something uncanny, and becoming frightened, turned her head away and called her daughter, who was asleep. They searched the house, but, of course, found no one.

In the morning Mrs. Rogers' niece, Mrs. Hildreth, who lived in the neighborhood, called to see her aunt. Mrs. Wilson related her experience of the night before and asked if the apparition resembled Mr. Rogers. Mrs. Hildreth replied emphatically that it did not, but that it agreed exactly with Mr. Tisdale, Mrs. Rogers' first husband.

Mrs. Rogers had come to Roslindale after marrying Mr. Rogers, and Mrs. Hildreth is the only person in that vicinity who had ever seen Mr. Tisdale; and in Mrs. Rogers' house there was no portrait of him nor anything suggestive of his personal appearance.

Mrs. F. E. Hildreth added her signed testimony to that of Mrs. Wilson.

A nurse I know, Margot Moser of Jamaica, Long Island, New York, told me of seeing the same apparition her patient saw. She also wrote her account for Dr. Karlis Osis for his survey *Deathbed Observations by Physicians and Nurses*. It is a particularly nice case because the ghost presented such well-defined features that her son was later recognized by the resemblance.

Mrs. Moser told me:

In the winter of 1948–49 I nursed a very sick old lady, Mrs. Rosa B. She was a very clever, well-educated, and highly-cultured immigrant from Odessa, Russia, who had lived for many years in New York City. She was residing at that time at the Savoy Plaza Hotel on Fifth Avenue, and up to the last she was mentally competent.

Early one afternoon I had put my patient to bed for a nap and was sitting at my little table beside the window writing in her chart. I was facing her bed, the door at my back. Mrs. B. had been asleep, but suddenly I saw her sit up and wave happily, her face all smiles. I turned my head toward the door, thinking one of her daughters had come in; but much to my surprise it was an elderly lady I had never seen before. She had a striking resemblance to my patient—the same light blue eyes, but a longer nose and heavier chin. I could see her very clearly for it was bright daylight; the window shades were only slightly lowered. The visitor walked toward my patient, bent down, and, as far as I can remember, they kissed each other. But then, as I got up and walked toward the bed, she was gone.

Mrs. B. looked very pleased. She took my hand and said, "It is my sister!" Then she slept peacefully again. I saw the same apparition twice later on, but never as clearly and always from another room. But every time she came the patient was obviously elated.

At Mrs. B.'s funeral service some weeks later, I positively identified a gentleman as being the son of the apparition, because he had his mother's nose and chin and looked so much like her. I asked one of the daughters about it, and she said that he was her cousin.

This account was first published in my book *The Enigma of Out-of-Body Travel.* (Garrett Publications, 1965.)

A collective hallucination, in which various members of a family all see the apparition the dying person sees, is something pretty special. Miss Emma Pearson, as quoted by F.W.H. Myers in *Human Personality and Its Survival of Bodily Death*, wrote the S.P.R. that her aunt, Miss Harriet Pearson, was taken very ill at Brighton, England, in November, 1864. The sick woman craved to be back in her own home in London, where she and her sister Ann (who had died some years previously) had spent practically all their lives; and Miss Emma accordingly had her moved home. Her account of what then happened goes as follows:

Her two nieces (Mrs. Coppinger and Mrs. John Pearson), Eliza Quinton the housekeeper, and myself did the nursing between us. She became worse and worse. On the night of December 23, Mrs. John Pearson was sitting up with her, while Mrs. Coppinger and I lay down in the adjoining room, leaving the door ajar to hear any sound from the next room. We were neither of us asleep, and suddenly we both started up in bed, as we saw someone pass the door, wrapped up in an old shawl, having a wig with three curls each side, and an old black cap. Mrs. Coppinger called to me, "Emma, get up, it is old Aunt Ann!" I said, "So it is; then Aunt Harriet will die today!" As we jumped up, Mrs. John Pearson came rushing out of Aunt Harriet's room, saying, "That was old Aunt Ann. Where has she gone?" I said to soothe her, "Perhaps it was Eliza come down to see how her old mistress is." Mrs. Coppinger ran upstairs and found Eliza asleep. Every room was searched—no one was there; and from that day to this no explanation has ever been given of this appearance, except that it was old Aunt Ann come to call her sister. Aunt Harriet died at 6 P.M. that day.

What of the dying woman? Yes, she knew old Aunt Ann had been there. She told everyone her sister had come for her, for she had seen her clearly.

Miss Pearson's statements were confirmed by Eliza Quinton, the housekeeper, who added, "We searched in every room but could not find anyone in the house." There wasn't anyone there . . . anyone visible, that is.

VII

PEAK IN DARIEN

Then felt I like some watcher of the skies
When a new planet swims into his ken;
Or like stout Cortez when with eagle eyes
He stared at the Pacific and all his men
Look'd at each other with a wild surmise
Silent, upon a peak in Darien.

—JOHN KEATS, "On First Looking
Into Chapman's Homer"

DARIEN, OF COURSE, is the name formerly given to the Isthmus of Panama. It was a Miss Frances Power Cobbe who originated the name "Peak in Darien" for the type of cases we will discuss in this chapter. Her concept was based on the belief that the spirits of dead relatives come to aid the dying and "take them away to another world," probably one they will happily greet with "a wild surmise." It is presumed that strong expectations alone can cause hallucinations. And thus when someone sees his deceased mother it's because he expected to. However, if the patient hallucinates a person about whose death he has not yet been informed, it excludes the possibility that he expected this individual to appear at his bedside, so in this case the hallucination would require a different explanation. The one then usually given by parapsychologists is that he has telepathically gained the information from the minds of those who do know.

A more comfortable explanation would be based on the idea that the surviving spirit has made a pilgrimage to the bedside of his friend or relative who is soon to join him. Many people prefer this idea. Sir William F. Barrett says in *Death-Bed Visions*, "The evidence of Visions of the Dying, when they appear to see and recognize some of their relatives of whose decease they were unaware, affords perhaps one of the strongest arguments in favor of survival."

Most of the outstanding cases of this type to occur before 1926 were gathered together and published by Barrett. The best authenticated of all these was related to him by his wife. It occurred when she was in attendance on a patient in the Mothers' Hospital at Clapton, of which she was one of the obstetric surgeons.

Lady Barrett received an urgent message from the resident medical officer to come to a patient, Mrs. B., who was in labor and suffering from serious heart failure. She went at once, and the child was delivered safely, though the mother was dying at the time. The mother suddenly began to look eagerly toward one part of the room, a smile illuminating her whole countenance. "Oh, lovely, lovely," she said. When asked what she saw she replied, "Lovely brightness—wonderful beings." Then she saw her father and said, "Oh, he's so glad I'm coming; he's so glad."

Her baby was brought for her to see. She looked at it with interest and said, "Do you think I ought to stay for baby's sake?" Then turning toward the vision again, she said, "I can't—I can't stay; if you could see what I do, you would know I can't stay."

After Lady Barrett left, the patient said in the presence of her mother and her husband and the matron of the hospital, Miriam Castle, "Oh, why there's Vida." She referred to a sister, who had been an invalid for some years and of whose death three weeks previously she had not been told because of her own illness. Her mother, Mary C. Clark, wrote for the record that they had made it a special point when visiting her to put off their mourning so that she wouldn't know. She says, "All her letters were also kept by request until her husband had seen who they might be from before letting her see them. This precaution was taken lest outside friends might possibly allude to the recent bereavement in writing to her, unaware of the very dangerous state of her health."

Her mother reported Mrs. B. as saying on the day she died, January 12, 1924, "Oh, it is lovely and bright; you cannot see as I can." She fixed her eyes on one particular spot, saying, "Oh, God, forgive me for anything I have done wrong." After that she said, "I can see Father; he wants me, he is so lonely." Then she said with a rather

puzzled expression, "He has Vida with him." Turning to her
mother she said, "Vida is with him." Then she said, "You do want
me, Dad; I'm coming."

If this were an isolated case, a mere casual coincidence might perhaps account for it, but it is only one of a considerable group of
similar instances. An explanation of chance coincidence thus becomes incredible. Professor Hyslop said this as he published the following account in *Psychical Research and the Resurrection*. It came
from the distinguished Unitarian minister, Dr. Minot J. Savage, who
investigated it personally.

There were two little girls named Jennie and Edith, one about
eight years of age and the other but a little older. They were school-
mates and intimate friends. In June, 1889, both were taken ill with
diphtheria. At noon on Wednesday Jennie died. Then the parents of
Edith, and her physician as well, took particular pains to keep from
her the fact that her little playmate was gone. They feared the effect
of the knowledge on her own condition. To prove that she did not
know, it may be mentioned that on Saturday, June 8, at noon, just
before she became unconscious, she selected two of her photographs
to be sent to Jennie, and also told her attendants to bid her good-
bye. If her subsequent knowledge of Jennie's death could be attributed to telepathy from her parents, why wasn't it in operation then?

The report goes on: "She died at half past six o'clock on the evening of Saturday, June 8. She had roused and bidden her friends
good-bye, and was talking of dying, and seemed to have no fear. She
appeared to see one and another of the friends she knew were dead.
So far it was like other similar cases. But now suddenly, and with
every appearance of surprise, she turned to her father and exclaimed,
'Why, papa, I am going to take Jennie with me!' Then she added,
'Why, papa! You didn't tell me that Jennie was here!' And immediately she reached out her arms as if in welcome and said, 'Oh, Jennie,
I'm so glad you are here!' "

The following is another account which tends to discount the
telepathy theory . . . at least telepathy with anyone known to the
deceased. Some kind of mind reading at a distance involving information exchanged between strangers would have to be the explanation if this case is to be explained as telepathy.

73

Mr. Hensleigh Wedgwood (the cousin and brother-in-law of Charles Darwin, and himself a well-known savant) reported this case to the *Spectator* in 1882. He says:

> Between forty and fifty years ago a young girl, a near connection of mine, was dying of consumption. She had lain for some days in a prostrate condition taking no notice of anything, when she opened her eyes, and looking upwards, said slowly, "Susan . . . and Jane . . . and Ellen," as if recognizing the presence of her three sisters, who had previously died of the same disease. Then after a short pause she continued, "and Edward too!" naming a brother then supposed to be alive and well in India—as if surprised at seeing him in the company. She said no more, and sank shortly afterwards. In the course of the post, letters came from India announcing the death of Edward, from an accident a week or two previous to the death of his sister.
>
> This was told me by an elder sister who nursed the dying girl and was present at her bedside at the time of the apparent vision.

You read about Peak in Darien cases and you think, "How fascinating!" But it hardly dawns on you that you might discover one close to home. Yet when I was talking to my friend Karl Romer about my search for good current material for this book, he dropped a beauty right in my lap. "Why, I know a woman who had an experience just like that," he said, and he told me about Maxine—I'd better not use the rest of her real name because we haven't been able to contact her to get her permission—who lived in Anaheim, California. She had what is practically a double Peak in Darien happening while in the hospital delivering a baby.

Regaining consciousness in her room, Maxine saw her father standing in an upper corner of the room near the ceiling, holding an infant in his arms. He spoke to her, saying, "Don't worry. I'll take care of the baby." Then he disappeared.

Maxine immediately rang for a nurse and asked about her baby. She was told it was doing fine. Given one excuse after another every time she inquired, she grew more and more suspicious that her vision

74

of her father must have meant something very important. Finally she insisted to her husband that he tell her the truth, no matter how painful it might be to her. Then he told her that the baby had been stillborn, and that her father had died suddenly while she was in the hospital.

Karl Romer and his wife are friends of mine of many years' standing. He is a serious-minded electronics engineer who would no more make up a thing like this than he would rob a bank. And he heard Maxine's personal account of her experience, shortly after it occurred.

Another modern incident involving California people was reported in *Coronet* magazine (April, 1949), when Natalie Kalmus, pioneer developer of technicolor, related what happened when she was at the bedside of her dying sister Eleanor. Eleanor had been promised that no drugs would be administered to ease her last hours because she was not afraid to die and was convinced that death would be a beautiful experience. Miss Kalmus described Eleanor's final scene:

"I sat on her bed and took her hand. It was on fire. Then she seemed to rise up in bed almost to a sitting position.

" 'Natalie,' she said, 'There are so many of them. There's Fred . . . and Ruth . . . What's she doing here? Oh, I know!' "

An electric shock went through Natalie. Ruth was their cousin who had died suddenly the week before. But Eleanor had not been told of Ruth's sudden death.

"Chill after chill went up and down my spine," says Natalie. "I felt on the verge of some powerful, almost frightening knowledge. She had murmured Ruth's name.

"Her voice was so surprisingly clear. 'It's so confusing! So many of them!' Suddenly her arms stretched out happily as when she had welcomed me. 'I'm going up,' she said."

Immediately afterward, death came for Eleanor. De Witt Miller, who used this account in *You Do Take It With You* added, "In view of the stubbornly ineradicable fact that the cumulative evidence of innumerable cases indicates that the moment of death is often a time of glad reunion, I have come to the conclusion that it is."

VIII

GUARDIAN ANGELS

GUARDIAN ANGELS COME in assorted sizes, colors, and garb, the least likely of which are flowing white robes and wings. No, instead they more frequently appear as a loving husband or wife or mother or father who has died and still seems to have an interest in those left behind.

Several people have given me their personal accounts of the help they believe they have received from spirits, and indeed it is difficult to doubt their stories because they subsequently have confirmed the information they have learned supernormally. There are a few cases of this sort which have already been published, one of the best known being an incident reported in *Across the Line* by Anice Terhune, widow of dog-lover Albert Payson Terhune. The author of many books about dogs had himself written a statement before his death in 1942 in which he wondered what comes after. "Is it annihilation?" he asked, or is it a personal and very real future life? "The last named," he stated firmly, "is my own rock-fast belief."

After Terhune's death Anice, who had been married to him for forty happy years, had to force herself to carry on with certain business commitments. One thing which particularly worried her was that she could not locate some very important papers which her lawyers were pressuring her to find—the pedigrees of all the collies in her kennels. She had looked everywhere to no avail, and then finally had slumped at her husband's desk, dejected and worried.

Just then, she writes: "Bert's voice—dear and familiar—suddenly startled me. It came clear, distinct and natural. 'Look *behind* you, little girl!' he said. 'They're all there.'" He repeated this, and she turned around. Then her hand seemed drawn to a drawer into which she had previously looked fruitlessly. But this time, down in the midst of a packet of papers, she found the ones she wanted.

Shortly after this Anice Terhune visited the friend of a friend, who did automatic writing and got messages for her from her husband. Eventually she learned this means of communication herself, and through it she received much encouragement, as well as a good bit of evidence. Through the writing Bert insisted, "If you love me, tell the fact of my actually living to everyone we know."

She did better than that. She told it to the world.

It isn't just husbands who serve as guardian angels. Mothers are very good at it also. Josephine Conte of Tucson, Arizona, had no belief whatever in an afterlife when her mother, Francesca Polizzi, who had died in 1950, took her welfare in charge. While impressed, Josephine wasn't in the least convinced by a dream she had in 1952. Jo had had several fibroid tumors removed, and the doctor had told her she would never be able to have a child. He had even said he'd help her adopt one if she wished.

Since she had no hope of becoming pregnant, she was rather surprised one night by a dream in which she saw her mother crocheting a baby blanket. She asked her who it was for and was told, "For you. You're going to have a baby." Jo didn't believe it then, but shortly afterward she began to experience the symptoms of pregnancy, and in January, 1953, she gave birth to Francine, named in honor of Mrs. Polizzi.

Her precognitive dream was interesting, but Jo still wasn't convinced that her mother had survived death. After all, her own subconscious mind may have observed the symptoms of pregnancy before her conscious mind did, and have taken the means of a dream to inform her. But one night early in May, 1962, certain events occurred that drastically changed her thinking.

"I woke up and went to the bathroom," Jo told me. "When I returned and started to get back into bed, my mother was suddenly sitting beside me on the edge of the bed. I panicked, of course, and she reached out and took my hand because I was shaking so badly. She was as real looking and felt as warm to the touch as she ever had in life. She was dressed in the usual type of drab, dark dress that she had always preferred. Her hair was in a bun, exactly as she had worn it when she passed on. She seemed at rest, happy and peaceful, very loving, her natural self. And she was as real and solid as she had ever been in her life. She spoke softly, telling me not to be frightened, and soon I began to get over my alarm and to listen to what she was saying. She had come to offer me an entirely new and different experience.

" 'You have had a hard life,' she said, 'and you deserve a rest. Come with me.'

"I had loved my mother so much," Jo went on. "She was my right arm, and I was certainly tempted to join her. But my little son Joe was only two years old, and my daughter Francine was nine, so I said no to her. She said, 'All right, honey,' and she disappeared."

The next night at about the same time Jo's mother appeared to her in the same way, and again the following night. And each time the same thing happened. Mrs. Polizzi asked if she wouldn't like to join her in her realm. And Jo said once again, "Mama, you know I would love to, but Joe is only two years old. I can't leave such a baby." The third night Jo promised, "After I've raised the kids, I'll be glad to come with you." This time her mother took both her hands, and looked at her seriously. "All right," she said, "if you insist you want to stay there, then you'll have to see a doctor. You're sick."

Jo Conte promised to do that and went to sleep. She was actually feeling fine, and might not have followed through with it; but the next morning when she awoke she found the telephone in her hand. It was not a bedside phone. She'd had to get up and walk over to the breakfast bar for it, and this she did not remember doing. Trying to understand what was going on, she recalled her midnight promise and decided that her mother was making sure the call was made. So she phoned her doctor for an appointment.

When Dr. Donald F. Griess asked her how she felt, she said, "I feel fine, but just came for a check-up." People don't often tell their physicians that their deceased mother had urged them to get medical attention.

When the doctor examined Jo, he found a cyst under her left arm. It had been there for years. In fact, fifteen years before, when she lived in Brooklyn, New York, a doctor had discovered it. He had told her then it was nothing to worry about and just to leave it alone. She was so convinced that she should leave it alone that when Dr. Griess said, "I think I'll remove that," she replied, "Oh, no you don't."

It was a slight operation that could be done right there in his office, but Jo was very opposed to it. "The doctor had to practically strap me down in order to do it," she says. "All the while he was removing it he was telling me he would show me what a cyst looked like. In fact, after he removed it he started to slice it in order to let me see how they look inside."

But then she saw the expression on his face change. "I think I'll send this for a biopsy," he said.

"Why, if it's just a cyst?" she asked. He explained that sometimes they were known to change and become malignant and that this didn't look good to him. So he sent a sample to the laboratory. It was returned with a positive report—a very rare type of cancer. Jo then had to go to the hospital to have adjoining lymph nodes and tissue removed. Fortunately, she recovered completely. And she gave thanks all the while to her mother, who had made a "believer" out of her.

Best-selling British novelist Ursula Bloom had a somewhat similar experience, receiving a warning from her dead mother that may have saved her from going blind. She had been suffering violent headaches, and a specialist said he could numb the affected part of the head permanently. She agreed to such an operation.

"That night," Ursula said, "a medium friend, who had not been in touch for three weeks, rang up and told me in detail what I had done. My mother wanted to warn me, she said—if I had the operation I would go blind."

Miss Bloom's doctor assured her there was no possibility of blindness, so she decided to go ahead anyway.

"But the medium kept ringing," she said. "Mother would not let her be. Finally I asked, 'Will my mother hear what I tell you?' She said yes, so I passed on a message.

" 'Look here,' I said, 'I can't live in this pain. For the first time I have been offered release from it. If it is dangerous, then prove it.' "

Later that very day the novelist was invited to meet someone who had been cured of migraine by such an operation. But the woman was blind.

"It was the result, I learned, of a slip during the operation—by the same specialist! I cancelled my appointment immediately and rang the medium. She was very calm. 'Good,' she said. 'Your mother has managed to explain.' There were no more messages, then or ever since."

Miss Bloom's headaches were later cured by other means. She ended her statement: "Life after death? I could never get more positive proof. I am as skeptical as ever of so-called evidence—but what other explanation can there be?"

Deloris Sanders, another of my Tucson, Arizona, friends, may be one of those psychics who acquired unusual talents because of a blow on the head. We have no way of knowing if she had the ability normally before her third birthday, but since the automobile accident in which she was then involved she has been exhibiting ESP as a matter of habit. In her family there has been an unusual pattern of tragic automobile accidents in which the men were killed.

Deloris was born in 1932 in Terre Haute, Indiana, to Herbert and Rose Hart. When she was three she was riding in an automobile which was badly damaged when hit by another car. Her grandfather, who was driving, was severely injured and her great-grandfather, sitting beside him in front, was killed instantly. Deloris, in the back seat, had the top of her head almost lifted off by a sheet of window glass. Taken to St. Anthony's Hospital, she was expected to die momentarily. But she survived, with no memory of the past for about two months, and she was paralyzed from the waist down. Fortunately she was able to learn to walk again and achieved complete mobility.

For several days after the accident she was in such critical condition that she was kept isolated in a hospital room with no one but nurses to look after her. Even her parents weren't allowed to see her. Yet she says that a lady stayed there with her all the time. This lady just stood at the foot of the bed with her hands on the white metal rail and beamed on her, encouraging her with her love to get well.

"She never touched me," Deloris recalls. "But she smiled at me and sent me her healing love to the extent that I felt as if I was wrapped in it, like in a warm blanket. I only saw her during the crisis, but I have never forgotten what she looked like."

Deloris's mother, who gave me her independent testimony relating to this incident, said she was surprised to learn that someone had been allowed into the room, when the child's own parents were refused admittance; but Deloris kept asking for the nice lady she insisted had been visiting her. The nurses assured Mrs. Hart that no one had been in there. Finally, the little girl was asked to tell what this lady looked like. She described someone quite small, with black hair, brown eyes and light skin. This was an exact description of her father's mother, Belle Hart, who had died when her son was about fifteen years old. Belle had been quite petite, no more than four feet eleven inches tall, weighing about ninety-eight pounds. Deloris has since seen a picture of this grandmother, whom she definitely identified as her hospital lady. She had never seen any likeness of her grandmother before her hospital experience, because her father's only picture of his mother had always been kept in a trunk with other mementos.

After Deloris grew up she married Ernie Sanders of Tucson and had two sons, Gary and Mark. On October 21, 1962, when Mark, the youngest boy, was ten years old, Ernie and Mark were both killed instantly in an automobile accident on the Nogales Highway.

Gary Sanders has apparently inherited his mother's psychic abilities. He is a great huntsman, and one cold day about six months after the accident, when he was fourteen years old, he was javalina hunting with two older men in the mountains above the town of Safford. "He hadn't listened to me," says Deloris, "and wasn't dressed warmly enough." During the hunt he became separated from his companions and was lost. After he had been wandering around in circles for what seemed hours, the sun set and it began to snow. Gary was frightened, and he sat down on a rock to reconnoiter.

Suddenly, about twenty feet in front of him near a tree he saw a man standing. It wasn't one of the hunters, for no gun was visible. Gary walked toward him for help and soon was close enough to recognize his father.

"Come with me, son," said Ernie's ghost, reaching out his hand. The boy took it and walked alongside him until they found their way back to his companions. His father made no footprints on the snow. When they were within three or four feet of the other hunters, who had been searching for Gary, Ernie disappeared, but not before he had told the boy to tell his mother not to grieve because he was all right.

Gary was so appalled and frightened by his experience that it was some time before he got up nerve to tell his mother about it. But she, of course, understood. She feels her husband's presence often, although she hasn't actually seen him as her son did.

Famous Hollywood actress Doris Day was bereft when her husband, Marty Melcher, died suddenly of a heart attack a few years ago.

"I was totally and completely lost without Marty," she said. "I hated everyone and everything. I turned my back on everyone who loved me. I even hated God for what He had done." The man who had masterminded her career for fifteen years, had just arranged for the *Doris Day Show*, a TV package with CBS, when he died. After that, Doris recalls, "I didn't want to do the show." She refused to begin work on it until, she says, "Marty came to me and told me what I had to do—I had to go on. After that, there was a great awakening and my heart was no longer heavy." Doing the show was the best therapy in the world for her, she admitted. "I found that gradually the heartbreak went away."

Now she believes Marty's alive in another world and still guides her career. He advises her just as he did when he was alive. "I benefit just as much from his wisdom and guidance today as I did when he was physically with me," she said.

Another show business personality who admits to getting help in curious ways is actor Peter Sellers, who is a natural psychic. He told the London *Sunday Express* that he clearly hears a spirit voice that guides him, and that he recognizes it as his mother's. Peg, he said, who passed on in 1967, "comes through frequently now, giving me help and advice. Of course we were so close that the bond couldn't possibly have been broken by her passing. We talk just as if she were still alive."

To conclude our guardian angels, we have a heartwarming story involving a young boy who was able to save another child from what might have been a death similar to his own. Susan K. Fine of Park Forest, Illinois, tells me that this miracle occurred when she was seven years old and lived in Midland, Michigan. During one afternoon in 1953 she and some little friends had been telling ghost stories, so that night she was too afraid to sleep. She crept to the top of the steep, narrow stairway, hoping her parents might let her come down with them.

At the head of the stairs her foot caught on the front of her robe and she started to fall; but as her head and shoulders lurched forward, she felt a hand grip her left arm and pull her backward until she was sitting on the top step.

"Don't hold me so hard," she complained, thinking it was her father who had saved her from the fall. "You're hurting me, Daddy."

Her father, James Davis, was downstairs. He came running when he heard her cry, calling, "What's the matter, Sue?" If it was not her father who had caught her, then who was it? She turned around quickly, but she could see no one behind her, and the pressure on her arm let up. She had a swollen red mark there, however, to prove that she had been caught and held in a very strong grip.

It was not until five years later, says Susan, that she learned the rest of her story. An elderly lady, Mrs. Sasse, visited their home for a sentimental look, saying that her father had built the place some eighty years previously and that she had grown up there. As the woman toured the house, she paused at the stairway. "How I hate those steps!" she said. "They killed my brother."

Mrs. Sasse then told them that her brother, a husky twelve-year-old, had been recovering from an infectious illness. Starting downstairs for a drink of water, he tripped on the steps and fell, breaking his neck.

Susan noticed that her father's face paled as Mrs. Sasse talked. Then, since what he had tried to tell himself was an illusion had been confirmed, he revealed to Susan what he had seen on the night she almost fell when she was seven years old. "As I looked up the stairs," he said, "I saw a young boy behind you. He was smiling; but when you turned to see who it was, he vanished."

To confirm Susan's story, her brother, Timothy "Jay" Davis of Elgin Academy, Elgin, Illinois, wrote me as follows: "I have read my sister's account of what happened to her on the stairs when we were children. We talked about it a lot while I was growing up. My father doesn't like to discuss it, but when I asked him if it was true, he said it was."

It looks as if this little spirit boy may have remained in the house for some time, possibly because he enjoyed the company of the children in the family. At least, he was there when he was needed to perform his guardian angel stint.

There are undoubtedly many who couldn't care less for this sort of afterlife activity. They may be off buzzing about somewhere on their own pursuits. But from the evidence in this chapter, if you have recently lost someone who loves you very much, it seems a reasonable assumption that he or she will continue to be around to help out whenever it is necessary. Even if they are unable to produce physical phenomena, they may frequently be sending you helpful thoughts when you need them.

IX

MOMENTS MUSICAL

IT IS NOT difficult, is it, to surmise that if a great composer died and still continued to remain the conscious entity he had been on earth, he might be interested in letting us know about it? What better way than to try to send a composition from the "other side" that had enough of his characteristics that there could be no doubt it was his work? If we are to believe the records, there seems to have been just such effort on the part of deceased composers to get their messages of continued existence through to us. The only problem is that they have no means to use but the body and mind of an earth person, and that may cause complications. It certainly would be difficult if they used someone with musical training who already had his own notions about what to do with his hands on a keyboard. Perhaps that is why mostly untrained people are the recipients of this largesse from beyond.

Apparently the hands can be controlled on the piano keys in the same way that they are when automatic writing is done on the typewriter, or by pen or pencil. A spontaneous instance of this occurred to the mother of a close friend of mine. Mrs. Irene H., a musician of almost professional caliber, was sitting at her piano one day, playing one of her own light, popular compositions. She was in a good mood and so was her music as she happily sat there whiling away some time. Suddenly she felt a tremendous pressure on both her hands and they started playing a funeral dirge. There was no reason for it that Irene knew of, but she could not control her hands; they were being forced to play solemn and melancholy music at an extremely slow pace. After a few moments the pressure on her hands was released and she was able to resume her own tempo. An hour later a bulletin came over the radio that the submarine *Thresher* had been lost with all on board.

Hands grasped or minds guided by some unseen force are today producing some highly interesting compositions. There are several persons in various parts of the world becoming known publicly because, without musical educations and while in something like trance conditions, they are composing and playing music quite beyond their normal talents.

A New Zealand housewife in her thirties named Shirley Waklyn was featured in a Wellington newspaper, the *Dominion* in December, 1971, because she maintained that the various pieces of music she has written over the past ten years have been composed at the insistence of someone "on the other side." Shirley, who is clairvoyant, plays on a piano once owned by a well-known "dead" composer, L. D. Austin. Whether or not it is Austin who produces the compositions through her is not stated, but she had no musical training and cannot even read her own scores. "Notation means nothing to me," she said. "I feel as if I'm paralyzed, that something within me is taken over." She gets a whole concept of what is going to happen in a flash, but "I have to really work at getting it down," she says.

Shirley submitted her second psychic piece to a film producer in 1961. It was accepted, professionally scored and included in an Australian ballet.

Asked for the purpose behind her inspired music, Shirley said, "I feel it is given as proof there is life hereafter."

Others are said to be receiving the attention of much more famous composers. The best known of these is a British woman named Rosemary Brown, who describes some of her communicants in her book *Unfinished Symphonies:*

> The first time I saw Franz Liszt, who died in 1886, I was about seven years old. All he said then, speaking slowly because

I was a child, was that when he had lived in this world he had been a composer and a pianist. He then told me: "When you grow up I will come back and give you music."

Today Liszt is the leader of a group of famous composers who visit me at my home in England and give me their new compositions. The others are Chopin, Schubert, Beethoven, Bach, Brahms, Schumann, Debussy, Grieg, Berlioz, and Rachmaninoff. Others, such as Albert Schweitzer, appear briefly, give me a little music, then don't return for a long time. (Mozart, for example, has been just three times.) But after six years of work I have today, in drawers and cupboards, some four hundred pieces of music—songs, piano pieces, some incomplete string quartets, the beginning of an opera, as well as some partly completed concertos and symphonies.

Rosemary Brown seems to be just a typical middle-class housewife, but she has been strongly psychic all her life, and this began to show exciting results when her music appeared. The work involved has been tremendous, she says, because she had a very limited musical education. She knew little about how to write down notes or how to orchestrate. There has also been the problem of the controversy she aroused. When her first long-playing record was launched in May, 1970, it consisted of eight different composers' "other side" music, and critics have been arguing about it ever since. She has been consistently investigated, and her words and music have been put through countless examinations. She has voluntarily taken musical tests, intelligence tests, psychological tests, psychic tests—every test imaginable.

Most people who criticize her compositions are convinced that she must have had a very thorough musical education when she was young. Fortunately, having lived in the same house all her life makes it easier for her to refute this. Those who wish to check on the facts of her personal history can do so with her doctor and family friends who have known her all her life.

She says:

> One musician suggested that I had actually had prolonged and advanced musical training, and then suffered from amnesia,

which caused me to forget this alleged training. My family doctor was able to dismiss this as complete nonsense, and most of the facts concerning my life can be—and have been—quite easily checked.

Anyone knowledgeable about music realizes that I would have to be very near a musical genius to have achieved all this alone, and most of the non-musical skeptics do not realize how very difficult it is to compose. Perhaps most competent musicians with a flair for extemporizing can take any ordinary song and play it with a classical flavor—even though that would be impossible for me to do as I cannot extemporize at all. But actually *composing* in different composers' styles—well, that is quite another thing.

Though not all of the music I have written down is superb —the composers are limited by my limitations at present—and the difficulties of transmission—I would surely have had to be a very brilliant musician indeed to have written all those different styles of music myself.

The fact that while the music is like that of say, Liszt or Chopin, it is not always *good* Liszt or Chopin, makes most critics, unfamiliar with the problems and difficulties of mediumship, think the music does not come from the great composers themselves. Uninformed critics tend to have opinions such as Thelma Foreshaw of the Sydney (Australia) *Morning Herald*, who had "a jolly good laugh at old Rosemary" who was undoubtedly "divinely crazed" because she thought she had a "cozy association with great minds in the hereafter."

Much more objective and encouraging are the statements of such musicians as Hephzibah Menuhin, who said of Mrs. Brown: "There is no question but that she is a very sincere woman. The music is absolutely in the style of these composers." Composer Richard Rodney Bennett said: "I've no doubt she's psychic. She's told me things about myself she just couldn't have known about. I was having trouble with a piece of music and she passed along Debussy's recommendation—which worked. . . . A lot of people can improvise but you couldn't fake music like this without years of training. I couldn't have faked some of the Beethoven myself."

Why does something as controversial as this come at all? Sir

Donald Tovey, a distinguished musician, composer, and musical critic who died in 1940 has written an explanation through Rosemary: "We are not transmitting music to Rosemary Brown simply for the sake of offering possible pleasure in listening thereto; it is the implications relevant to this phenomenon which we hope will stimulate sensible and sensitive interest and stir many who are intelligent and impartial to consider and explore the unknown regions of man's mind and psyche.

"When man has plumbed the mysterious depth of his veiled consciousness he will then be able to soar to correspondingly greater heights."

Jesse Shepard, later known as Francis Grierson, under which name he wrote a number of popular books, was for a long time famous as "the musical medium." He did not write down his compositions, but for many years he played "marvelous instantaneous compositions on the piano" purporting to come through the control of deceased composers. Born in England but reared in the United States, he performed for the famous of this country and the crowned heads of Europe in the latter part of the last century and the first part of this century and won wide acclaim for many years. Vincent Gaddis says in "Jesse Shepard the Musical Medium" in *Fate* (June, 1972):

> Whatever the source of his inspiration, Shepard was a master pianist whose improvisations left his listeners dumbfounded. Varied in style, emotionally powerful, his music sometimes had a delicate lilting beauty; at other times it was haunting, primitive. His renditions roamed the world and the centuries. With processions of chords, he evoked the antiquity of Egypt, the mystery of India, the agelessness of China and the sophistication of the West.

Unlike Rosemary Brown, Shepard did not commit his music to paper. But when he played he did purport to be under the control of many of the same composers. Prince Adam Wisniewski wrote of his Liszt impersonations in *Vessillo Spiritista*:

> Notwithstanding this extraordinarily complex technique, the harmony was admirable, such as no one present had ever known

paralleled even by Liszt himself, whom I personally knew and in whom passion and delicacy were united. In the circle were musicians who, like myself, had heard the greatest pianists in Europe, but we can say that we never heard such truly supernatural execution.

Mozart and Berlioz also contributed to the enjoyment of the listeners at this concert, and then came Chopin. He entertained with the expressive tones that distinguish his compositions, and played first a fantasia followed by haunting and exquisite melodies "with a pianissimo of diminishing notes and tones full of despair—a prayer to God for Poland."

That Chopin really gets around . . . if we are to believe all we read about him these days. According to Jim Kenner in "Chopin Guides Her Hands" (*Fate*, March, 1973), Mrs. Karin Harms, an eighty-year-old woman of Copenhagen, has been in contact with Chopin for about nine years. This amazing woman took piano lessons for only three months, and that was forty-eight years ago; but she now plays intricate etudes, polonaises, mazurkas, sonatas and other complicated works—"all Chopinesque music which requires subtlety and technical skill."

Mrs. Harms told Kenner that Chopin talks to her. "We practice together," she said, "and he dictates his compositions to me. Since I cannot read or write regular musical notes, we have worked out a system of letters which I am able to translate into music."

Mrs. Harms presented several recitals in Denmark in 1971 and 1972 which, Kenner says, "left critics amazed. They say that her pieces seem to be authentically those of the great Polish-French composer who died in 1849."

Kenner goes on: "Hans Voigt, music critic for the country's leading daily newspaper, *Berlingske Tidende*, told me, 'Mrs. Harms knows quite a lot of the ways in which Chopin treated his music, the way he expressed himself in music. And after all, this cannot be a fraud from her side. The concerts she has given were not static. There was something there from the inspiration of Chopin, something more than herself. She certainly seemed sincere to me.' "

"Seen entirely pianistically," wrote Hans Voigt in his critique published in the *Berlingske Tidende*, "Mrs. Harms' presentation was impressive in many ways. Chopin's melodic phraseology, tonality and certain sides of the emotional quality which mark his productions were remarkably well performed."

The Copenhagen daily, *Politiken*, commented, "Chopin was unmistakable in these works."

In addition, music critic Borge Friis said, "I have listened to Mrs. Harms playing the piano and her style is indeed Chopin-like. She has musical talent and she interprets Chopin well. The audiences at her solo concerts were deeply impressed. It is certainly amazing that she can play this way with only three months of formal piano lessons. I've been a critic for many years now and I must admit that I've never come across a case like this before."

What better way for a former composer or musician to be a guardian angel to someone on earth than to help him with his homework? Some claim that many brilliant children are prodigies because they have attracted the attention of a spirit with like interests and have his aid while practicing.

Nicolo Paganini (1782–1840) was said to have been able to compose difficult violin pieces while standing on the stage apparently in trance. Perhaps because he once had this ability, he now likes to encourage those on earth with similar talents. Or perhaps he was attached for another reason to Florizel von Reuter, eighty-two-year-old American violinist and composer, conductor and music teacher, who began life as a violin prodigy. Before Florizel's birth, his mother wanted more than anything for him to become a famous musician, preferably a violinist. The name best known to her was Paganini, so she implored his spirit to guide her unborn child. According to the late British newspaperman Hannen Swaffer, quoted in *Psychic News* (May 20, 1972), "She besought him night and day to influence her baby." When the child was born she dedicated him to the ideal for which she had striven. Florizel accepted the responsibility from his earliest youth, amazing his teachers, not only with his skill but also with his feats of memory. He often spoke of someone who was with him when he practiced. "Some old master is always listening," he said. "I mustn't disappoint him."

Von Reuter said in his book *Psychical Experiences of a Musician* that it was not until he was thirty that he began his search for survival evidence. One of his first spirit communicators was Paganini, who spoke at a voice sitting. Florizel was told: "There is a great violinist present who wants to greet the young man. He says his name is Paganini." Then the great violinist, purporting to speak, thanked Florizel's mother for having influenced him to become interested in the child and his music.

Mrs. von Reuter, also present at the séance, said, "Florizel plays all your twenty-four caprices."

"I know," was the answer. "I have often been present in concerts where he has performed them."

Florizel von Reuter says he doesn't doubt it for a moment. Sometimes when he has been playing the violin he has felt his hands moved to a better fingering than the one he had in mind, and he knew it was Paganini helping him.

So now our famous composers are not only attempting to get their music through to us, but being our guardian angels as well! There is more to come. If they are still hanging around and wanting to make their presence known, might one not attempt to get some kind of a message through that would help to find a lost composition? Wouldn't he be likely to think that would bring good evidence of his continued activity and interest?

There are a number of people who believe this was once accomplished by a man who had been dead for many years.

Composer Robert Schumann (1819–1856) not only believed he received inspiration from his predecessors during his music writing career while on earth, but he apparently continued his interest in his compositions after his death. The finding of a lost manuscript of his is an interesting story which brings at least enough evidence of spirit communication to engage our interest.

For many years a group of some thirty people had been sitting regularly in London in an effort to communicate. They were led by Baron Erik Palmstierna, who was Swedish Minister to the Court of St. James from 1920 to 1937. The two strongest mediums of this circle were Adila Fachiri and her sister, Jelly (pronounced Yaley) d'Arànyi, both famous violinists of the day. (If it were generally known how many groups of prominent people have sat, and for that matter, are sitting today attempting spirit communication, probably the whole public attitude toward the subject would change. It would be the "in" thing to do. Certainly in many communities it is the literati who are the most active in developing their psychic abilities. The usual picture of frustrated widows and kookie cranks as the only participants in such activity is highly limited and undiscerning.)

Baron Palmstierna has written in *Horizons of Immortality* that it had been discovered by accident that Adila Fachiri possessed "the rare gift of transmitting spiritual waves in a waking state and fully conscious, never falling into a trance." It was through her interest and devotion to the task that messages were received, and replies were frequently given even to mental questions which had not been spoken orally. The usual means of communication indulged in by the group was a sort of homemade Ouija board. Letters of the alphabet had been drawn in a circle; and a small glass placed in the center was used as a pointer, working when the hands of two or three members of the group were touching it. This is one of the most laborious means of communication, but it was apparently preferred by the spirits who were active with the Palmstierna circle.

Because of the prominence of the members of this group and their interest in cultural pursuits, music and art figured largely in the conversations between worlds. It was in March, 1933, that the first message purporting to come from Robert Schumann was received. To me it seems very fitting that Schumann would be the one who has been able to give psychical literature one of its best illustrations of evidence for communication from the world of spirit. This is because the careful check I have made of the history of his illness indicates that he himself had become increasingly mediumistic during his lifetime. Yet because he succumbed at the early age of forty-four to a brain tumor, he has gone down in history as the famous composer who went insane. As his illness increased and the pressure on his brain became more and more intolerable, it is his psychic experiences that have always been quoted as presumptive support of the theory that he was crazy.

Robert Alexander Schumann was one of the most lovable men in the history of music. Daniel G. Mason said of him in an article in

The International Cyclopedia of Music and Musicians: "Everything about him wins our admiring affection; the fresh youthful note in his music, with its heaven-soaring melodies, clashing harmonies, and rushing rhythms; the impetuous, uncalculating generosity of his nature, as shown in his letters as well as his music; his very weaknesses —such as the frequent ineffectiveness of his writing for orchestra, the unhealthy subjectivity of his temperament, even his tragic loss of mental power in middle life and early death; and above all, his ardent loyalty to his great fellow-musicians. If all the world loves a lover, then no one can help loving Schumann."

While quite young he had met Clara Wieck, the daughter of his piano teacher, and from then on his love for her was the ruling force of his life—except for his passion for music. Yet his wife was also one of his biggest problems. Although he loved her dearly, their marriage was not an unqualified success. Because of an injury to one of his fingers, Clara was a better and more successful concert pianist than he. Neither was it easy for him to make a living with his musical work. As time went on he retired increasingly into himself. In 1854, his forty-fourth year, his health failed altogether, and in his misery he threw himself into the Rhine River. He was rescued, but, aware of the mental condition he was in, he had himself committed to an asylum, where he died in Clara's arms, July 29, 1856.

Clara's arms had been otherwise occupied for some time, if rumor is to be believed. Just six months before Robert's decline began, the Schumanns had met that rising young genius, Johannes Brahms. He was the protégé of Joseph Joachim, one of the world's foremost violinists, who was the reigning celebrity of Schumann's day. When Joseph Joachim brought Brahms to visit the Schumanns at Dusseldorf, Johannes and Clara clicked at once. Whether or not they became lovers during Robert Schumann's lifetime, less than a year after Schumann was incarcerated in the asylum they went on a five-day pleasure trip with only Clara's maid to chaperone them. In the years that followed, whenever they traveled together, Brahms's shoes were always seen outside Clara's door at night. In those days people raised eyebrows at such behavior.

A number of books which describe Schumann's life and music all point out the various psychic experiences he had as evidence of his approaching insanity. Their writers obviously didn't know that such experiences are everyday occurrences with those who have mediumistic talents, and so they always refer to such incidents as his deranged hallucinations. The fact that an autopsy revealed an osseous growth that had exerted increasing pressure on his brain has been thought to prove that his mind was affected.

Robert Schumann's first psychic episode to be reported occurred as early as 1839, when news of his brother's serious illness reached him in Vienna and he returned to Leipzig. He wrote to Clara that while on the train en route he heard a whole choral of trumpets, and he later learned that his brother had died at just that time. This event, which would be considered evidence of supernormal knowledge by many of us, was referred to by one of his biographers as "the first of the aural hallucinations." Later he started attending Spiritualist meetings on occasion. Then he began to insist that the deceased Beethoven was trying to communicate with him by raps. Beethoven identified himself by knocks in the rhythm of the figure that begins his Fifth Symphony—*da, da, da, dum.*

Schumann frequently became oblivious to everything that was going on about him. A mild trance state? Then he began to hear premonitory voices. Soon he was "peopling his own private world with phantasms which became increasingly evil." We cannot insist that this was not his insidious insanity creeping up on him. Yet again, those who have psychic powers without realizing it and knowing how to protect themselves have sometimes given evidence of having become possessed, or at least influenced, by malevolent entities. I sometimes wonder if many who are adjudged insane might not just be so innocently psychic that they are unable to control voices which they are legitimately hearing.

The final musical composition of Schumann's life, a theme on which he wrote five variations for the piano, was sung to him in a dream by Schubert and Mendelssohn. Schumann did not hesitate to announce this fact, and since he threw himself into the Rhine shortly afterward, his biographers have avidly added it to the list of his curious mental aberrations. Yet Johannes Brahms thought enough of the theme to select it as the subject for his Four-Hand Schumann

Piano Variations, Opus 23. It bears a subtitle *Geisterthema*—The Spirits' Theme.

Back now to Baron Palmstierna's circle, meeting in London some eighty years later. Is it surprising that Schumann, a spirit who while on earth had experiences of the type I have mentioned, would now still be interested when activity of a similar nature was attempted? His old friend, the violinist Joseph Joachim was also busy communicating with this group because Adila Fachiri and Jelly d'Arànyi were his grandnieces. And if Schumann were to attempt to reveal his presence, what better way than to offer information known to no one present, in the hopes that it could be verified as evidence? The great composer therefore declared his hope that Jelly should find and ultimately play a work of his own for the violin which had not been published or performed and apparently was lost. It was his only violin concerto and was, as he recalled, in D Minor. Although it was not one of his best compositions, he said, he was very keen to hear it. Unfortunately, he was able to give, at the most, only clues as to how to go about locating it.

Members of the group immediately became intrigued with the mystery. They inquired everywhere they could possibly think of in London, but nobody there had ever heard of such a work by Schumann. About two weeks later Schumann offered his first clue: "Tell Tovey, Museum Weimar."

Professor Sir Donald Tovey, a well-known music critic of the day, was not at Weimar, however. He was located fairly easily in Edinburgh. He replied to Jelly's letter that although he had heard of such a concerto, he knew nothing about it. "It might have been destroyed," he concluded.

The spirits would have none of that. They continued their urgings to find the manuscript. Joseph Joachim suggested the *Hochschule für Musik* in Berlin as a likely place to look for the concerto. When asked why Schumann had spoken of Weimar, Joachim replied with characteristic gentleness, "My dear *kind* [child], we do not know everything."

When a query sent to the Hochschule Museum of Music was not answered, the spirits said it had not been delivered because the principal was away on a holiday.

Following the clues provided was a slow process, and lack of results was disheartening, but the communicants did not let up in their interest, even when the humans became discouraged. On August 22, 1933, a message was received by Mrs. Fachiri, who was vacationing in Scotland with her family at the same time that Baron Palmstierna was in Sweden. The statement was: "Remember to write to Palmstierna, reminding him to go and look up in Berlin the work of Schumann. He is so anxious for you to find it." When Adila asked for more directions which might help the Baron locate it, the spirit said: "We do not know where it is. There are several places where it may be. Do not think we know everything!"

The Baron found it! Inquiring in Berlin, he learned that the Schumann manuscripts had been moved from the Hochschule, but it was not known where they had been taken. A fortunate hint which he received from an unknown source led him to institute a search in the archives of another Berlin museum, now known as the *Deutsche Staatsbibliothek*, and there the lost manuscript was finally located. Then there was a lot of trouble getting it released, and when the permission finally came it was too late for Jelly to be the first to play it. Hitler saw to that. Violinist Yehudi Menuhin was by then also eager to introduce the work, but the Nazis refused permission to either Menuhin or d'Arànyi, giving it to Georg Kulenkampff to perform. Accompanied by the Berlin Philharmonic, he introduced the concerto on November 26, 1937, and Telefunken soon afterward released a record of his performance. Menuhin has since made a lovely recording of Schumann's lone violin concerto, with Sir John Barbirolli and the New York Philharmonic Orchestra, and has defended it staunchly, playing it in concerts all over the world.

After the circle members were successful in locating and releasing the manuscript, they did not mind their role becoming public. They felt that their success vindicated their efforts. When it was revealed that the Palmstierna circle had been responsible for discovering the lost manuscript a "big fuss" was made over it, according to Davidson Taylor in *Modern Music* for January, 1938. Some of this fuss was because of the purported interest the deceased Schumann took in the concerto's discovery. More of the fuss was because critics were inclined to quibble about the use of the word "lost" in reference to the work. It was not lost, according to Abraham Veinus in *The Concerto*—it merely "lay dormant." How long it might have lain dormant had not someone made a point to locate it, cannot be conjectured, but Veinus would probably not care had it never been discovered. He refers to it as "Schumann's most inspired failure," quite below his usual standard, a thoroughly uneven work.

My friend, the noted concert violinist Joan Field, says that Schumann naturally wrote better for the piano than the violin. She told me, "His writing for strings *was* awkward." Still, even Veinus admitted that the work in question contained an "heroic pattern unusual in his music." Because Veinus thinks of Schumann as having been far gone in his illness during the thirteen days in 1853 when he wrote the D Minor Concerto, he does not hesitate to speak of "the infelicities in the score—lapses in genuine inspiration." Yet he added, "It is a great inspiration as yet unmoulded into great music; nevertheless there are a few moments which no one with a sensitivity for important music would willingly forego."

The reason it had been tucked away on the shelves of the archives for so long was because violinist Joseph Joachim had also thought of it as a work composed during Schumann's mental collapse. Joachim put it tactfully, merely saying that he sensed a "certain fatigue" in the concerto. But he obviously did not think it worthy of public performance.

Instead of being an evidence of his illness, perhaps this concerto was actually a bit too modern for Schumann's contemporaries. Some of his earlier works, with the "unconventional harshness of their frequently dissonant harmonies" were a great stumbling block for Schumann's friends to accept. They greatly preferred the suave and clear Mendelssohn to him. Perhaps Schumann was right when, via the glass pointer and alphabet, he defended the concerto from the aspersions cast on it as being unbalanced. He said then that the criticism was only due to its being ahead of its time.

We cannot be sure, of course, that the spirit of Robert Schumann was the inspiration for the search instituted by this group. Yet why else would the circle have suddenly become so interested in digging out an unknown work as good as lost to the memory of contemporary persons? Whence came the impulse to insist that the group unearth an unknown piece of music which had been buried for the greater part of a century? Who in either world could have desired such a consummation more than the composer of the lost work himself?

X

CROSS CORRESPONDENCES

Some of the best evidence of continuity of thought purporting to exist after death is what are called cross correspondences, or a variety of messages on the same subject which have come through several mediums. I, myself, have had on a few occasions a simpler form of this, or what can more correctly be called "cross references." One that is rather interesting, a simple example of a message received from one sensitive and then confirmed by another, occurred to me in the winter of 1965 when I was in the state of Washington investigating the mediumship of Keith Milton Rhinehart. I spent most of my time in Seattle at Rhinehart's Aquarian Foundation, where I attended evening séances, development groups, and Sunday message services.

I have already given an account of this in my book *Confessions of a Psychic*, but it should also be mentioned here. On the night of Saturday, December 4, I had been invited by a club entirely independent from the Aquarian Foundation to lecture to their branch in Olympia, Washington. After the talk some of us were invited to the home of one of the members of the sponsoring organization for coffee, cake, and conversation. A man named Sam Miller, who was unknown to any of these people, apparently having attended the lecture by chance, accompanied us. He came with us, he declared, because of a mission he felt he must accomplish.

"I have something important to tell you about yourself," he advised me. So I sat down to talk with him about one of my favorite subjects, me. He asked for a deck of cards. The host didn't have any, and so, while my attention was turned to someone else, Sam Miller left for a moment. I later learned that he had made the host take him next door, where they awoke the neighbors to borrow a deck of cards!

When Sam returned he had me cut the deck several times, then he laid out some cards in front of me. After that he hardly looked at them, but began to rattle off the following statement, which I recorded: "Something completely different is going to happen to you. It will be good fortune for you and for others. It will put you in touch with forces and things of great moment and will concern large groups of people. It will change your entire life. Unusual forces are surrounding you. They have been gathering for quite some time.

"This thing that will happen to you is completely unusual. It will be the turning point of your life. It has been building up. Watch for it and don't be frightened when it happens. Follow through on it. A man will be associated with it."

To this day I don't know of any especially exciting and wonderful event in which a man was associated with me—well, actually, I do —but I mean one that could be the answer to this prediction. It could still happen, however. There is no time limit on it. The message itself, however, was confirmed in an interesting cross correspondence the following day.

I arrived back in Seattle from Olympia about 2 A.M. The next morning I awoke late and just had time to rush to the Aquarian Foundation for the church service. At no time did I talk to anyone about my message of the night before. The couple who had accompanied me to Olympia was scientifically oriented in their thinking and did not attend that church. Between 2 A.M. and 10 A.M. they were not likely to have spoken of my personal experience, least of all to anyone connected with Keith Rhinehart's group, and they have assured me they did not.

The prophecy of the night before was exciting enough that it was still in my mind, and so my question on my billet for the message service involved it. I happened to pick up a pencil with exceptionally light green lead, and the card, which is still in my possession, is almost indecipherable unless held very close to the eyes. My request was: "To my Guides. Explain Sam Miller's message."

The good spirit doctor who allegedly used the entranced Rhinehart for a sounding apparatus answered my question in this manner: "I sense as though the thing you have wondered about from your guides is very unusually accurate. There is a message you have received only within the past twenty-four hours and you couldn't believe it because it is too good."

I asked, "Is it true?"

"Of course it's true and a wonderful thing," the medium replied, adding, "You sometimes doubt too much."

Some of the things I had observed at the message services of Keith Milton Rhinehart had rather tended to indicate that his performance then was not fraudulent. One cannot guarantee anything about any medium who purports to produce physical phenomena in pitch dark, but Keith's Sunday message services were conducted in the light and his eyes were carefully bandaged. I know that most mediums who bandage their eyes leave a small viewpoint through which they can see. They work this so cleverly that it is not perceptible to witnesses, but it is almost invariably done so that they can read the billets. I have often checked Keith's bandages myself, however, and during the months I had observed him I don't think he was peeking. But even if he had been, the word "message" here was written so lightly that I doubt if he could have deciphered it without close scrutiny. Yet he spoke of my message, gave the fact that it had been recently received, which I did not indicate in my question, and stated that it was too good to be true, my exact reaction. So this was definitely a cross reference, or cross correspondence of a simple sort, from one medium and then from another.

Of course, instead of being proof that a surviving entity was giving me a message, this could more simply be explained as an example of telepathy—that the second medium was reading thoughts planted in my mind by the first one.

A cross reference of similar type involved the wonderful psychic and healer Olga Worrall and Arthur Ford. Let us review the story as it was told by the Reverend Canon William V. Rauscher, Rector of Christ Episcopal Church, Woodbury, New Jersey, in the first issue of *Spiritual Frontiers*, the quarterly journal of Spiritual Frontiers Fellowship. Olga and her late husband Ambrose Worrall always set aside a period as a quiet time each evening at nine o'clock, when they sent healing prayers to all those who "tuned in" to them. On the evening of Saturday, August 24, 1968, the Baltimore-based Worralls were visiting in Philadelphia, and among those sitting with them were the Reverend Robert J. Lewis and Canon Rauscher.

Olga began by giving a message to Father Lewis. "Bob," she said, "there is a Father John present. He is standing right by you. Do you know a Father John?"

Lewis did know a Father John. He had been the late vicar of All Saints, Hershey, Pennsylvania.

Father John, said Olga, was telling Father Lewis, "You are going to have your own church very soon." She added that Father John said, "You don't have a complete say now in your position, but you will."

Canon Rauscher explains that unknown to the Worralls, the Reverend Canon Gerald R. Minchin, the rector of St. Mary's Episcopal Church, Haddon Heights, where Father Lewis was the associate, had come to Lewis four days before and told him that he had decided to retire in December. He had not yet notified the bishop or the senior warden.

Olga went on, "Now they are placing a church right down over your head . . . just like that . . . right down over your head."

Six days after this sitting the senior warden came to Father Lewis and said that he had been informed by the canon of his retirement. He pledged his support to Lewis and had a conference with him about the possibility of his being called to be the rector of St. Mary's.

After this long buildup, here comes the cross reference, which Canon Rauscher deliberately hoped to receive as a test. Before Father Lewis's new position had been confirmed, Rauscher arranged a sitting with Arthur Ford for himself and Father Lewis, to see if this information received from Olga Worrall might be confirmed. It was. As soon as Ford went into trance, Fletcher, his control, congratulated Lewis on his new position.

Rauscher points out that it is quite unusual that an assistant such as Father Lewis should be offered the key position in an Episcopal church, but it is even more unusual that the event was seen in advance by two different psychics.

The above are extremely simple cross references. Those which are known as genuine cross correspondences are vastly more complicated. And the best of them are considered to be the nearest thing we have to scientific evidence for post-death survival of the human consciousness. Most of the classic cases came in the early part of this century purportedly from a specific group of recently deceased members of the Society for Psychical Research, London, who said they were trying to find a way to communicate the fact of their survival in a manner that would eliminate the possibility of telepathy by the subconscious minds of the mediums from minds of those still living.

These apparently all came about through the efforts of the spirit of Frederick W. H. Myers, poet, classical scholar, and one of the founders of the S.P.R. After his death in 1901, for many years mediums associated with the S.P.R. received messages purporting to come from him and a group of his close lifetime friends from Cambridge University, which included Professor Henry Sidgwick, Edmund Gurney and others.

Myers realized that for any communicator merely to say through a medium, "I am Myers," or "I am Henry Sidgwick" is no proof at all of identity. And if he says, "Do you remember this or that?" the answer from the sitter would have to be, "Yes, and because I do it is simpler to say that the medium got it telepathically from my living mind rather than from the dead."

In an effort to overcome these difficulties, the "other side group," as they came to be called, devised a method of demonstrating not only their continued existence but also their power to plan. They attempted to produce written messages which would show evidence of an obvious design which was not in any living mind. A group of mediums in various parts of the world who did automatic writing (and thus were referred to as automatists) began to receive highly complicated messages purporting to come from Myers, Gurney, Sidgwick, and others. When these various scripts produced by these automatists were compared, it was seen that certain classical references seemed to indicate a continuing stream of thought. It was the initial alertness of Miss Alice Johnson, secretary to the S.P.R. at the time, in discovering that a lot of material was coming through these various mediums that claimed to be from Myers and seemed to be related to the same general theses of classical antiquity, which caused the putting together of this information and the eventual deduction that coherent messages were being sent.

As an example of how this was done: a bit of Greek or Latin poetry may be given through one automatist, and a supplementary bit, not simply an echo of the first, is given to another automatist. "Thus," explains Dr. Gardner Murphy in "An Outline of Survival Evidence," "as Mrs. Verrall automatically gives a description of a painting which represents Pope Leo I at the gates of Rome, pleading with Attila not to sack the city, another message is given to Mrs. Holland, five thousand miles away in India, in the words: '*Ava Roma Immortalis*. How could I make it any clearer without giving her the clue?' In 'cross correspondences' . . . it is not repetition of motifs, but the development of complementary and related associations, that points to a common psychological origin for the many automatisms."

After Miss Johnson's discovery, an intensive study of the scripts of these automatists was undertaken by investigators for the S.P.R. and eventually the system of cross correspondences was recognized as the most comprehensive technique so far undertaken by any spirits in an effort to prove survival.

The investigating group consisted of, among others, Mrs. Eleänor (Nora) Sidgwick, widow of Henry, her brother Arthur James, 1st Earl of Balfour, Mr. J. G. Piddington, and Miss Johnson. Fortunately they were all persons of exceptional acumen, patience, and capacity for hard work, for it was a tricky business.

There were about twelve scattered automatists involved, who were referred to as the "this side group." They were all evidently quite powerful sensitives. The first of these was Mrs. Margaret Verrall, a lecturer in classics at Newnham College, Cambridge, and wife of Dr. Arthur W. Verrall, a well-known Cambridge classical scholar. Both Verralls were members of the Council of the S.P.R. She had been doing automatic writing for some years before her husband died in

1912; then, after his death, he apparently joined the "other side group" and became one of the band of communicators.

Miss Helen Verrall, Margaret's daughter, who afterwards became Mrs. W. H. Salter and was, with her husband, a lifelong active worker in the field of psychical research, also learned to be an automatist, and some of the cross correspondence scripts came through her.

Alice Kipling, sister of the famous author Rudyard Kipling, went to India at the age of sixteen and later married a British Army officer, John Fleming. A talented amateur poet, Mrs. Fleming first began automatic writing in 1893 for her own amusement, producing mostly verse during the first ten years. Then she read F.W.H. Myers's *Human Personality and Its Survival of Bodily Death*, which had been published posthumously. Beginning to realize from it that there might be something of interest in her scripts, she wrote to the S.P.R. and enclosed some of the material she had produced in India. From the beginning she used the pseudonym "Mrs. Holland" because of her fear of the ridicule of her family, who were set against such "foolishness."

Shortly after she read Myers's great work, "Mrs. Holland's" scripts changed in character. Where they had been mostly poetry before, they were now prose purporting to come from Myers, Gurney, Sidgwick and others. It is natural to suspect that her reading of Myers's book had put the idea into her subconscious mind to communicate with him and his friends. The fact that she received from them a lot of information she had no normal way of knowing somewhat helps to refute this argument. Also, her scripts revealed the personalities and characters of these men whom she had not known in life.

Myers, continuing to be as beautifully articulate, if wordy, after death as before, explained his condition through "Mrs. Holland's" scripts as follows:

> To believe that the mere act of death enables a spirit to understand the whole mystery of death is as absurd as to imagine that the act of birth enables an infant to understand the whole mystery of life. I am still groping, surmising, conjecturing.

The experience is different for each one of us. . . . One was here lately who could not believe that he was dead; he accepted the new conditions as a certain stage in the treatment of his illness. . . . It may be that those who die suddenly suffer no prolonged obscuration of consciousness, but for my own experience the unconsciousness was exceedingly prolonged. . . . If it were possible for the soul to die back into earth life again I should die from sheer yearning to reach you, to tell you that all we imagine is not half wonderful enough for the truth, that immortality, instead of being a beautiful dream, is the one, the only reality, the strong golden thread on which all the illusions of all the lives are strung. . . . The reality is infinitely more wonderful than our most daring conjectures. . . . Does any of this reach you, reach anyone, or am I only wailing as the wind wails—wordless and unheeded?

In one of "Mrs. Holland's" earliest scripts, the communicating Myers wrote a letter to Mrs. Verrall, of whom "Mrs. Holland" had never heard. He said: "My dear Mrs. Verrall, I am very anxious to speak to some of the old friends, Miss J. and to A. W." There followed a long description of an elderly gentleman who was obviously Mr. A. W. Verrall. Then he wrote:

It is like entrusting a message on which infinite importance depends to a sleeping person. Get a proof, try for a proof if you feel this is a waste of time. . . . Send this to Mrs. Verrall, 5 Selwyn Gardens, Cambridge.

This was among the scripts "Mrs. Holland" sent Miss Johnson, who recognized that the description was very appropriate to Dr. Verrall. She also knew that the address was perfectly correct. So she sent the message onward. When Mrs. Verrall read the script, she supported Miss Johnson in her enthusiasm for it. So "Mrs. Holland" was accepted as one of the "this side group."

Two other primary mediums involved were Mrs. Willett and Mrs. Leonore Piper. "Willett" was the pseudonym for Mrs. Winifred Coombe-Tennant, a London woman of such prominence that she was to serve as a delegate to the Assembly of the League of Nations in 1922. In her early girlhood she had discovered that she possessed the power of automatic writing, but having no one to guide or advise her, she soon gave up the practice. After the death of her daughter in 1907, she became interested again, and her correspondence with Mrs. Verrall led her to begin to produce scripts which were found to be interrelated with those of several others of the group of automatists.

Mrs. Piper of Boston was the only American who participated in the S.P.R. cross correspondences. She was one of the greatest mediums who ever lived, and her integrity was checked frequently by investigators and discovered to be above reproach. Once she was even watched by private detectives to see if she was making surreptitious inquiries for the purpose of obtaining information which might later appear to be supernormally acquired. The result of this investigation was completely satisfactory; not the slightest indication of anything underhanded or dishonest was found.

Lesser known mediums of the "this side group" were a Mrs. Forbes and a brother and his sisters who were identified only as "the Macs."

H. F. Saltmarsh in *Evidence of Personal Survival from Cross Correspondences* wrote: "Now Myers, as an experienced psychical researcher, was fully aware of the difficulty of eliminating the possibility of explaining away evidential messages by telepathy or clairvoyance." Although much material purporting to be evidence of personal survival involves information known to the deceased, it is incapable of verification unless some living person also knows it, or has known it in the past and possibly forgotten it. Yet if this is true, then the information could be said to come by telepathy from the living person's mind—and parapsychologists, being strictly objective, have to make that presumption.

"In these circumstances," says Saltmarsh, "it is hard to imagine any possible evidence which could bring unequivocal proof of survival. Now Myers, as I have said, was fully aware of all this, and what makes these experiments so peculiarly interesting is that if we take the statements of the communicators at their face value, it looks as though his surviving spirit had invented a means of getting over the difficulty and had endeavored to carry it out."

What Myers contrived, then, was most ingenious. The statements made in the script of one writer were by no means a verbatim reproduction of the statements made in the script of another, but they seemed to represent different aspects of the same idea, and one supplemented or complemented the other. There was neither a mechanical verbatim reproduction of phrases, nor even the same idea expressed in different ways such as might result from direct telepathy between the writers. A fragmentary utterance in one script, which taken alone had apparently no particular point or meaning, and another fragmentary utterance in another, equally without meaning taken by itself, when put together were found to supplement one another, and then it became apparent that one coherent idea underlay both, but it was only partially expressed in each.

It may be looked at like this, Saltmarsh goes on: "Two people are each given one piece of a jigsaw puzzle. Taken separately each piece is meaningless, nor will they fit each other. A third person is then given a third piece, and when the pieces are all brought together, it is found that they not only fit each other, but that when fitted they exhibit a coherent picture showing evidence of design and purpose."

Telepathy between the mediums or the sitters, when there were sitters, would not explain this, quite obviously, for none of them is able to understand the meaning of his own particular fragment. Thus they wouldn't be able to convey among themselves telepathically what they were doing. The puzzle had to be solved by an independent investigator, for frequently the mediums involved did not even know that other mediums were in any way sharing their experience.

Saltmarsh concludes that when reading the reports of the cases and the scripts of the various automatists, one can hardly help feeling that it was indeed Myers, Gurney, Sidgwick and the rest, who once had lived on earth and worked enthusiastically for psychical research, continuing their labors from the other side, and making strenuous endeavors to prove their identity.

Cross correspondences are so complicated that it is difficult to condense them so that a fairly adequate picture may be presented. Most, involving as they do reference to classical and literary topics and in some instances their evidential value turning upon some subtle point of classical scholarship or literary criticism, their full strength can hardly be appreciated by a reader who is not versed in these subjects. But the whole point is that Myers, Sidgwick, *et al.* were so versed, and it is their continued ability to remember and to think that they were trying to prove. They were working against almost insurmountable difficulties, as they did not hesitate to mention.

The fact that they managed to get anything at all into the minds of the mediums was amazing, for as they, and so many other communicators, have made plain, the actual efforts involved from their side were extreme. Myers explained it to "Mrs. Holland": "The nearest simile I can find to express the difficulties of sending a message—is that I appear to be standing behind a sheet of frosted glass which blurs sight and deadens sounds—dictating feebly to a reluctant and somewhat obtuse secretary."

Both Myers and Gurney exhibited a tendency to scold the automatist unmercifully, and somewhat unfairly. Hers was a hard job, too. It is difficult to make the mind a blank so that it can be communicated through. Those who don't go into an actual trance find that their own minds want to get into the act and think about what is being written. They want to evaluate what is coming, to criticize, to judge, sometimes even to glory in it. Sitting there keeping yourself half asleep is awesomely tedious.

Despite all the problems, some curiously interesting material was received. The Medici Tombs Case is a good illustration of how the scripts of the various automatists were interrelated on one theme. Beginning in November, 1906, there appeared in "Mrs. Holland's" scripts reference to shadows, death and sleep, dawn, evening and morning, and in two cases the name Margaret was written, signifying a cross correspondence with Mrs. Verrall. On January 21, 1907, in Mrs. Verrall's script, laurels and laurel wreath were mentioned several times.

The following is from the waking stage of Mrs. Piper's trance of February 26, 1907, at which Mr. Piddington was the sitter.

"Morehead. Morehead or some such name or word. Laurel for laurel."

"Say that again," said Piddington.

"For laurel. I say that I gave her that for laurel. Good-bye."

A few moments later Mrs. Piper looked at Piddington with an

113

expression of disgust and alarm and said: "There are . . . a nigger. Oh, dear. You go out. I don't like you at all. Dead." Later on came, "Well, I think it was something about laurel wreaths."

At a sitting the next day Mrs. Piper stated, "I gave Mrs. V. laurel wreaths."

On March 17, Miss Helen Verrall's script had: "Alexander's tomb . . . laurel leaves . . . are emblem laurels for the victor's brow."

"Mrs. Holland" on March 27 wrote: "Darkness, light and shadow, Alexander Moor's head."

On October 7, 1908, the Mac script contained, "Dig a grave among the laurels."

Thus we have a set of topics interconnected, but with little apparent meaning. Light and shadow, death and sleep might be associated normally, but laurels, Morehead or Moor's head, and Alexander did not seem to fit at all.

Then after the lapse of nearly two years, the clue came through a different automatist—Mrs. Willett. On June 10, 1910, her script contained the words: "Laurentian tombs, Dawn and Twilight."

July 8, 1910, in Mrs. Piper's trance, the subject had again been referred to in the words: Meditation, sleeping dead, laurels.

It was not until 1912 that the riddle was solved, when it was seen that the whole series of references pointed to the Medici tombs. The laurel was the special emblem of Lorenzo, the Magnificent.

On the tomb of Lorenzo, Duke of Urbino, there is a figure known as *Il Pensieroso* ("meditation" in Mrs. Piper's script) of which Elizabeth Barrett Browning wrote, "with everlasting shadow on his face"; also, two recumbent figures representing Dawn and Twilight, or Morning and Evening. On the tomb of Giuliano, Duc de Nemours there are two figures representing Day and Night.

Now Alessandro de Medici, the most infamous of the family, was the son of Clement VII and a mulatto slave. In his portrait he is shown as having woolly hair, thick lips and a generally African-Negro-like appearance. He was known as *Il Moro* (the Moor). It is therefore quite correct for him to be referred to as Alexander, Moor's Head. He was murdered and his body secretly placed in the tomb of Lorenzo, Duke of Urbino. This tomb may therefore be called Alexander's tomb.

"Laurel" is the key word in this Medici case, laurels being the special emblem of the family. There is further confirmation in the mention of the word "nigger" a few moments later. There is no possible association outside of the Medici Tombs between the name Morehead, laurel and nigger, but there is a very close connection if the name was instead meant to be "Moor's head" because of Alessandro de Medici, *Il Moro*.

I warned you cross correspondences were complicated. Most of the other great historical ones are even worse, and much too involved even to try to summarize here. But for those who have had time to decipher them, their very complexity has brought evidence of some kind of supernormal activity that seemed to involve surviving intelligences.

XI

OUIJAS AND SUCH

THE SIMPLEST MEANS for private individuals to attempt spirit communication is table tipping. It achieved a great vogue shortly after the time of the Hydesville Rappings in the mid-nineteenth century, when Spiritualism had its beginnings, and it is still used as a party game today. If a person who is highly psychic has his hands on it, a heavy table has been known to tip or even to lift up into the air. I have some photographs taken recently with infrared flash camera by Roger Vogelsang of Grand Haven, Michigan, showing a table clearly levitated by supernormal means. Levitation, while it gives evidence of some psychokinetic force we cannot yet explain, does not do anything to prove survival, however. But a rumpusing little table tapping its foot may do so.

To make this work, several people sit around a table. Any size can be used, even a sturdy card table, but you might as well make it as easy as you can for the invisible tipper, so use the smallest one you have. Each person places his hands lightly on it, and then everyone sits waiting for it to make some response. There are two schools of thought about whether or not to be quiet. Some people prefer to sing or to chatter innocently rather than to sit still. It seems to work either way if it is going to work at all. If the combination of persons doesn't cause the table to begin moving, change one or two for someone else. A different group of sitters might be more successful.

Eventually small raps may be heard in the table, or it may rise up on two legs. I have also seen tables raise three legs into the air and stand on just one. Sometimes they go skittering across the floor; on occasion a table may attempt to climb on the lap of one of the ladies present as if coaxing her to pet it. If it does stand up on its hind legs, give it a code by which it may rap answers, and then as it comes down and all legs hit the floor, it is responding. Tell it one rap alone will mean "Yes," two "No," and three "I don't know." Then inform it that it can spell out words for you by rapping at the letter it wants as you repeat the alphabet. It raps by dropping to the floor at the desired letter, then rearing back up ready for the next letter. Some tables prefer to bump at every letter of the alphabet and remain still at the right one, but this is a silly waste of effort for all concerned.

Cynics will tell you that this activity is caused purposefully by one member of the group who moves the table by conscious pressure of his hands. Others say the action comes from someone's subconscious mind, which moves his hands and manipulates the table without his conscious knowledge. It has never been conclusively shown just how it really works, but if the people seated around the table have no appreciable psi faculty, there will be no reaction whatever and the table will stay quiet as an inaminate object should. The fact nevertheless remains that some psychic people do receive evidential information from a tipping table.

As I reported in *How to Develop Your ESP*, I know a group of attractive young matrons in Bal Harbour, Florida, an exclusive suburb of Miami, who believe one of their members' uncle communicates with them via a tipping card table. They meet, or used to meet when I knew them, regularly for luncheon, meditation, and then a rap session. This alleged uncle has accurately predicted, among other things that came true, most of the successful candidates in a forthcoming election.

A case which brings a simple kind of evidence and is almost a classic in the table-tipping department is the story of Benja.

F.W.H. Myers says in *Human Personality and Its Survival of Bodily Death* that the case of Benja stands alone as a narrative of a direct experiment—a test message planned before death, and communicated after death, by a man who held that the hope of an assurance of his continued presence was worth at least a resolute effort, whatever its result might be.

"We may say that the information was certainly not possessed supraliminally by any living person," concludes Myers. And he adds that it is "what purports to be the successful accomplishment of an experiment which everyone may make—which everyone *ought* to make; for, small as may be the chances of success, a few score of distinct successes would establish a presumption of man's survival which the common sense of mankind would refuse to explain away." The incident also indicates a continued perception on the part of the deceased of the efforts made by friends to communicate with him.

This is from *Proceedings* S.P.R., Vol. VIII, pp. 248–51.

Mrs. William A. Finney of Rockland, Massachusetts, writes to psychical researcher Richard Hodgson to tell him of her experience. She says that her brother Benja had conversed with her freely for some months before his death on the subject of spirit communion and such matters, and one morning he requested her to bring him a piece of brick, and also pen and ink. He made two marks on one side of the brick and one on the other with ink. He then broke it into two pieces, retaining a piece weighing one and a half ounces, and handing the other piece, weighing about two and a quarter ounces, to his sister. He told her to take care of it, that he would hide his piece of brick and then after his death he would try to tell her where it was hidden. He said that she could then compare them together and it would be a test that he could return and communicate. She could be sure her own mind could not have any influence in the matter, as she would not know where he had put it.

For months after his death Mrs. Finney and her mother anticipated a message from Benja, but got nothing satisfactory. Then they began sitting at a small table at home, and at last it began tipping, purporting to be Benja communicating. By their repeating the alphabet, and the table tipping when they got to certain letters, the following message was given: "You will find that piece of brick in the cabinet under the tomahawk—Benja."

Mrs. Finney went to a cabinet in which her brother had kept souvenirs. It had not been touched since his death. She unlocked it and looked on the shelf directly under the tomahawk. There she found a Triton shell about ten inches long, lying so that its opening was entirely concealed. Deep in the recess of the shell, wrapped in folds of soft paper, and held in by gummed tape, was Benja's piece of brick.

At the time they made their pact, her brother had also given Mrs. Finney a sealed letter, saying he would try to tell her its contents from the spirit world. When she received the directions for finding the brick, she also was told that the contents of the letter were: "Julia, do right and be happy—Benja." When she opened the letter she found that this indeed was the message written therein.

Since Mrs. Finney's mother and other witnesses to this event had died, she appended a character witness from the Reverend C. Y. deNormandie of Kingston, Canada. She sent the pieces of brick and the shell to Dr. Hodgson.

A Frenchman invented the planchette in 1853. It is a piece of light wood on rollers to which a pencil is attached. It is much easier to use than a tipping table, but it is difficult because the writing is usually so large that huge rolls of paper must be provided.

Margaret Cameron received the material she published in the book *The Seven Purposes* via planchette and a big roll of blank wallpaper, called lining paper, which she spread out all over a table. She wrote in her Introduction about it:

> Twenty-five years or more ago my attention was attracted to the entertaining possibilities of a planchette, and, like other young persons, I played with one at intervals for several years. Like others, also, I speculated concerning the source of the remarkable statements sometimes obtained in this way, but the assumption that these statements were dictated by disembodied personalities always seemed to me rather absurd.

Nonetheless, as time went on Margaret Cameron became convinced that she was communicating with deceased friends, not only because of the excellent philosophy they gave her but because of certain specific bits of information that brought evidence. Writing during the early part of 1918, they stated the time of the ending of the First World War and predicted that a greater, more terrible, more encompassing war would not be long in coming because of conditions in Germany. They also told her small things such as when letters would arrive, that a lost muff had been found, and the winners of elections.

"Open the door of spiritual force to forces here," her communicants said, "and we can always help. That is what we hope to establish as a recognized truth in your life there . . . a force as yet unknown to science is operating between the planes, and can be developed and used in your life there."

Hensleigh Wedgwood was an enthusiastic psychical researcher of the old days. He worked closely with a lady merely identified as Mrs. R., who used the planchette and received ostensible communications from deceased persons. When he asked for evidence, sometimes curious things were forthcoming. A few months before his death, Mr. Wedgwood sent his friend F.W.H. Myers the record of messages he and Mrs. R. had received on March 22 and 23, 1891. At the top of the script was the crude drawing of a woman in a medieval cap. She was tied to a stake as if she were about to be burned. Myers published this report in a monograph titled *The Subliminal Consciousness* in 1894.

The scripts started off with the initials A.G. and the date 1605. Then they continued, "A.G. condemned March 1605. Condemned to the fear and the fire. A.G., A. Grimbold."

Wedgwood asked, "For what crime?"

"Accomplice. Robbery and murder."

"Accomplice with whom?"

"Harrison and Bradshaw. I was old Mrs. Clarke's servant. Harrison was my lover. The fire should have been for him. I never meant them to kill her."

Subsequent questioning drew out the story that Harrison had promised to marry Alice Grimbold if she would help him steal money from a coffer in the bedroom of tightfisted old Mrs. Clarke, who ran the inn where she worked. Harrison got off because he had powerful friends. She was tried in Leicester. She said, "I died a thousand times with fear before it came to the fire. Which was the most real—the dreams or the end? It was long since; but there is a righteous Judge. I was afraid of agony, but I did not repent. I loved the evil and it clave to me. I repent now, and this is part of the work I am given to atone. Alice Grimbold, servant at the inn." She also gave the name of the inn as the Blue Boar and mentioned Adam Bonus, a friend of Harrison's.

Wedgwood, who knew nothing about this case, dug in old volumes and records until he found in the *History of Leicester*, a rare old book located in the British Museum, the following account:

An event occurred in the month of March, 1605, which has acquired more than ordinary importance: we refer to the murder of Mrs. Clarke, landlady of the Blue Boar Inn, by her servants. . . . In 1604, a man named Harrison, who had fled from Staffordshire in consequence of having done bodily injury to a person named Philip, came to Leicester; the Blue Boar being the first inn he approached, he resolved to lodge there, and slept there three nights.

During his stay he "fell into speech with a maid in the house, in the way of marriage, whereupon she told him her mistress had a great store of money in her house, and bade him come again some night, and bring a secret friend with him whom she might trust, and there would be means made to get some of the money."

Accordingly, Harrison "went his way," and at Lichfield met with Adam Bonus, and Bonus further made one Edward Bradshaw acquainted therewith.

Harrison and Bradshaw came to Leicester together on the first of February, 1605, and that night lodged at John Webster's house: on Saturday, 2nd February, they removed with their horses to the Blue Boar, where they slept; and on Sunday they remained together at the inn all day.

In the evening, about ten o'clock, one of the female servants (Alice Grimbold, a native of Peckleton) went with her companion with some provender for the horses, to the stable, whither they were followed by the man. Alice Grimbold then went to the well to fetch some water for the horses, and on returning to the stable with it, found her fellow-servant bound therein; when Harrison immediately laid hands on her, and secured her also. . . .

They then unbound Grimbold (as she stated) and took her into the house with them, and obtained her mistress's keys from her, Bradshaw having bound Mrs. Clarke while Harrison secured the servants in the stable. The latter in his examination confessed that he had done this, and added that the "big maid," (meaning Grimbold), after she was unbound, went with them, apparently on compulsion, into her mistress's parlor, where they opened three coffers . . . the third having six or seven bags of gold and silver therein.

The robbers took most of the money (amounting, as was variously estimated by them, to . . . not less than £250—more probably £500), but left some upon the bedstead for their female accomplice. Bradshaw then murdered Mrs. Clarke, fastened Grimbold in the chimney . . . Grimbold would gladly (according to her own confession) have gone away with them, but they swore by "God's wounds" they would hang her, and themselves, too, if she attempted to do so.

The murder was discovered the next day and Harrison's friend Bonus was examined on Monday, February 4, before the justices and coroners. He had played no part in the robbery, but seems to have incriminated Bradshaw in it.

The trial took place on March 25. Bradshaw was sentenced to hang, and Alice Grimbold was sentenced to be burned at the stake for the crime of petty treason and accomplice to murder. For some strange reason, perhaps his "powerful friends," Harrison was allowed to go free though he had planned the crime and directed it.

Wedgwood later learned that the same story could be found in an old book published in 1653 by Sir Roger Twisden. But neither he nor Mrs. R. had ever had access to it any more than they had to the book from the British Museum.

Mr. Wedgwood wrote to Myers: "I am rather impressed by the fact that A.G. communicated with us in March, so near the anniversary of her trial and condemnation, and probably that of her awful death. . . ." He added that he had never been in Leicester or the neighborhood, and had last been in the British Museum when he was twelve years old.

Edmond P. Gibson in "The Alice Grimbold Case," (*Tomorrow,*

Winter, 1954), points out that those who exclusively hold to theories of clairvoyance and retrocognition (supernormal knowledge of the past), might seek to explain the Grimbold case by the assumption that Wedgwood and Mrs. R. acquired the Grimbold material by extrasensory means from existing books or historic memory. There certainly is no evidence to suggest that either of them had normal access to the facts at any time, the only verification being found in rare and obscure volumes. Gibson states:

> If one weighs the evidence without bias, taking all of it into account, it seems possible that the communication was the purposeful act of Alice Grimbold herself, confessing her sins, and thus seeking to free herself from a guilt that had lasted almost three centuries.

I am sure there is no need to define a Ouija board to modern readers. It has been around since 1893, and few homes have been without one at one time or another, although it has usually been considered a strange toy. It has also been the means for some famous sensitives to discover their psychic abilities. Many who have no idea that they have such talents have begun to receive messages that were highly challenging and interesting, and it has led to their further development toward controlled mediumship.

For most people, little but childish prattle is received, and they soon lose interest. When challenging material does come, however, it may intrigue your interest, and there is the possibility you may get "hooked" on it. In that case be wary, for there are dangers lurking in that innocent-looking board. No professional medium I know will use a Ouija board. They insist this is because negative or malicious "earthbound" spirit influences are so often attracted to such a simple means of communication. These may cause all kinds of trouble if they are encouraged. Of course, psychologists say the communications come from your own subconscious mind, but whatever the source of the words, taking them too seriously is not warranted. It is not advised that anyone who is not a developed psychic and who knows nothing about protecting himself ever sit alone or in a twosome with a Ouija board. You are vulnerable unless you are aware of the possible problems to which you may be exposing yourselves.

An attractive young acquaintance of mine in Miami, Florida, had begun to communicate with someone on her Ouija board who called himself her sweetheart. He told her he loved her and would remain with her always. He insisted she talk to him on the board as frequently as possible. Because of all the love stuff he wrote, she was intrigued, and would sit and chat with him by the hour. I warned her against it, but she did not listen.

This girl was popular and had many dates. One afternoon a group of young people went to the beach together. There they met a Cuban youth, whom they invited home with them. While drinking beer and having fun in Ann's apartment, they decided to play with Ouija. The invisible boy friend immediately began to communicate, but he was quite unhappy because she was letting other men work the board with her. All his answers to the questions proffered by the men contained fluent profanity . . . words I am sure Ann did not use herself.

Instead of being turned off by this, they decided to test their communicant to see if any supernormal knowledge could be produced. So they asked the Cuban boy to think of a question in Spanish and not to state orally what it was. Then the board answered his question, also in Spanish. It was correct! They had to give up using the Ouija, however, because the profanity became worse, accompanied by violent threats of bodily harm to the men. Ann finally realized that any lover who was so vulgar was not her type, so she put away the board for good.

Some Ouijas have eschewed twaddle and profanity and have produced much interesting material. The most famous and also the most controversial of all was the Patience Worth case, which has had several books written about it and has been mentioned in nearly every psychic source book since then. Mrs. John H. Curran of St. Louis, wife of the former Immigration Commissioner for Missouri, was the medium, and her writing began on the Ouija board. She later developed her psychic abilities so that the words could be spoken through her mouth. The alleged communicant was a woman who said she had lived in the early seventeenth century in England and had migrated to the United States with the pilgrims. She spoke in the idiom of that period. Mrs. Curran, who loved to play the piano, was not educated beyond high-school level in anything but music, and she read very little. Still, over a period of nearly twenty-five years, Patience Worth gave through her a staggering amount of poetry, novels, parables and other literary forms, all written briskly and with a great amount of wit and humor.

It is usual for those who are using the Ouija to have someone else watch the indicator and write down the letters to which it points. The sitters can thus keep their eyes closed in an effort to try to prove it is not their subconscious minds performing. Some of the most interesting material received under test conditions came through a powerful sensitive known either as Hester Travers Smith or Hester Dowden, because she was the daughter of Edward Dowden, a famous Shakespearean scholar of Dublin University. She used to produce fascinating material when both she and the other person sitting with her at the board wore opaque black satin masks which completely shut off their vision. As another precaution, the recorder would always note the letters silently, so that the masked writers could have no inkling of what was being spelled out under their hands. Oddly enough, Mrs. Travers Smith and a friend once tried the board with their eyes open and the well-trained pointer would not budge. When they put on their masks, the words came instantly!

Sir William Barrett presided over the circle of six to eight friends who used to meet twice weekly with Mrs. Travers Smith, and he kept careful watch of all that occurred. On one occasion he turned the board around so that the familiar location of the letters could not be sensed. Another time he used separate cards for the alphabet, mixed them up and spread them helter-skelter under a sheet of glass, but these precautions made no difference to the speed and sureness of the indicator as it moved swiftly from letter to letter and made sense of its writing. The movement was sometimes so fast that the recorder had to resort to shorthand. Sir William himself sat at the board blind-folded, and was startled by the vigor with which the pointer under his fingers went to work.

An interesting bit of evidence brought on one occasion was reported by Barrett in *On the Threshold of the Unseen.* Here is the account of it as it was originally written up by Hester Travers Smith:

> On the evening of the day on which news had come that the Lusitania was reported sinking, Mr. Lennox Robinson and I sat at the Ouija board; the Rev. Savill Hicks taking the record. We *did not know* that Sir Hugh Lane was on board. We were both personal friends of his, and knew he was in America, but had no idea he was coming back so soon.
>
> Our usual "control" came and then the words "Pray for the soul of Hugh Lane." I asked, "Who is speaking?" The reply was, "I am Hugh Lane." He gave us an account of the sinking of the ship and said it was a "peaceful end to an exciting life." At this point we heard the stop-press evening paper called in the street and Mr. Robinson ran down and bought a paper. I went out of the room to meet him, and he pointed to the name of Sir Hugh Lane among the passengers. We were both much disturbed but continued the sitting. Sir Hugh gave me messages for mutual friends and ended this sitting by saying, "I did not suffer. I was drowned and felt nothing."
>
> At subsequent sittings he spoke of his will, but never mentioned the codicil now in dispute. He hoped no memorial would be erected to him in the shape of a gallery or otherwise, but was anxious about his pictures. The messages were always coherent and evidential and always came through Mr. Robinson and me.

Barrett says of it, "This is a very evidential case, for no information of the *death* of Sir Hugh Lane was given until some days later."

A case which has none of the authentication we have come to expect from such as Hester comes to us from W. F. Neech in *No Living Person Could Have Known.* Mr. Neech attributed the source of most of his accounts, but he somehow failed to do so in the following instance. But it is such a good story . . . and it names names, so it may very likely be just as authentic as any of the others. We can't become so arbitrary that we will accept only cases sponsored by the S.P.R. or the A.S.P.R. or Sir William Barrett. Neech reports that the death of Judge Dahl of Frederikstad, Norway, had been predicted a year in advance . . . by a Ouija board.

It was the evening of August 8, 1933, that the judge's daughter, Mrs. Ingeborg, sat before the board with a friend, Mrs. Stolt-Neilsen. They were in Judge Dahl's home. I never heard of a Ouija using code before, but it's a great idea for procuring evidence. The one used in this story had A being represented by the numeral 1, B:2, C:3, etc. About sixty numbers were received, and Mrs. Ingeborg and her friend were instructed by their communicant to seal them in an envelope which was not to be opened until one year had passed.

Months later Judge Dahl, his daughter and her children went swimming at a beach on the Isle of Hankoe. The judge, a strong swimmer, plunged into the water and swam a short distance from shore. Suddenly he stopped and shouted to Mrs. Ingeborg that he had cramps in both legs. She swam out and saved him, but brought him back to shore unconscious. A doctor who was summoned was unable to revive him, and in the midst of his efforts the judge died.

Some time later Mrs. Ingeborg and her friend Mrs. Stolt-Neilsen recalled the Ouija board message and retrieved it from where they had placed it the year before. They saw that the envelope was marked, "Open August 8, 1934." This, they realized with astonishment, was the day on which Judge Dahl had died.

When they opened the envelope and uncoded the message, it read: "In the month of August, 1934, Judge Dahl will be killed in an accident."

It is a very odd thing, but as we go on in this book we will find that a great many communications have to do with predictions of the date or manner of death. Apparently those on the other side don't think of it as quite the tragedy we do.

Gustav Gumpert and a friend were determined to make a calm and objective experiment as they hunched over a Ouija board one snowy night in the winter of 1960. But, Gumpert says in "Did I Speak with Angels?" (*Fate*, April, 1961) "Actually, we were about to get the shock of our lives; for we received a series of messages that reversed our opinion on the chances of communicating with a world beyond the senses."

They did not believe that what they began to receive could have come out of either of their minds, for it was in a language neither of them knew—"one no man has ever spoken." The first part of the message, in English, said, "This is Raphael." And then they received a brilliant lecture on occult philosophy. This, of course, brought them no evidence, and they weren't convinced at all that one of the archangels of the ancient Hebrews' angelic hierarchy was speaking with them. They challenged the communicator to give them proof beyond any question.

Then they received what seemed to be a string of nonsense syllables: ECA RAFAEL OD VADAN I OD IAODPIL T AI. But a certain precision of the movements of the pointer aroused their suspicion. So they let it go on and received another string of similar words.

Both the sitters were linguists, speaking eight languages between the two of them and having some smattering of several others. And Gumpert had always been interested in linguistics and cryptograms. Perhaps this is why they were chosen for such a message. I know if one like it had come to me I would have thrown it out as junk—not being so perceptive about languages and puzzles.

Gumpert recalled that he had somewhere read about a strange language that had been discovered in England centuries before by Dr. John Dee, court astrologer to Queen Elizabeth, and that it was supposed to have been spoken by an angel. Gumpert had not seen any samples of this hidden language, but on the basis of a pure hunch he began to search for the original writings received in this peculiar tongue. He found it in a very old volume published in 1659, in which there were thirteen pages of the language. But there was no dictionary for the words. How were they to find out what they meant? Gumpert writes, "We decided to prepare a dictionary, rather than look through the whole thirteen pages for each word. It took three days to compile the dictionary. When completed, it consisted of eight hundred entries. In the course of the work we discovered that the language had genuine syntax and logical structure. The verbs were conjugated and the nouns declined."

They also found that some of the words went back to the most ancient recorded speech. Here is the translation of the first message they received: "Therefore Raphael exists, and Truth exists, and the Everlasting God dwells amongst you. Mighty is the Lord in His creations. He is the world, in which He operates, and it is His servant."

Gumpert and his friend have continued their conversations with their angelic friend and to the date the article was written they had received enough material to fill forty pages of typescript. It outlined an amazing system of occult philosophy.

One of the many interesting answers to the questions asked the angel was the following:

Q: Is there life after death?
A: Time has no beginning or ending, nor do you. It is as though you walked through a series of rooms. Each room is there and continues to exist after you depart from it. Before you enter, it is the future; and after you leave, it is the past. But the room is always there—it is you who change. You will always continue, for you are a great circle that begins nowhere and ends nowhere.

During the time I lived in Coral Gables, Florida, an acquaintance dropped in occasionally who had no interest whatever in ESP or related subjects. He stated firmly, "My rabbi says there's no life after death, and that's good enough for me." Although I doubt if many rabbis are that arbitrary about it, he was.

Once when this man happened by I got out the Ouija board to entertain him, and he endured it out of curiosity as to how it worked. He soon had it all figured out. "You push it," he asserted.

My denial was to no avail, so I invented a new technique of Ouija operation—placing my hand lightly on top of his hand which was on the indicator. The little pointer began to race across the board, but as I had purposely sat at the back of it so that he could be the one to see what was going on, I did not observe what was spelled. In fact, I just presumed it was making nonsense as it usually does when getting warmed up. After it stopped writing, the man took his hand off the pointer and sat and stared at me. Finally he said, "Do you know what happened?"

"No," I replied. "Did it spell anything that made sense?"

"It wrote the name of a dead uncle of mine and gave me greetings from him," he said. He didn't want to work the board any more after that. He seemed a bit disconcerted, actually. Before he left, however, he had arrived at an explanation that satisfied him.

"You pushed it," he said.

XII

AUTOMATIC WRITING

As was indicated in the last chapter, many persons who start out by using the tipping table or the Ouija board continue their purported correspondence with spirits by means of automatic writing with a pencil, pen or typewriter. In fact, they are often instructed to do so by their communicant. I was. On the Ouija, I had started getting what seemed to indicate the possibility that my mother was in touch with me from wherever it is out in space that she now resides. Then I was told, "Get a pencil," and my efforts at automatic writing began. Although I now receive reams of inspirational material automatically on the typewriter, I have never gotten much that brought any real evidence, and so cannot personally contribute anything to this chapter. Fortunately, plenty of other people have.

Probably as good a discussion of automatic writing and its problems as is available was given by William Oliver Stevens in *Psychics and Common Sense:*

> Usually, what is "received" by the common run of automatists is their own ideas, prejudices, ignorances, and hopes finding expression under a pencil which they believe is being moved by a spirit agency. Publishers are beset by earnest ladies with bales of manuscript under their arms who believe that their "inspired" writings should be given to the world in print. Often

this pathetic conviction arises from the illustrious names—the great ones of the past—which are attached to the scripts. That circumstance alone should put the manuscript under suspicion if not make it ridiculous, especially when Abraham Lincoln or William James—he seems the favorite—or the prophet Hosea, expresses exactly the political and moral sentiments of the person holding the pencil, listening by the inner ear, or working the Ouija board, and all in the same style.

Stevens is right that William James is said to be the most active spirit of all, for many who do automatic writing will tell you he has written through them. I myself have a spirit entity who communicates with me who calls himself James, and has admitted to being the famous William. It is well known that the original William James was scientifically interested in the subject of communication while he was on earth, so perhaps his interest has maintained. I don't claim that great man as my correspondent, however. I just call my communicant James and delight in his company whenever he has time to bestow it on me. And I especially appreciate the philosophy he gives me, which is in no way similar to my own previous beliefs. It will soon be published as *The Book of James* by G. P. Putnam's Sons.

Psychologists say that automatic writing is produced entirely by the subconscious mind. They are most often correct, but they fail to take into consideration the occasional excellent material that has brought information which transcends the subconscious mind, such as the following:

Dr. A. A. Liebeault of Nancy, France, discovered a psychic of ability by the process of hypnotizing her for a malady. Mlle. B., the niece of a French family from New Orleans who had come to stay for some time in Nancy for business reasons, had been treated by Dr. Liebeault for slight anemia and a nervous cough contracted in Coblenz, Germany, where she was teaching in a high school. He easily induced somnambulism and she was cured in two sittings. But her hypnotic trances suggested psychic trances to Mlle. B., and she endeavored to put herself into a mediumistic state so that she could receive automatic writing. At the end of two months she had become a remarkable writing medium.

"I have myself," says Dr. Liebeault, "seen her rapidly writing page after page of what she called 'messages'—all in well chosen language and with no erasures, while at the same time she maintained conversation with the people near her. An odd thing was that she had no knowledge whatever of what she was writing. 'It must be a spirit,' she would say, 'which guides my hand; it is certainly not I.'"

Dr. Liebeault continues:

> One day—it was, I think, February 7, 1868, about 8 A.M., when just about to seat herself at table for breakfast, she felt a kind of need, an impulse which prompted her to write . . . and she rushed off at once to her large notebook, where she wrote in pencil, with feverish haste, certain undecipherable words. She wrote the same words again and again on the pages which followed, and at last, as her agitation diminished, it was possible to read that a person called Marguerite was thus announcing her death.
>
> The family at once assumed that a young lady of that name, a friend of Mlle. B.'s, and her companion and colleague in the Coblenz High School, must have just expired. Mlle. B. wrote to a young English lady who was also a teacher in that same school. She gave some other reason for writing; taking care not to reveal the true motive of the letter. By return of post we received an answer in English, from which they copied for me the essential part. . . . It expressed the surprise of the English lady at the receipt of Mlle. B.'s unexpected and apparently motiveless letter. But at the same time the English correspondent made haste to announce to Mlle. B. that their common friend, Marguerite, had died on February 7 at about 8 A.M. Moreover, the letter contained a little square piece of printed paper: the announcement of death sent round to friends.

Dr. Liebeault didn't believe there could have been any deceit here involved, and he based his conviction on the honor of the girl's family, "which has always appeared to me to be absolutely above suspicion."

F.W.H. Myers, who first published this case in *Human Personality and Its Survival of Bodily Death*, wrote that while formerly of the opinion that this was "an example of spontaneous telepathic impulse proceeding directly from a dying person, I now regard it as more probably due to the action of the spirit after bodily death."

Another whose automatic writings frequently brought evidence of identity was Geraldine Cummins, an Irish automatist who first developed her abilities with Heather Dowden's group in Dublin. Ever objective and critical of her own work, she stated in *Mind in Life and Death:* "My interest in psychical research was increased, I think, through my background of medical science. My grandfather was a physician, my father Professor of Medicine at the National University, Ireland, his two brothers were professors in special medical subjects at universities. Two brothers and two sisters of mine are members of the medical profession.

"We were, therefore, brought up in an analytical atmosphere and with a kind of religious respect for exact truthful statement in scientific research; there was to be no loading of the dice for emotional or personal reasons. I am still what I described myself at the age of seven, 'a very curious person'; that is to say a person who wants to know the truth however disagreeable it may be. The greatest of all mysteries, that of life and death, has since then been a challenge to my insatiable curiosity. . . ."

For many years, Edith Beatrice Gibbes, or E.B.G. as she was known in the records, was companion and helper to Geraldine Cummins in her psychical work. Miss Cummins says, "During our study of psychic or paranormal phenomena I was the specimen in the laboratory, the automatist or medium, and E.B.G. for the most part the investigator." Very careful reports were always made for the Society for Psychical Research; so practically everything in her cited cases has been, as she expressed it, "approved by the highest accepted authority in the field of Psychic Science." Because of the rigid conditions on which the society insists as a protection against fraud and irrational credulity, the Cummins' reports of paranormal phenomena, she states, were as correct and accurate as it was possible to make them, and they were authenticated as genuine only after being submitted to rigorous scientific examination.

On November 18, 1924, a case of automatic writing began which was to continue for over a year, involving the efforts of a spirit to bring evidence of his existence to his wife. It began when Miss

Cummins' control Astor wrote: "There is someone here newly dead, I think, anxious to get a message through. He has only just passed over."

Miss Gibbes, who talked to the communicants and handled the pages as the entranced Miss Cummins covered them with automatic script, said, "Please ask him to speak." The writing then changed: "Is this the earth? How queer. I thought I was dead. Is my wife there?"

E.B.G.: We don't know who you are.

SPIRIT: Surely you see me?

E.B.G.: No, we can't.

S: Then perhaps if I tell you who I am, you will tell my wife I am alive.

E.B.G.: Yes, please tell us who you are.

S: Henry is my Christian name.

E.B.G.: That isn't sufficient.

S: Try and listen now (Here the pencil hesitated a little, making only a tiny movement. Then the following was written and underlined.) Bois. Horswich. Did you get my name?

E.B.G.: Yes, that is clear.

S: The place I lived in. Write to Highfield; my wife lives there.

E.B.G.: I wonder if we have your name correctly?

S: Yes, Henry Bois, Bois. (The pencil then gyrated as if there were some difficulty and again the word "Bois" was written.)

E.B.G.: All right, your name is clear. I will try to trace you at that address.

S: Yes, yes. Horswich. Tell her I am alive. I know how she is grieving. Tell my wife her husband will be watching for her and give her my love. I am in dimness but don't tell her that. I feel this is only the beginning. I have faith. I know I shall find Heaven and my God eventually.

E.B.G.: I don't know where this place is that you mention but I will try to trace it.

S: England. Horswich. It's not a foreign name. I am English.

E.B.G.: We would like now to see if there is anyone else here who would care to speak, so I must ask you to come again.

S: Yes, please let me come again. I am so relieved to feel the earth has not stopped. I thought everything had stopped at first. Good-bye.

135

It seemed apparent that some obstruction checked the writing of the name "Bois," but no attention was paid to it at the time. When Miss Cummins learned of the message from Henry Bois, she remarked that it must be the invention of her subconscious mind because she had known a Henry Bois who lived in India. She therefore assumed the whole message to be fictitious. Miss Gibbes nonetheless consulted a railway guide book and discovered that a town of the name of Horswich existed in Cheshire. She wrote the postmaster there, but he replied that no one by the name of Henry Bois had lived there.

The communicant came back about a month later and more or less repeated himself. A few additional points of interest were mentioned, however. He said he had lived on Highfield Road, and then he wrote: "Horswick, Scotland. I am confused. Find my wife. Let her know I am alive. She thinks I am dead. I am not dead at all."

A few days later, strangely enough, a letter was received from the postmaster at Horswick, Scotland. Apparently the postmaster in Horswich, Cheshire had forwarded the letter of inquiry to him. (This was a *long* time ago.) The Scottish postmaster replied that there was no Bois there, but a Boyce on Heathfield Road. This Boyce family, when appealed to by Miss Gibbes, replied curtly that they had never known a Henry in the family.

After Bois wrote the second time, F.W.H. Myers, said to be a regular communicator of Miss Cummins', apparently tried to get through but had difficulty. At another time he was asked whether he had spoken on the previous occasion. He wrote:

> I tried to speak through the old man [Astor] but it was very confusing. Someone else was trying to talk, too, who said he had not been able to give you his name properly, or something like that. Anyway, I tried to get my message through in spite of him and the other influences.

Little attention was paid to this at the time. Eventually, however, they realized that the spelling "Boyce" might have been suggested to Miss Cummins' mind, but because she had known a Henry "Bois" the name had been written that way. Perhaps the man was actually trying to write "Boyce." Possibly also when thinking about getting his message through the medium the name of the other town in Scotland had occurred to him. In a flash, his thought was communicated to the brain of the sensitive. He would seem to have confirmed this view, for he quickly followed up the word "Scotland" by the remark that he was confused. Probably he realized this slip but was powerless to arrest its passage. "This," says Miss Gibbes, "may be an example of *unintentional thought-transference* (from the dead to the living). It may often account for errors in communications for which the medium gets the blame."

If there was a Boyce family in Horswick, perhaps there was a Henry Boyce family in Horswich, Cheshire, so Miss Gibbes wrote there asking for information concerning him. The widow of Henry Boyce answered by return mail, saying that her husband of that name had died there on November 13, 1924. The problem was solved.

Since what he originally said had checked out, it seemed sensible to get into further touch with Henry Boyce to see if more evidence could be obtained. So E.B.G. asked Astor to bring him if possible, and he came again on October 8, 1925. He wrote:

> A queer place this, all misty. I am puzzled. Is any friend of mine here? I know that this light of yours means the world and the people living in it. I think I spoke to you before, but my memory has all gone to pieces—I mean of the earth. I am quite sane and clear in my mind, in fact, I can think a hundredfold quicker than when I was alive. But you human beings are just like stone effigies to me now, so cold and grey and silent.

Miss Gibbes asked if he were the same person who had spoken to them before and he replied, "I am called Henry Boyce. You are a stranger to me. But in that time of terror just after my death, your face appeared to me in this mist and I thanked God for it."

E.B.G. added a footnote: "This is the first time anyone has ever thanked God for the sight of my face!"

She asked him to tell something about himself and he said among other things that he had been retired from his business for a long time. He wasn't actually ill very long before he died, however. He never was a great talker. His profession was handling money, buying and selling for a good part of his life. He recalled his childhood most clearly. "I remember being brought up very strictly and the little Highlander my mother made of me. The kilt I didn't like a bit, but it was the fashion in those days." He also said, "I was a serious mind and I didn't care for newfangled ideas." He and his wife were devoted to each other though they never said very much. "She didn't know how much I loved her. If you ever meet her tell her this."

The writing then became very faint as Henry Boyce left. After a short pause Astor wrote as follows:

> He slipped away. He was a person of no great interest, I think. He seemed not to have lived to be very old. I think he must have died in the fifties. . . .
> E.B.G.: Can you describe him?
> He seems to have been about medium height . . . quite a pleasing appearance . . . dark, but he was dim to me.

It was obviously somewhat difficult to formulate a letter to the widow inquiring as to the accuracy of these details without explaining the reason for so doing. Even when intense love exists between parties concerned, the idea that the dead may possibly still be alive is distasteful to some people. Miss Gibbes feared a rebuff and yet was very anxious to receive the cooperation of the widow. The letter she wrote was friendly. It enumerated various remarks Boyce had made, but she explained her query by saying that she was anxious to trace someone answering to that description. After four days, the widow replied—guardedly asking the reason for it, but saying that "all the questions could be replied to." Then Miss Gibbes wrote again, assuring her that her efforts were entirely disinterested and giving her a banker's reference. The following is a copy of Mrs. Boyce's reply:

> 2, Highfield Road
> Horswich
> October 15, 1925.

DEAR MADAM,
    In reply to your letter of the 14th October. You will quite understand why I wanted to know who I was answering your

questions to, about one whom I dearly loved and have a great respect to his memory.

My husband was a great sufferer from arthritis, he was ailing two years, and kept on going to business . . . he started out one Monday morning and only got a few yards down the road, he could not walk any further, I had to get him back home, and he never went to business again, it crippled him up so much that I had everything to do for him for eight years. . . . On November 10th, 1924, he was not very well, so I called in the Doctor and he told me it was a gastric ulcer that had burst in the stomach, and he gradually went worse, and died three days after, November 13th, 1924, he was fifty-five years of age when he died.

I cannot say that he was a great talker, but he was a great reader, and enjoyed a good conversation with anyone, and would talk on most subjects. He was not a very serious man and did not care altogether for some of the new ideas, he was medium height, dark, and of a very pleasing appearance. I do not know that he ever wore Highland kilts, but as a boy he wore velvet suits.

I am anxiously waiting for a reply to these questions to know if I am the right person you are seeking.

Miss Gibbes, elated at all the points of corroboration, replied to the above gently informing the writer that she thought she had received a message from her dead husband. To this the widow unfortunately did not reply. "I fear she was disappointed," says E.B.G., adding:

. . . it seems hardly probable that the mind of the psychic would wander into the mind of a woman unknown to her who lived 190 miles away, and gather the fact that her late husband (among other things) refused to admit that he was "dead." For it subsequently transpired that the widow declined to believe in the continued existence of her husband. It seems reasonable therefore to postulate that the communications purporting to come from Henry Boyce can only be accounted for on the assumption of the spiritistic hypothesis. What is more natural than that this discarnate entity actually saw Miss Cummins' psychic "light" and "went straight for it"? Under difficult conditions he identified himself giving his correct name and address.

It is curious that while most persons who die apparently have no desire to make the effort to reveal their continued existence, or if they do, find conditions too difficult to make it possible, an occasional individual is persistent enough that he is absolutely determined to get his message through. And he may find various means of doing so. Such a one started with the hand of a medium, Mme. d'Esperance, on the morning of April 23, 1890, as she was sitting in an office writing business letters. She found that her hand had of its own accord written in large, distinct letters, the name Sven Stromberg. At the time she was only vexed at the hindrance, for she had to write a new letter. Later she wondered where the name had come from, and mentioned it to Mr. Matthew Fidler in a letter to him in England.

Some two months later Walter, Mme. d'Esperance's control, wrote through her: "There's a man called Stromberg who wants you to tell his people he's dead. Died in Wisconsin, I think he said, on March 13. I think he said he lived in Jemland. Is there such a place? He had a wife and half a dozen bairns."

Mr. Fidler wondered if this might be the same Stromberg who had written his name in the medium's letter. He said, "If he died in Jemland he must give us his wife's address."

"No, he died in America, but his people lived in Jemland."

"All right," said Mr. Fidler. "Get me the address and I'll write to them."

Mme. d'Esperance was a world-renowned medium, and at the time a group of Russian experts were visiting her because they were interested in some experiments for photographing materialized spirit forms. The day after this conversation their preparations were ready and the photographer wished to try the light. Mme. d'Esperance, in her account of this episode, says:

"While he tried it he asked me to sit in my accustomed seat, and the magnesium light flashed. In that fraction of a second I distinctly felt something touching my head. Before I could speak someone cried out, 'There was a man's face behind you.' When the plate was developed and a print made, sure enough, there appeared the face of a man calm and placid in contrast with mine, for the intense light had caused me to make a grimace. No one took much interest except Mr. Fidler who asked Walter if he knew who had been photographed.

" 'Yes,' Walter replied, 'that's the Stromberg I told you about. It wasn't Wisconsin he died at, but New Stockholm, and it was the thirty-first of March, not the thirteenth. I knew there was a three and a one but could not remember which way about. His people live in Stroms Stocking, or a name like it, in Jemtland. He went from there in '86, I think he said, got married and had three children—not six —then died, universally respected and lamented, and all the rest of it.'

" 'What does he want me to do about it?' asked Mr. Fidler. 'Shall I send his photo to his wife?'

" 'How dense you are!' complained Walter. 'I told you his people in Jemtland don't know he's dead. His wife does, I guess. He wants them to know all about the universal respect and lamentation.'

" 'It's the wife's business to tell them,' said Mr. Fidler, 'but if it will please him I'll write, or at least make some inquiries.' "

Walter suggested that the photograph be sent to Jemtland, and so Fidler wrote to the clergyman of the parish of Strom, asking if a man named Sven Stromberg had lived there and emigrated to America about 1886. Mr. Fidler also looked on maps for a place called New Stockholm in the United States, but it was not to be found. He then wrote to a friend who was the Swedish consul in Winnipeg, Canada, for information.

When a letter came from Jemtland, a pastor there replied that he had searched all the record books but found that no one of that name had ever lived there. There was a Sven Ersson who had married and gone to America about that time, and there were other Svens, but no Sven Stromberg.

Not dismayed, Fidler continued his investigation for over a year. He was ultimately to uncover the facts that New Stockholm was in Canada, and that Sven Ersson of Strom Socken parish in Jemtland, Sweden, had married Sara Kaiser, and had emigrated to Canada where he had taken the name of Stromberg. He purchased land in a place later to be called New Stockholm; he had three children and died on March 31, 1890. His wife and the clergyman who had attended him said that his last request had been that his old friends in Sweden be informed of his demise. This had not been done, however. A letter had been written but not mailed, for the nearest post office was twenty-four miles distant.

Mr. Fidler sent the photograph to Jemtland where it was seen by many. It was nailed up in the town hall with the request that anyone who recognized it would sign their names under it. It was returned with many signatures and remarks, many of them having reference to the moustache he wore, which they had not seen on him as a young man before his emigration.

This story with all its details was published in Scandinavia, France, Germany and Canada, as well as in several English-language magazines. It comes to us by way of Ernesto Bozzano's *Animism and Spiritism*. Although the actual documents supporting it are not at hand, it is so similar to the Henry Boyce case of Miss Cummins' that it has to be given consideration.

The preceding could almost be called "drop-in" cases involving automatic writing. There have been others in which concerted efforts by several persons over long periods of time have produced spectacular results. Certain events of this nature have been immortalized in two books by Frederick Bligh Bond: *The Gate of Remembrance* and *The Company of Avalon*, which tell of research at Glastonbury Abbey directed by automatic writing purporting to come from the deceased monks who had lived there.

The site of this abbey was an island surrounded by marshland, which was probably used as a burial ground by the Celts as early as the third century B.C. Called the "Isle of Glass" originally, it later became known as Avalon and figured in the legends of King Arthur. Glastonbury Tor, a nearby hill, is encircled by terraces which may have been spiral pathways for Druid processions. There is much more conjectural history involving Glastonbury, even including the supposition that Jesus was once there. All who have visited the place have remarked about the mystical feeling the surroundings impart.

In the early sixteenth century Glastonbury Abbey was the richest and most imposing in England. When Henry VIII split with Rome, he set about systematically disbanding and destroying the monasteries of his country. Glastonbury was demolished in 1539; its wealth was removed to Henry's treasury; its monks were dispersed, and its land was auctioned off to the highest bidder. "An engaging sidelight," adds Eleanor Touhey Smith in *Psychic People*, "is that one of the purchasers was John Horner, immortalized as 'Little Jack Horner sat in a corner, eating his Christmas pie.' That pie was Glastonbury."

There was nothing but neglect and pillaging of the ruins for the next three hundred and fifty years as the property passed into successive private hands. During this time all the buildings except the abbot's kitchen were torn down, and only a few arches and other fragments remained. This was the condition at Glastonbury when ecclesiastical architect Frederick Bligh Bond joined the Somerset Archaeological and Natural History Society in 1903. He was not an archeologist, but he had steeped himself in the history of the abbey and its environs. Glastonbury became his obsession and he was convinced that "in that hidden landscape" there was a link with the earliest history of the British Church. He converted the society to his way of thinking, and they persuaded the Church of England, represented by the Bishop of Bath, to buy the land when it was up for auction in 1907, and to put it under their management. Bond was appointed Director of Excavations in the month of May, 1908. He immediately began studying all that was left of the ruined structure, hoping to be able to restore the lost sites of many of the buildings that had been part of the original abbey. But he soon found himself up a blind alley in his excavations because the sites of the lost chapels lay deep beneath the ground, and there were no records of their remains to work from.

Bond had a friend, a former British army captain, "a high-minded English gentleman" named John Allen Bartlett. Although he had begun his career as a soldier, graduating from Sandhurst, he later resigned from the army and became a professional song writer, devoting himself largely to composing lyrics for music written by his wife. He also did automatic writing occasionally, but always spontaneously.

When Bond found himself unable to discover where the remains of his beloved abbey were, he and Bartlett decided, as a wild chance, to see if the gift of automatic writing might be of service to them. The technique they worked out was for Bartlett to hold the pencil, while Bond, who asked the questions, rested the fingers of one of his hands on the back of his friend's writing hand. When the records of their sittings were finally published, the pseudonym John Alleyne was used for Bartlett.

The script that began to come, a patchwork of monkish Latin, archaic and modern English, was in small, difficult to decipher handwriting, purporting to be written by spirits who had in their lifetimes been connected with the abbey.

When this automatic script was published, its authenticity was ridiculed. One American critic called its language "improbable Latin and impossible English." But, says William Oliver Stevens in *Psychics and Common Sense*, "the Latin was probable enough and the English possible enough to furnish specific information about the abbey's lost chapels and other structural details." Measurements were given, accurate descriptions of locations were written giving the sites of the missing chapels, and even rough outline drawings were made.

It is interesting that as time went on Bartlett, who was no artist, came to do a series of drawings in great detail that turned out to be highly finished pictures. They were said to be scenes of the old abbey, both inside and out, together with portraits of some of its personnel from the period just before its destruction. Bartlett would find himself going into half trances and then have the strange experience of seeing scenes before his eyes of the abbey as it used to be. As the visions became clearer, he felt impelled to draw them. He would fix them before his eyes on a sheet of paper and trace their outlines, almost against his will, with his left hand, and at great speed. Afterward, he would consciously, with his right hand (with which he normally wrote), add the colors as he remembered them, usually in pastels.

Bond, in *The Gate of Remembrance*, tells of their first experience communicating. The question he asked was: "Can you tell us anything about Glastonbury?"

144

J.A.'s fingers began to move, and one or two lines of small irregular writing were traced on the paper. He did not see what was written, nor did F.B.B. decipher it until complete. The agreed method was to remain passive, avoid concentration of the mind on the subject of the writing, and to talk casually of other and indifferent matters, and this was done. The writing turned out to be a sort of abstract dictum—viz: "All knowledge is eternal and is available to mental sympathy. . . ."

After a short time a line drawing was made which when examined proved to be a fairly correct outline of the main features of the Abbey Church traced by a single continuous line. Down the middle of the plan were written the words: "Gulielmus Monachus." A lot more came at that first sitting, and when asked which abbot did this, the answer came, "Ricardus Whitting." Richard Whiting was the last abbot of Glastonbury. He was executed by order of Henry VIII on November 15, 1539.

Another introduced himself as Johannes Bryant, and he became the most frequent communicator, revealing himself as a fat, good-natured monk. He was friendly and eager to assist them to reinter the abbey, for he had helped build it and he loved it—the Edgar Chapel particularly. Johannes called himself a "lap . . . mason," which he translated as "lapidator . . . stonemason." He also obligingly reported information from other monks who had lived there centuries before his time. They told about some of the older structures of the abbey.

Johannes wrote in language such as the following:

> Johannes wold speke. There is somewhat gone from us. The olde foundations were left and they did add to them. The walls at an angle were put in by Abbot Beere when he builded the chappell and enlarged the windowes. We have told ye of the high windowes and the arche under wych the tombe of Edgar one on either side—the Elder and the Younger. The arch was ycarven very faire and panellae did rise to ye roofe, and ye volte over the Est window was ydonne in fanne worke: likewise the eastern part of ye choire was in fannes wyth a great arch as soe it was donne with panellae between.

A good description of Johannes was apparently given by one of his fellows:

> He ever loved the woods and the pleasant places which lie without our house. It was good, for he learnt in the temple of nature much that he would never hear in choro. His herte was of the country and he heard it calling without the walls and the Abbot winked at it for he knew full well that it was good for him. He went a-fishing, did Johannes, and tarried oft in lanes to listen to the birds and to watch the shadows lengthening over all the woods of Mere.
>
> He loved them well, and many times no fish had he, for that he had forgot them . . . but we cared not, for he came with talk and pleasant converse, as nutbrown ale, and it was well. . . .

It was not until 1918 that the help that had been received from spirit agency was made public, when *The Gate of Remembrance* was published. Then for the first time the full story of the finding of the Edgar and Loretto Chapels was made known. Though he had achieved striking success in discovering the sites of buildings buried and lost for centuries, Bond's revelation of the source of his information aroused a storm of controversy. The furor was not only among the local clergy but even caused by one of F.B.B.'s clerical friends, who rushed into print with a flock of misstatements to denounce his book.

Or, as William Kenawell less extravagantly says in "Frederick Bligh Bond's Psychic Search," (*Tomorrow*, Summer, 1962), "Needless to say, the scholarly and ecclesiastical worlds raised their reserved and cultivated eyebrows. Perhaps these orthodox powers would have been content to let this one pass but Mr. Bond had to press his good fortune, as usual, to the wall; book followed book, article followed article, speeches and statements came in profusion. Bond, never a master of discretion, became more reckless in his claims until he was relieved of his official position as director of excavations. Matters became much tangled and bitter until finally Mr. Bond was permitted on the Abbey grounds only as a common tourist."

For the rest of his life, Bond apparently was so defensive about his phenomenal experiences that he continually rubbed others the wrong way. In 1926 he came to America to lecture and stayed to work with the American Society for Psychical Research, but his arrogance and pride hurt his success here. His heart still belonged to Glastonbury. "The last twenty-five years of his life," says Kenawell, "were spent in almost hourly expectation that the scholarly world and the Church would vindicate his work and the theories on which much of them were based. Each spring during these years, he expected that he would once again be called upon to resume his digging on the grounds of his Abbey. The expectant hope was pitiful in its trust and simplicity. His written pleas to the great among scholars, Churchmen, and nobility all met with polite but firm refusals."

Bond's last years were spent in Dolgelley, Wales, as a recluse dependent for financial support on friends. He died there in 1945 at the age of eighty-two. His bravery in admitting the source of the fantastic information he received must be respected, even if his disposition was not the most kindly. Unfortunately, he lived before his time, and was judged by the closed-minded standards that even now often still prevail.

Eleanor Touhey Smith, who surely must have been there, writes:

> Today, the scant excavation carried on at Glastonbury is sporadic and entirely scientific in manner. Little spadework is evident to the casual visitor. The broad, carefully tended lawns form a tranquil base for the few arches and fragmentary structures which rise serenely toward the sky framed by Glastonbury Tor in the background. . . . The gatekeeper, who also sells books and other mementos, will assure the visitor that any day now the archeologists will announce some startling discovery which will prove to scholars that the legends about the Isle of Glass, Avalon, or Glastonbury are historical fact.

It is doubtful if he ever points out that many of the excavations already in evidence were revealed by monks many centuries in their graves.

Yet certainly they, themselves, would appreciate it if he did. They were eager for their status as discarnate individuals still retaining memory and identity to be recognized. As the script of March 23, 1919, specifically states: "Is it not clear and patent to you now that there is a great cloud of witnesses who dwell beyond your ken and yet in your midst as raindrops in an all-pervading ocean of spirit; not absorbed in Nirvana, as the Esoterics assert, nor lost to a sense of Personality and Individuality, but actual individual drops. . . ?"

Unfortunately, there are those who are going to insist that it is still not "clear and patent." So what else can communicators do to try to prove their continued existence? Why not write automatically in their very own handwriting? That should be a real clincher.

XIII

HANDWRITING EXPERTS

WE HAVE MET the Oxford-educated medium Stainton Moses before. He was a man of great integrity. According to James Hyslop, "not a man has ever been able to question or to whisper about him a single breath of suspicion." It was only after Moses' death that a series of chances led Frederic Myers to discover additional proofs of the veracity of the following case.

During Moses' lifetime, one Sunday night a spirit (whom Myers later gave the pseudonym of Blanche Abercromby) began to write through his hand. She had died on that very Sunday afternoon at a country home some two hundred miles from London. Of her illness and death Moses knew absolutely nothing, but she wrote that she "had just quitted the body."

A few days later Stainton's hand was again controlled and a few lines were given purporting to come from Blanche Abercromby. She asserted that her script was in her very own handwriting, as a proof of her identity. There is no reason to suppose that Moses had ever seen her handwriting, for he had only met her once casually at a séance. Since the facts she gave were private, he mentioned the correspondence to no one, and gummed down the pages of writing in his notebook, marking them "private matter."

When after the death of Reverend Moses his documents were examined, F.W.H. Myers obtained permission from the executors to open these sealed pages. To his astonishment he found the communication to be from Blanche Abercromby, a woman he had known. When he compared the handwriting of the script with letters from her while on earth, he found the resemblance to be incontestable.

Myers submitted the communication to the lady's son and also to a handwriting expert, and both affirmed that the writing by the spirit and that by the lady while living were from the same person. Numerous peculiarities were found common to the two, and the contents of the automatic script were also characteristic of the deceased. The ordinary handwriting of Mr. Moses was quite different from that which usually came in his automatic script, and both were totally unlike the calligraphy of Mrs. Abercromby.

A more recent experience of this sort also occurred to a woman who had no previous evidence of psychic ability, Grace Rosher. This Englishwoman is an artist of such caliber that her miniature portraits have been shown in the Royal Academy in London. She is not given to sudden flights of fancy, is honest, independent, and has a good sense of humor. She had no knowledge of, or interest in, automatic writing or any kind of alleged communication with spirits. "In fact," she says in her book *Beyond the Horizon*, "I was quite definitely prejudiced against anything of that kind, and had no wish to investigate the subject."

Yet one day as Grace was sitting at her desk with pen in hand, pausing to decide what to write next, her pen took it upon itself to make a statement. It wrote, as if of its own volition, "With love from Gordon." Thus began one of the most curious correspondences of all time, for Gordon Burdick had been Miss Rosher's fiance who had died four days before, on September 20, 1957.

The romance between Grace Rosher and Burdick had been a longtime, long-distance affair, lasting forty years. When Grace was in her twenties, she had left her English home to visit in Vancouver, Canada. There she met Gordon Burdick, director of a shipping salvage firm. They fell in love and became engaged, but because of family interests they had to be separated. Grace returned to England, and Burdick remained in Canada. They wrote carefully restrained love notes to each other across the distance, but one thing after another came up to delay their marriage all those years.

Finally it was actually arranged for Gordon to come to London so that they could tie the nuptial knot, but a week before he was to sail he died. It was while Grace was penning the sad news to a cousin that the automatic writing from Gordon began.

At first Grace Rosher suspected that her own subconscious mind was writing the lines, but as time went on the messages became more and more complex, and Grace became more and more confused about their origin. As both parties gained more facility at their task, the script grew to look just like Gordon's. And even more odd, the communicator soon learned to write when Grace's hand was not even gripping the pen. She made a fist and leaned the pen against the outside of her thumb. Some force from her body, with no guidance from her hand, made the pen move, and soon entire pages of manuscript were being written in what appeared to be Burdick's own handwriting. (I well know that certain individuals have attempted to disprove this story by showing that it is possible to hold a pen in that curious position and actually write of your own volition. That they can also produce handwriting in any way similar to that of another specific person's has not been indicated.)

Grace kept her automatic writing a secret for some time, because, quite frankly, she was still not sure her own mind was not playing tricks on her. But gradually she began talking of it to some of her friends. Eventually the word reached the London *Mirror*, which sent an incredulous reporter and an equally unbelieving cameraman to investigate, and a handwriting expert named F. T. Hilliger to give the writing a careful examination.

Even in front of these witnesses the pen moved as usual. Apparently the spirit of Gordon Burdick had no stage fright. In his small backhand, completely different from Grace's bold forward slant, the pen wrote, as previously, with only the back of her thumb touching it. The photographer got pictures of the pen in action. The reporter took notes of everything that occurred. Both of them were amazed, and they didn't hesitate to say so.

The handwriting expert studied samples of Burdick's letters before his death and compared them with the automatic script. He found them so similar that he wrote, "On a purely scientific basis this is impossible.

"Forgery and copying must be ruled out because they require laborious care—and this message was written with speed. I picked twenty handwriting characteristics which repeat themselves in the letters Gordon wrote during his lifetime. Sixteen of them are reproduced consistently in the writing that has just occurred on these pages. That fact is staggering but conclusive."

Finally, we have a surprising instance of automatic writing that came upside down and backwards. As reported by Robert Dale Owen in *Footfalls on the Boundary of Another World*, the story begins, "In a beautiful country residence, at no great distance from London, in one of the prettiest portions of England, live a gentleman and his wife, whom I shall designate as Mr. and Mrs. W. They have been married sixteen years, but have no children." The couple were well known to Mr. Owen, and he received the report about the unusual writing within just a few days of its occurrence.

Four or five years before the incident an old gentleman over eighty came to live with them, and Mrs. W. tended him with the anxious affection of a daughter. When he died she mourned him as if she had lost a father. Mr. Owen says:

> In such a frame of mind as this, and feeling more than usually depressed, Mrs. W. went one morning, not long after her old friend's death, into her garden, in search of some distraction from the grief that oppressed her. She had been there but a few minutes, when she felt a strong impulse to return to the house and write. . . . On one or two occasions previously she had sat down, out of curiosity, to see if her hand would write automatically; a few unintelligible figures or unimportant words having been the only result.
>
> On the present occasion, however, the impulse to write, gradually increasing, and attended with a nervous and uneasy sensation in the right arm, became so strong that she yielded to it; and, returning to the house and picking up a sheet of note paper and a small portfolio, she sat down on the steps of the front door, put the portfolio on her knee, with the sheet of

note paper across it, and placed her hand, with a pencil, at the upper left-hand corner, as one usually begins to write. After a time the hand was gradually drawn to the lower right-hand corner, and began to write *backward*; completing the first line near the left-hand edge of the sheet, then commencing a second line, and finally a third, both on the right, and completing the writing near to where she had first put down her pencil. Not only was the last letter in the sentence written first, and so on until the commencing letter was written last, but each separate letter was written backward, or inversely; the pencil going over the lines which composed each letter from right to left.

Owen says:

> Mrs. W. stated to me that (as may well be conceived) she had not the slightest perception of what her hand was writing; no idea passing through her mind at the time. When her hand stopped, she read the sentence as she would have read what any other person had written for her. The handwriting was cramped and awkward, but . . . legible enough. The sentence read thus:
>
> "Ye are sorrowing as one without hope. Cast thy burden upon God, and He will help thee."

Mrs. W. told Owen that if an angel from heaven had suddenly appeared to her and pronounced the words, her astonishment could hardly have been greater. After a time she again took the pencil in hand and tried deliberately to write something backward. But the simplest word, of three or four letters, was too much for her.

Then the question rose in her mind as to who had written this to her. Naturally she thought it was her aged friend who had just died. Yet, desiring further assurance, she silently prayed that the spirit who had written this sentence through her hand might also be allowed to sign its name. Then she placed her pencil at the foot of the paper, confidently expecting the name of the friend she had recently lost.

Instead, the initials R.G.D. were subscribed. These initials were those of a young man who, eighteen years before, had sought her hand in marriage. Although she had long known and highly esteemed him, she had rejected him, "not experiencing for him any sentiment warmer than friendship, and perhaps having other preferences."

He had accepted her refusal in good spirit, but had never married. Twelve years later he had died, and although Mrs. W. was sorry, she had put him out of her mind in recent years and seldom thought of him. Thus she was quite surprised to see his initials appended to her curious communication.

This occurred on the afternoon of Tuesday, March 1, 1859. A little more than a month afterward, one afternoon while sitting in her parlor reading, she suddenly heard, apparently coming from a small sidetable near her, three distinct raps. She listened; and again there came the same sounds. Uncertain as to whether it might not be some accidental knocking, she said, "If it be a spirit who announces himself, will he repeat the sound?" Whereupon the sounds were instantly and still more distinctly rapped. She then said, "If I take pencil and paper, can I be informed who it is?" Immediately there were three raps, as if of assent, and when she sat down to write, her hand, writing backward as before, formed the same initials, "R.G.D."

Then she asked, "For what purpose were these sounds?" And the reply, again written backward, was "To show you that we are thinking and working for you."

Nor was this all. Ten days later, Mrs. W. happening to call to mind that R.G.D. had once presented her with a beautiful black Newfoundland dog, thought to herself, "How much I should like to have just such an animal now." To one of her servants who was near at the time, she said, "I wish I had a fine large Newfoundland for a walking companion."

The next morning after breakfast, a gentleman was announced who proved to be a complete stranger, a surveyor from a neighboring town. He led a noble black Newfoundland, as high as the table. He said he had taken the liberty to call because he felt assured that in her the dog would find a kind mistress. She accepted joyfully.

Mrs. W. told Owen that she had made sure, to an absolute certainty, that the servant girl to whom she had spoken on the matter had not mentioned her wish to have a dog to anyone. And so she felt that her sudden acquisition of one was supernormal, to say the least.

Owen says that those who were as well acquainted with Mrs. W.

as he was knew that uprightness and conscientiousness were marked traits in her character, and that the above incidents may be relied on confidently as the exact truth. He had them direct from Mrs. W. herself just a few days after they occurred, and then she kindly gave him the original manuscript of the two communications.

"The circumstances, taken in connection, are, of their kind, among the most extraordinary with which I am acquainted," said Robert Owen, adding that Mrs. W., until then a skeptic about the reality of any direct contact with another world, confessed to him that her doubts were removed, that she felt comforted and tranquilized, and that she accepted the indications thus given to her, unsought, unlooked for, as sufficient assurance that she was under spiritual protection—thought of, cared for, even from beyond the tomb.

XIV

POSSESSION

THE CONCEPT OF possession is as old as mankind is old, and it is still predominant in primitive cultures. Possession by their gods is a practice of many religions, such as Vodun, or Voodoo. Siberian shamans and their American Indian counterparts actually offer themselves to spirits who will possess them, as do spiritualistic mediums of all countries. And when those entranced do not bring messages, and are not ecstatic as when possessed by angels or gods, but instead are miserable and even maniacal, then the possession is attributed to demons.

St. Anthony said: "We walk in the midst of demons, who give us evil thoughts; and also in the midst of good angels. When these latter are especially present, there is no disturbance, no contention, no clamor, but something so calm and gentle it fills the soul with gladness."

Obsessing or possessing spirits are frequently mentioned in the Bible—both Old and New Testaments. In I Samuel 16:23, the Good Book reads: "David took an harp, and played with his hand: so Saul was refreshed, and was well, and the evil spirit departed from him." Matthew 10:1: "Jesus gave his twelve disciples power against unclean spirits, to cast them out." Mark 1:39: "Jesus preached . . . and cast out devils." Luke 8:27, 29, 36: "A certain man which had devils a long time. . . . Jesus had commanded the unclean spirit to come out

of the man. . . . He that was possessed of the devils was healed."
Acts 19:12: "The evil spirits went out of them."

In Mark 9:17, 21, 25–27 the story is told of the man who brought
his son to Jesus, saying, "Master, I have brought unto thee my son,
which hath a dumb spirit. . . . And he asked his father: How long is
it ago since this came unto him? And he said, Of a child. . . . Jesus
rebuked the foul spirit, saying unto him, Thou deaf and dumb spirit,
I charge thee, come out of him, and enter no more into him. And the
spirit cried, and rent him sore, and came out of him and he was as one
dead; insomuch that many said, He is dead. But Jesus took him by
the hand, and lifted him up; and he arose."

In ancient or primitive or modern settings, no matter who is
credited with being the possessor—angel, demon or spirit—the possessed person has similar symptoms and acts the same way. In today's world there are circumstances that render the problems posed
by possession more acute. The rise of an interest in Ouija boards as
an ostensible means of communicating with spirits by those who are
uninstructed in proper protective techniques and the wild growth of
magic and witchcraft make the acknowledgment of the possibility of
various forms of possession, or obsession, imperative. And they even
suggest the need for information about exorcism, as the novel *The
Exorcist* has so adequately pointed out.

The Reverend John Nicola, assistant director of the National
Shrine of the Immaculate Conception in Washington, D.C., and one
of the nation's foremost experts on exorcism, has been asked to be
the technical consultant to the movie version of author William
Peter Blatty's best-selling novel. He has agreed to do this because
he thinks we must stay alert about such things.

The church, Father Nicola says, keeps quiet about exorcism cases,
probably because it "is afraid of being laughed at by a scientific society. It is afraid of sensationalism and hysteria.

"But, then again, the church could be too sensitive on the subject.
It may be that we are letting people rot in institutions as being in-
curably insane, when actually they are diabolically possessed and
could benefit from an exorcism."

Psychic magazine (February, 1973) states that when investigating
a case, Father Nicola, who has four master's degrees—philosophy,

theology, classical languages, and educational psychology—follows a "principle of scientific economy" by eliminating possible reasons for a supernatural phenomenon. First he eliminates fraud as a possibility (and he says that about 98 percent of his investigations unearth only frauds). Then comes a search for an explanation in the natural, physical sciences. Then he explores the various areas of parapsychology—telepathy, ESP, and psychokinesis. It is then, and only then, that he will give serious consideration to performing an exorcism.

Of course, we can, as most people do, ignore all thought of such a repugnant idea as possession and just relegate the symptoms to hysteria or madness, but I advise against it if we're to face the realities of life. We live in an age remarkable for its mechanical and scientific improvements, but nobody can say that we have been advanced philosophically by accepting materialism. And now that materialism is . . . hopefully . . . on its way out, we must find answers to life which will not be inadequate or false, but which will be meaningful and true to the evidence of experience, as behaviorism and materialism never were.

Let us, then, discuss the idea of possession as it applies to our topic, not as involving gods or demons, but intervening spirits. As Cambridge professor R. H. Thouless, an eminent British psychical researcher for many years, says in the *Journal* of the Society for Psychical Research (September, 1972), "While it must be admitted that the idea of incorporeal personal agencies causing harm to human beings does not belong to the climate of current opinion, it is not self-evidently absurd." This is especially valid when it is considered that the few well-reported cases we have of possession seem to bring evidence of a weird kind for the continued existence of the deceased entity who claims to be doing the possessing.

In *My Occult Diary* Hungarian newspaperman Cornelius Tabori tells of a most peculiar incident he investigated: Iris Farczady, seventeen years old, of a decent middle-class Hungarian family, two years previously, had suddenly changed into a Spanish charwoman. Her father, Geroe Farczady, was a chemical engineer, a Unitarian from Transylvania. Her mother was the daughter of a distinguished Viennese officer who had been an aide-de-camp to Archduke Friedrich.

The family lived in a pleasant well-built villa on a quiet little street in a garden suburb of Budapest on the western, hilly side of the Danube.

On the afternoon of April 29, 1935, Tabori visited the home to learn what he could of the case. When he told the girl's mother what he wanted, she said: "You are looking for Iris? Iris is dead. She left us in August, 1933. Where is she? Only God knows. Iris has disappeared. She who now lives with us is called Lucia—a woman from Madrid."

"I stared at her," writes Tabori. "She was so calm, so matter of fact. I felt a little chilly. But she smiled."

"No, I am not a Spiritualist! Nor am I crazy. Look at me. I pride myself on being an enlightened, level-headed woman. I try to lead a civilized life—but I seem to have been chosen for some special experience."

She went on to tell the investigator that her daughter Iris had been an excellent pupil with a wonderful future, but she was often ailing. Then one night when there was a flu epidemic she fell seriously ill. Suddenly she gave a deep long sigh and her mother feared that she had died. "I bent over her," she said, "but I could feel her breathing. I touched her breast; I heard her heartbeat. I felt relieved and scolded myself for my stupidity. Iris was alive, of course, I thought. But I was wrong. Iris was dead. Her body remained with us, but the spirit had disappeared. We only discovered this the next morning."

When the girl awoke the following day she began to shout in some foreign language, jumped from her bed and tried to rush out of the house. She did not understand when the family talked to her; she just kept crying and shrieking. When they discovered that she spoke only Spanish, they began to teach her German so they could communicate with her. In a few months she had learned enough that she was able to tell her story. The girl herself related it to Tabori in heavily accented German:

"I am a Madrilena, and a pious Catholic. I was married to a day laborer named Pedro Salvio at seventeen and I died in August, 1933, at the age of forty of tuberculosis. I didn't love my husband, but I bore him fourteen children. I was terribly sorry for the children when I had to die."

Skeptical about all this, Tabori asked the mother if it were true that Iris knew no Spanish at all.

"But my dear sir," replied Mrs. Farczady, "can't you understand that she is not my daughter? She isn't Iris, she's Lucia, a Spanish woman. Iris didn't speak a word of Spanish and we never discussed anything in our family that was connected with Spain. But now that's all we hear. You must realize that Iris is dead—that this person you are talking to is Lucia, the Madrid charwoman."

"But her body, her face, her hands," Tabori argued, "they are Iris Farczady's. . . ."

"Yes," the mother interrupted. "The body of my darling Iris remained with us—but the soul of Lucia moved into it. She is changing more and more every month. Lucia has quite a different temperament. My little Iris was a sad, serious, melancholy girl, a deeply artistic and thoughtful creature. Lucia, on the other hand, is full of life and gaiety. She dances passionate dances and sings Spanish folk songs."

"Is this true?" Tabori asked the girl in German.

"All that the señora says is true," she replied. "When I looked into the mirror for the first time after I came here, I was shocked. What had happened to me? I have become such a young girl! And where were my black eyes? My thick, dark hair which came down to my hips?" Now, she said, she is quite pleased that in her new life she has become such a pretty young girl. She had been a worn-out, middle-aged woman and now she was reborn to a new youth.

When Tabori checked with other members of the family, they told how strange their life had been to the Spanish girl at first . . . how surprised she was, for instance, when she saw the Budapest tram cars, so different from those of Madrid. She was taken to Iris's school, but knew none of her former classmates, although they recognized her as Iris. She had visited Dr. Tibor Huempfner, the Hungarian professor and Cistercian monk. She amazed him with her knowledge of Spanish churches, the details of the buildings and their decorations. She was introduced to a Spanish teacher, who was surprised to hear the perfect Madrid dialect she spoke.

Tabori also interviewed Iris' father at his work. He said, "Of course, she is my daughter. At least outwardly. What happened inside her—I certainly cannot discover. I only feel deeply sorry that the beautiful career, the promising studies of my Iris were all abandoned. I had expected and hoped so much of her." He said she didn't like it if he called her Iris now. "I must certainly admit that before she fell ill she was rather irritable and moody. Now she is calm, interested in housework and sometimes produces extraordinary dishes. With milk, butter and vegetables she can prepare wonderful titbits."

The girl's sister Rene said, "Now she's become used to us and loves us dearly. Only she can't forget her former life, her work. Every day, early in the morning, she sets to work, cleans the house, washes the dishes, does the laundry, scrubs the floor. . . ."

"Well," concludes Tabori, "that's all I could discover. There is no explanation, no easy solution. Are they all pretending? But why? Perhaps a psychologist could explain the matter. I've only recorded what I have seen and heard."

There have been occasions when someone is said to be taken over by the spirit of a local person who recently died, and then the likeness of personality, appearance, and actions is easily identified. A modern case illustrates this perfectly. It also is one which brings what would seem to be fairly authenticating evidence. Dr. Giovanni Scambia of Catanzaro in Calabria, Italy, made a meticulous report for the Associazione di Recherche Psychique, and from it, as published in *La Ricerca Psichico* for June, 1939, comes the following story by way of *Fate* magazine (April, 1953).

At the age of seventeen Maria Talarico, the second of six children in a family in the village of Siano, suddenly became someone else. She said she was a man who was identified and recognized as Giuseppe (Pepe) Veraldi, a young bricklayer of Catanzaro. Three years before, on February 13, 1936, this young man had been found dead beneath a high bridge over the River Corace. Because he had recently had an unfortunate love affair, at the inquest it was decided that he had committed suicide by jumping from the bridge, but his relatives were not convinced of this and were sure he had been murdered.

On January 5, 1939, three years later, Maria Talarico, a healthy and popular young woman, walked across this bridge and apparently picked up Pepe's spirit, for when she returned home she was seized by a strange fit or frenzy and then declared herself to be Pepe. In a voice deeper than usual she demanded that her mother be brought, but when her own mother came she did not know her. She said, "You aren't my mother. My mother lives in Baracche Street in Catanzaro and her name is Catterina. I am Pepe."

When the news went abroad that Maria was insane, a number of physicians were called in to examine her, and Dr. Giovanni Scambia was one of them. He visited her fourteen times during the period of her derangement and kept careful records. During this time it was decided that Maria was actually possessed by the spirit of Pepe. She knew intimate facts about Pepe's life, but did not know her own relatives. And she continually insisted that Pepe had been murdered instead of having committed suicide. Maria-Pepe carefully set the stage to show how Pepe had been killed. She-he asked four men to play cards, and called them by the names of the four who had been Pepe's companions on the night of his death. And then Maria-Pepe accused them of murder. She-he cried out, "Abele, Toto, let me alone! Don't hit me like that! Help! Help! They are trying to kill me under the bridge!"

The next day Maria-Pepe awoke early and said, "My mother is on her way to visit me. She is almost at the bridge now." Soon she-he went to the door and greeted Catterina Veraldi, who arrived at seven o'clock. She-he embraced her, kissed her, and called her Mother. Mrs. Veraldi was surprised when the possessed girl climbed on her lap crying, "Mother, my Mother. It is Pepe. I haven't seen you for three years."

Maria-Pepe then told her the story that had been enacted the night before, of the murder under the bridge, and insisted that people should go to the bridge. There she-he climbed down the steep river bank, threw off most of Maria's clothes, and lay down on the ground, sprawled in the same spot and position that the dead man had been found. The body then became unconscious, and about ten minutes later Maria's own personality awoke and recognized her mother for the first time in days. Her mind was blank about the entire time the Pepe personality had been present. Even Dr. Scambia, who had attended Maria-Pepe daily for more than two weeks, was unrecognized.

Dr. Scambia believed it was a definite case of possession, the obvious motivation being Pepe's desire to clear his name of suicide and to lay the blame for his murder where it rightfully belonged. Perhaps he had attempted to take over other persons in his efforts to "come back," but had finally found in Maria the one who was receptive enough to allow him to possess her.

Edmond P. Gibson, the author of the article in *Fate*, "The Possession of Maria Talarico," says, "The scales seem weighted in favor of the hypothesis that the spirit of the dead man returned, temporarily invading Maria's body, and when he had explained his murder he abandoned her body and she was once again herself."

In comparison with an instance of temporary possession for a brief period of time, there are occasional cases where the possession may be continuous, coming and going for a long while, as illustrated in the Gifford-Thompson case. A goldsmith and engraver named Frederic L. Thompson of New York City suddenly found himself moved by a powerful compulsion to paint certain scenes which rose vividly into his mind. He had never been an artist, but when he attempted to put these down, they were very professional and very good. Also, they looked exactly like the pictures painted by Robert Swain Gifford, who had died about six months before. Thompson had known Gifford slightly, but he had no reason to expect that he should be so favored with his attentions.

Thompson later said of his experiences, "I remember having the impression that I was Mr. Gifford himself, and I would tell my wife before starting out that Mr. Gifford wanted to go sketching, although I did not know at that time that he had died early in the year." Often afterward while Thompson was occupied at his goldsmith's bench, he heard a voice urging him to get on with the sketching and painting. The influence began to cause serious interference with the engraver's regular occupation, for he would take journeys to other parts of the country under the influence of the impulse to paint certain scenes which were favorites of the deceased artist. During most of this time, Thompson continued to be aware of his own identity, yet on one occasion at least he had a period of complete amnesia when he did not remember a thing he had done while under the influence of the Gifford personality.

Sometime later, on being admitted to Gifford's studio by the painter's widow, Professor James Hyslop, who investigated this case and wrote about it in his *Contact With the Other World*, was startled to discover a group of unfinished paintings, left behind by Gifford, which bore such an uncanny and accurate resemblance in detail and treatment to Thompson's work while possessed that they might almost have been tracings or copies made one from the other. It should be pointed out that Thompson had at no time enjoyed access to the Gifford studio, and therefore never had seen these unfinished paintings.

The story of Lurancy Vennum was so carefully recorded and testimonies taken so soon after its occurrence, that it is the best documented possession case we have.

In Watseka, Illinois, in 1878, thirteen-year-old Mary Lurancy Vennum began to have what were called fits. It appeared that she went into trance and a procession of spirit oddballs took her over. One minute she might say she was Willie Canning, and she would talk and act like a fresh young man. A short time later she would claim to be an old woman named Katrina Hogan. Then she would sit with mussed hair and slatternly posture, actually looking like an old hag.

Dr. E. W. Stevens, a medical man who was also a Spiritualist, was brought in to investigate her condition. After calming her, he suggested she should try to find some strong spirit who could control her and keep the intruders away. The child mentioned the names of several deceased persons whom she said she could see. Then she indicated that there was one, Mary Roff, who particularly wanted to help her.

Mary Roff was a local girl who had died at the age of eighteen, when Lurancy was about fifteen months old. It was apparently decided that Mary should control the body of Lurancy until her reserves were strong enough that she could protect herself from the invasion of earthbound entities. So the transfer of ownership of the body of Lurancy Vennum was accomplished the next day. Lurancy's own consciousness disappeared and in its stead came the personality, mind, and memories of Mary Roff. For the next three months this child who looked like Lurancy Vennum spoke and acted and thought and remembered like this other girl who had died thirteen years before.

Obviously uncomfortable in the Vennum home after the change had been made, the girl was allowed to go and live with Mary's parents. There she knew everything and everyone Mary had known in the past. She recognized and called by name those who were friends of her family. She remembered scores, even hundreds of incidents that had transpired during Mary's life. One evening while the child was out in the yard, Mr. Roff suggested that his wife find a certain velvet headdress that Mary had worn the last year before she died. He told her to lay it out and say nothing about it, to see if it would be recognized. When Lurancy (as Mary) came in, she immediately exclaimed as she approached the stand where it lay, "Oh, there is my headdress I wore when my hair was short!" She then asked, "Ma, where is my box of letters? Have you got them yet?" Mrs. Roff dug out a box long stored in the attic. Examining it, the girl said, "Oh, Ma, here is a collar I tatted. Why didn't you show me my letters and things before?"

An on-the-spot report of the incidents of this case was eventually compiled by Dr. Richard Hodgson of the Society for Psychical Research. He went to Watseka about twelve years after the big event and interviewed members of both families and their friends. Objective as he was—and he was famous for falling over backwards to be critical—after his investigation, Hodgson felt impelled to suggest that there seemed a strong likelihood that the highly controversial occurrence he was recording had actually transpired as told to him.

When Hodgson visited Mrs. Minerva Alter, Mary Roff's sister, she assured him that the mannerisms and behavior of Lurancy Vennum when under the control of Mary Roff strikingly resembled those of her sister. The real Lurancy had known Mrs. Alter previously, having met her casually at school, but she knew her as "Mrs. Alter." While possessed by Mary she embraced Mrs. Alter affectionately and called her "Nervie," Mary's pet name for her.

Lurancy-Mary stayed at Mrs. Alter's home for a while, and almost every hour of the day some trifling incident of Mary's life was recalled by her. One morning she said, "Right over there by the currant bushes is where Allie greased the chicken's eye." This incident had happened several years before Mary's death. Mrs. Alter remembered very well their cousin Allie treating the sick chicken's eye with oil. At that time Allie lived in Peoria, Illinois, and Lurancy had never known her.

One morning Mrs. Alter asked the girl if she remembered a certain old dog they had owned. Lurancy replied, "Yes, he died over there," pointing out the exact spot where the pet had breathed his last. The Roff family considered accumulations of little things like this to be incontrovertible evidence that Mary was actually visiting them in this other body.

When the term of Mary's tenure was up, she declared that Lurancy was entirely healed and would now return to her body. This she did, after Mary took fond farewells of her friends and relatives. After Lurancy came back, she was well from then on. The Roffs and Vennums had become friends—this experience of sharing a daughter had, not surprisingly, brought them close together. For some years afterward, until Lurancy was married and had left home, whenever the parents visited together Lurancy would go into trance and abdicate temporarily in favor of Mary so that the older girl could have a chat with her mother and father.

A priceless story like this doesn't come along very often, and we are fortunate in having not only the report of Dr. Hodgson's interview, but a thorough account of the entire episode written by Dr. Stevens right at the time it happened. "The Watseka Wonder" is undoubtedly the best possession case on record.

There are others even more recent and more scientifically researched. We can thank Dr. Ian Stevenson of the University of Virginia for the Jasbir story, which he reported in *Twenty Cases Suggestive of Reincarnation*.

Jasbir, son of Sri Girdhari Lal Jat of Rasulpur, India, died of smallpox in the spring of 1954, when he was three-and-a-half years old. Instead of burying him immediately, as was the custom, his father and friends waited until morning, and by then the child was stirring again, feebly.

He slowly came back to consciousness; but he was not able to speak for some days, and it was weeks before he could express himself clearly. Then he spoke in a different dialect altogether. He stated firmly that he was Sobha Ram, son of Sri Shankar Lal Tyagi of Vehedi, and that he was a Brahmin. He would no longer eat the low-caste food served by his parents, who were Jats. He showed a remarkable transformation in behavior, acting haughty and unpleasant, and he would have starved himself had not a kind Brahmin neighbor undertaken to feed him. This she did for about a year-and-a-half, and then gradually Jasbir began to eat with his family again.

Among his memories of life in Vehedi, Jasbir told about how he had died. He said that he had eaten some poisoned sweets at a wedding procession and became giddy and fell off the chariot on which he was riding. He had suffered a head injury in the fall, and death had followed some hours later. When the little boy Jasbir was finally taken to Vehedi, he recognized all the people Sobha Ram would have known, and he gave a complete account of other information which was correct. The child was much happier in Vehedi, and so from time to time his family would let him go there to visit. Dr. Stevenson called on him twice, in 1961 and 1964, and interviewed most of the witnesses in the case. He believes the information he received to be genuine.

This is similar to the cases of memories of past lives that occur fairly frequently in India where reincarnation is a popular belief. Except that here, of course, the boy had definitely died at the age of three and had been possessed by the deceased entity. Dr. Stevenson believes the difference between reincarnation and possession lies in the extent of displacement of the primary personality achieved by the influence of the "entering" personality. The distinction he makes is this: "In short, if the previous personality seems to associate itself with the physical organism at the time of conception or during embryonic development, we speak of reincarnation; if the association between previous personality and physical organism only comes later, we speak of possession."

In most cases there seems to be no definite way to make the distinction as to just when the intruding spirit may enter the body, even possibly of a foetus, and so most reported instances giving evidence of reincarnation could possibly be cases of possession.

XV

DROP-INS

OCCASIONALLY, AS WE have seen, communicants like Henry Boyce, unknown to the sitters or mediums at home circles or séances, just seem to happen by, and then give dramatic evidence for survival. These have come to be known as "drop-ins."

A very good illustration of this was revealed by Maurice Johnson, a reporter for the *Psychic News*, London, in the November 13, 1971 issue. It is always valuable when any phenomena occur in the presence of newspaper reporters, for they know enough to track down whatever information may be available. In this case, Johnson wrote, "I was present at a home circle last week when a 'dead' girl, a complete stranger to all the sitters, gave her name and address and details of her passing which I have verified."

The circle met at the home of Sam and Hilda Patterson in Sunderland, and its medium was a natural psychic, Marion Jamieson of Mill Lane, Whitburn. During the meeting Mrs. Jamieson, in trance, said: "There is a young girl here giving her name as Ruth Heslop. She lives in Stoddard Street, South Shields, and was killed by a bomb in 1941 as she was crossing the marketplace to go to the air raid shelter after having been to the cinema. She says, 'You don't believe me, do you? My grave is in Harton Cemetery. It is beside the soldiers' graves.'"

Members of the circle went out in a group and found the girl's grave. Then the reporter took over the investigation. He learned the address from the caretaker and went to call on the girl's sister, Mrs. Grace Deakin. She confirmed that she'd had a sister named Ruth Heslop who had lived in Stoddard Street, that the girl had been killed by a bomb while crossing the marketplace. She also supplied the information that Ruth was with a friend named Gladys Stewart, who had been killed at the same time.

The reporter made it a special point not to mention what he had been told, in the hope that Ruth would come again at another home circle meeting. She did, and, among other bits of information, she reported that a friend had been with her and also killed at the same time and that her body was buried near her.

Contemporary British researcher Alan Gauld says in "A Series of 'Drop In' Communicators," *Proceedings* S.P.R. (July, 1971): "Cases of verified 'drop in' communicators . . . present obvious problems to anyone who wishes to explain away all apparently successful communications as due to the medium's exercising powers of ESP or 'Super-ESP.' On the other hand they can be given a perfectly natural, though perhaps entirely specious, explanation in terms of the survival hypothesis."

Gauld goes on: "'Drop in' communicators may represent themselves as wishing to assuage the grief of living friends, as brought along by persons in the next world who have previously communicated through the same medium, as lost in a kind of limbo where the medium is their only means of contact with others, as linked through common interests to people present, as altruistically trying to help, as simply 'dropping in' for a chat."

Gauld gave a number of instances of drop-in communicators who all made their appearance at a home circle which met at the house of a current member of the S.P.R. A Ouija board was the means of communication generally used. As an example of the simplest type of thing they got, there are the messages from one who said he was Edward Druce. What was originally written were such words as DRUCE HARTINGTON GRANTCHESTER RIVE XMAS. Later the additional information was given: UNIVERSITY LABORATORY OR LIBRARY. Research ascertained that a Mrs. Druce was still living in Hartington Drive, Cambridge, that Edward Druce had been a laboratory worker who had drowned himself in the River Granta at Christmas time some years previously. Druce communicated again over a dozen times, but the only further personal detail he gave was the correct Christian name of his wife.

Since no one present knew this man or his family, and since they seldom read the local newspaper where the account of his suicide had been printed long before, they felt secure that the information had not come from any of them.

The oldest drop-in case I found, dating from 1853, brought good evidence of identity, as reported by Robert Hare in *Experimental Investigation of the Spirit Manifestations*. At a home circle in the township of Waterford, New York, a communicator spoke through medium John Prosser, claiming to be the spirit of a Revolutionary War soldier who had been over a hundred years old when he died. Elisha Waters, a member of the circle, recorded the following conversation that took place with the old soldier:

"Now this is every word true I'm telling you. I'll tell ye, so that if you've a mind to take a little pains, you can find out that this is jest exactly as I tell it ye. I lived at Point Pleasant, New Jersey, and if you want to know, you jest ask if old Uncle John Chamberlain didn't speak the truth. . . ."

This spirit came another time and said: "My friends, I did not expect to speak with you again, but I want to give you this as a test. I died on Friday, the fifteenth day of January, 1847, and I was the father of eleven children. Now, if you've a mind to take a little pains, you will find this is all jest as I tell it ye. I don't talk as you do, but if you like to hear an old man, I will come again."

A letter addressed to the postmaster of Point Pleasant, New Jersey, brought the following reply:

"With pleasure I will give thee a correct account, for I have known him well for fifty years, and lived a neighbor to him. He deceased January fifteenth, 1847, aged one hundred and four years. He had seven children that lived to be married; three of them have deceased and left children. He has four daughters living at this time; three of them are neighbors to me; the oldest daughter is a widow, seventy-eight years old; three have husbands; one of them lives twenty miles from me. As they have very little learning, they request thee to correspond with me. . . ." Signed Thomas Cook.

Another old drop-in of quality dates from August, 1874, when W. Stainton Moses was visiting a friend, a medical man, on the Isle of Wight. Now Stainton Moses, a clergyman and teacher, was a man of such high repute that no one doubts his veracity. His psychic experiences began in 1872, and ranged, it is claimed, from automatic writing and trance speaking to levitation, the movement of heavy objects, passage of matter through matter, and the production of music without instruments of any kind.

At one sitting held by Moses, his doctor host, and guests Moses was entranced, and a singularly impetuous spirit spoke through him, giving his name as Abraham Florentine. He stated that he had been engaged in the War of 1812 in the United States but only lately had entered into the spiritual world, having died in Brooklyn, New York, on August 5, 1874, at the age of eighty-three years, one month, and seventeen days. No one present had ever heard of such a person, but Moses had had so many successes with his communication that he was confident, so he published the particulars in a London newspaper, asking that American journals please copy. Thus, if possible, the statement might be either verified or disproved.

In the course of time an American lawyer, a claims agent who had been auditing the claims of soldiers in New York, saw the paragraph and wrote to an American newspaper to say that he had come across the name A. Florentine. He said a full record of the person who made the claim could be obtained from the U.S. Adjutant General's office. Accordingly, the headquarters of the U.S. Army was written to, and an official reply was received, stating that a private named Abraham Florentine had served in the American war in the early part of the century.

Ultimately the widow of Abraham Florentine was found to be alive. A physician named Dr. Crowell discovered her address in Brooklyn and visited her. She stated that her husband had fought in the War of 1812, that he was a rather impetuous man, and had died in Brooklyn on August 5, 1874, and that his eighty-third birthday was on the previous June 8. He was therefore eighty-three years, one month, twenty-seven days old when he died. We can hardly be disturbed by the slight inaccuracy of seventeen for the number of days instead of twenty-seven. This mistake might easily have been made when Abraham Florentine's message was recorded. Or, for that matter, Florentine himself might have made a mistake. How many old men do you know who aren't a wee bit forgetful?

Journalist J. Cuming Walters gave a lecture on Sunday, April 1, 1923, the subject matter being material in his book *Some Proofs of Personal Identity*. He said that six persons were having a séance in a private room in Manchester, England, one summer evening when they were amused by a message beginning with the chorus of a humorous song. On inquiring, they were told the communicator's name was Frank Collins, and that years before he had been a member of a society to which Walters belonged. He gave the names of six other members of the society he had known, all of them recognizable. Another name Collins gave at a later visit was, he said, of his friend Richard Lawson. This name was also unknown to the sitters. Collins said he was a vocalist and had taken a prominent part in musical evenings and Christmas reunions. His favorite songs, he said, were old English ballads, and the lyrics out of Shakespeare's plays such as "Under the Greenwood Tree" and "Blow, Blow Thou Winter Wind." He was also extremely fond of Gilbert and Sullivan and his chief successes were "Take a Pair of Sparkling Eyes" and "A Wandering Minstrel."

When Collins volunteered all this information, Walters asked him if he was a professional singer, and he said that it had been the greatest disappointment of his life that he had not been able to join an opera company because he was lame and could not appear on the stage.

Walters found this so interesting that he pursued it, asking old-time members of his society if they remembered Frank Collins, but none of them did. Neither did the registers reveal a record of him or of a Richard Lawson. It was six months later when, Walters writes:

I went out of town with some friends. We lunched together some twenty miles away from Manchester. During an interval a lady among the company was asked if she remembered a certain Lancashire song written by Edwin Waugh. She said she did, and she sang it. When she finished, a very old gentleman, eighty years of age, seated next to me remarked, "I haven't heard that since Frank Collins sang it."

Walters naturally began questioning him and he revealed that Frank Collins had been a great singer, the life and soul of their Christmas parties, singing old Lancashire songs, Shakespeare songs, and later in his life Gilbert and Sullivan.

At this point the old gentleman called out to a friend on the other side of the table, "Do you remember that Gilbert and Sullivan night that Frank Collins gave us?"

"Yes," replied the other, "I remember how he sang 'Take a Pair of Sparkling Eyes.' I never heard it sung better."

"Aye," remarked the old gentleman next to Walters, "he ought to have gone on the stage."

"Why didn't he go on the stage?" asked Walters, still pretending to know nothing.

"Because he was lame," he answered. "It was the disappointment of his life. . . ."

Walters concluded his account with this:

> Nor was this quite the end of the matter. Some time later I was able to procure one of the earliest numbers of the society's journals, long ago out of print. I purchased it simply out of curiosity. What was my amazement to find in that volume a reference to Frank Collins and his singing of some Shakespeare songs at a Christmas supper, . . . and secondly, the name of Richard Lawson . . . who had joined the society the same year as himself. The whole case was now complete from beginning to end, and I have all the written and printed records, together with all the living witnesses, to testify to the truth of the story.
>
> It may, of course, be asked, "But what good was it?" No good at all from one point of view; that is, it was no good to Frank Collins, whom I have never heard of since, nor to his family, if any, whom I do not know; nor to his old friends, to whom I did not explain the reason of my interest.
>
> But there was a very decided gain all the same—the gain of evidence that the discarnate can and do communicate with us, that they remember, that they speak truthfully, and that their

personal identity can be demonstrated. And this was worth having for what it is, and for what it may lead to hereafter. . . .

A modern case to help give substantiation to some of these older stories is perhaps the best-documented account available, for it was carefully researched by Dr. Ian Stevenson. Dr. Stevenson, who had been for a long time the chairman of the Department of Neurology and Psychiatry, University of Virginia School of Medicine, wrote in the *Journal* A.S.P.R. (January, 1970):

> The medium of the present case was Frau P. Schütz, a non-professional trance medium who lives in Zurich, Switzerland. For many years (when her somewhat frail health has permitted) she has given regular sittings to a small private circle in Zurich. The sitting at which the "drop-in" communicator of this report manifested took place on February 2, 1962. Present, in addition to Frau Schütz, were Frau N. von Muralt (who was the organizer of the circle), and Herr and Frau Professor W. Brunner. . . . It was the sitters' custom to compare notes after the sittings and then to make a typed version combining the details of both sets of notes.

The typewritten copy was furnished to Dr. Stevenson. Translated from the German, it reads in part:

> MEDIUM: We are in a large meadow. Here comes a little lad. What do you want, child? Now he says: "Give my love to my mother."
> SITTER: What is his name?
> MEDIUM: He had an appendix. It doesn't bother him now. He is quite well. His name is Hans-Peter. He died in the children's hospital. . . . He had an Indian name . . . Pasona. . . . He has been here a long time. . . . He lived in the seventh district. . . . Oh, now he says, it wasn't only the appendix, it was an unusual illness with a lot of fever. But he has no trace of it now. He has dark hair and dark eyes. He has two brothers still living. They drink tea. Perhaps the father had something to do with tea? The little boy says, "Yes." He had drunk a lot of tea. He

sends love to his mother. "You have never known me," the lad
says. He's gone now.

This communicator never manifested again. The sitters were
intrigued and so they attempted to verify as much as they could.
Searching the telephone book of Zurich, they found the name
Passanah (not Pasona). When they got in touch with the Passanahs
a son verified that the family had a business of importing tea, drank a
lot of tea themselves, had lived in the seventh district of the city, and
had lost a boy child who had died of appendicitis many years earlier
in the Children's Hospital. The parents of the deceased child were
considerably upset by the telephone call from the sitters, so no attempt was made to pursue the matter further at that time. It was
later learned, when Dr. Stevenson came to Zurich and attempted to
verify more of the story, that Mr. John Passanah (the younger of the
two surviving sons of the family), who had done most of the talking
on the telephone earlier, had given some misinformation. The child
did not die of appendicitis at all, but from whooping cough and then
pneumonia. His name was Robert. The name Passanah is of Portu-
guese origin (not Indian), but the family had lived in India before
coming to Zurich.

Everything the child had said was correct except for two items, his
first name and the disease from which he died. And he had stated
that he had formerly had another name and therefore disavowed
"Hans-Peter" as his name when alive. On the second item, Dr.
Stevenson believes the sitters may have misheard the name of the
disease spoken by the medium, since the German word for appendicitis has its last three syllables in common with the German word for
pneumonia. "Thus a mishearing of the words for these diseases would
be easier in German than in English. This is not to deny that the
item was incorrect, but to try to understand why it was incorrect. A
mistake on the part of the communicator is certainly another possible
interpretation of this error."

We can only thank modern parapsychologists, just as we do the
early psychical researchers, for so carefully investigating the cases
that come to their attention. They cannot help but strengthen other

similar stories reported in newspapers and elsewhere that depend
only on the testimony of the narrator.

In this modern world even disc jockeys are not immune from sen-
sational psychic experiences. The dramatic story of what occurred at
an experimental group home séance was told by radio personality
Kenny Everett in *Destiny*, a monthly woman's magazine published
in London, in September, 1972. One weekend at their Surrey house
the Everetts and three male friends decided to try to communicate
by means of a Ouija-board-like apparatus consisting of an alphabet
and a glass on which certain persons lightly laid their fingers. The
glass then moved around and came to a stop over the letters, thus
spelling out words.

Soon activity began. A female name was written, and John, one of
the young men present, said he had just broken off his engagement
with a girl of that name. But she was alive and well, he said, so she
could not be the spirit purporting to communicate. She insisted she
was the very one. "Then when did you die?" he asked. "Noon today,"
came the reply. After more questions she said she had gassed herself
because of a fight with her mother. She said she still loved John and
wished they had not parted. Asked where her body was now, she
gave the address of a mortuary miles away.

"John had gone terribly white," said Everett. "If this was a joke he
thought it in very bad taste. The fantastic thing was that none of us,
apart from John, even knew the girl's name, let alone that she had
been engaged to him."

All five were by now badly shaken. They suggested that John call
the mortuary. "He did," said Everett, "and found every detail the
glass had given us about the girl was true. But no one in that room
could have known."

XVI

THE NON-PROFESSIONALS

Most people have a little bit of psychic ability and some have a fantastic amount of it. If these latter train themselves carefully and wish to work at producing their phenomena regularly, they become professional mediums.

In this chapter, however, we are talking about those with much innate talent who prefer not to make a business of it. The Worralls, and Harold Sherman, and others like them, have such a great amount of psi that they could easily have been professional mediums had they so chosen; but they will not take money for the help and healing they are able to give.

Orlando, Florida, medium Phyllis Schlemmer told me an experience which involved the non-professional talents of one of her students. Phyllis said that psychic ability runs in her family and that her grandmother was a genuine medium, but her grandmother's husband never would accept the reality of her gift. He argued with his wife about it a great deal. This grandfather, who was of Italian birth, once told Phyllis, "I am going to die, the worms are going to eat me, and there is no such thing as life after death." Two weeks later he made the transition—in August, 1968.

In November, 1968, Phyllis was holding a series of development classes in Cassadaza, Florida, and a couple joined who lived in Cocoa Beach. The woman, Carolyn Harmes, brought a sketch pad with her

179

the first night she came and drew a picture all during the quiet period. This was held in a dark room in which there was an infrared light so that everything was clearly visible.

When class was over Mrs. Harmes showed the picture she had drawn to everyone in the class to see if someone recognized it. When Phyllis saw it, she cried, "My God, it's my grandfather!" And it was indeed an excellent likeness. Mrs. Harmes, who had lived in Italy for five years, said that as she was drawing the sketch of the entity who was posing for it, he was cussing all the while in Italian, and saying over and over, "The old lady is right! The old lady is right!"

A somewhat similar story was published in *Fate* (March, 1961) by W. Tanna Rose of Los Angeles, California. If Ms. Rose is a professional medium, she did not say so in her report. She said that one day in October, 1928, a Mrs. Bennett came to her after church in Chicago looking very sad and woebegone because of her great need for money. She writes: "It was fall and her children needed warm clothes for the winter and she needed coal to keep her house warm, especially on Chicago's South Side, where the wind howls with fury. While she talked to me suddenly her husband built up behind her." This means that Ms. Rose saw an apparition that was so real that the man seemed actually to be standing there. He said to tell his wife how glad he was to see her. Mrs. Bennett broke into tears when she was given this message, saying, "Two years he has been gone, and I went everywhere trying to contact him."

The spirit husband then said, "As I was only three days sick with fever and passed on without regaining consciousness, I know I put you in a tough position. But today I have found this lady a proper go-between for you and me. Darling, I loved you sincerely and still do, and I want you to know that in the cubbyhole high up in the dining room there are some papers, three insurances all paid up before my passing into the spirit. Now, go on home, get a little ladder from the neighbors and get up there and take the policies and cash them. Then you and the children will have nothing to worry about anymore."

Mrs. Bennett shrieked. She said she knew about the cubbyhole, but had never seen her husband use it and didn't know he had. "I don't see why he never told me about this!" she exclaimed.

Through Tanna Rose her husband answered, "I had no idea my life would end so soon. I put the papers there when you went out to the store or somewhere."

In about a month Mrs. Bennett returned to see Ms. Rose, telling her that everything her spirit husband had declared was true and that she and her children were now well taken care of.

Harold Sherman, who has been one of this country's leading psychics and writers in the field for many years, wrote in his book *How to Make ESP Work for You* of a close friend who gave evidence through him that convinced his wife of his survival after death. Sherman said the incident occurred in 1958 when he and his wife were driving to Phoenix, Arizona, where he was to deliver a series of lectures. Harold began to have a strong impression while driving along that the spirit presence of his friend W.B. was in the car with them. He dictated to Mrs. Sherman the message he heard him speaking in his mind's ear. He writes:

> W.B. urged me to warn his wife, who had been running his business following his demise, not to have anything to do with a certain man who wanted to purchase an interest in the company.
>
> Not knowing anything about her business affairs, and never having heard of the other individual in question, nor even knowing the whereabouts of W.B.'s wife, I hesitated about writing to her. But again, the mental pressure was so strong that I finally addressed a letter to her permanent post office box number, for forwarding.

In a few days Harold had a telephone call from her from an East Coast city to tell him that the night before his letter arrived, she had been awakened by her husband. She saw him standing by her bedside, so real and lifelike that she felt she could have reached out and touched him. Then she distinctly heard him say to her, *"Kick that man out!"*

"The next morning," says Harold, "came my letter with the message: *'Have nothing to do with this man.'* She said she had had no reason to suspect that he wasn't the right sort, and had been seriously considering his offer, feeling that she should have a man in the business to help her. But these warnings had caused her to check more carefully, and her investigation had revealed that involvement with this man would have been ruinous. She ended by expressing appreciation for my passing on the message from W.B. She said she was writing me full details, which I have in my files."

In *Your Power to Heal* Harold Sherman tells an interesting story about Olga Worrall, the famous Baltimore psychic, and the evidence she was able to bring a grieving friend. In September, 1954, Olga and her late husband Ambrose were sitting in the silence one Sunday night, at their usual nine o'clock quiet period, when Olga received an impression that they would hear of the passing of an elderly person very close to them. They received a call Monday evening informing them that Mrs. Busick had died that afternoon at two o'clock while watching television. They were not surprised, for she had had a bad heart for some time. Sherman writes:

> The next morning Olga was strongly moved to call Mrs. Busick's daughter Ruth on the phone. She argued with herself that Ruth would be at her sister's house and, in any event, that she should not call so early in the morning. However, the urging would not stop. She decided to prove to herself that Ruth was not at home and dialed the number. Ruth promptly answered and expressed surprise at hearing Olga's voice. . . . Olga tried to console Ruth as much as she could, and Ruth finally cried, "Oh, if I could only be sure that Mommy is with Daddy, it would help!"

Almost at once, Ruth's father appeared before Olga. In another moment, her mother was by his side, looking rather frail but smiling. The father used his pet name for his daughter, saying to Olga, "Tell Deedee that I have Mother with me and I am going to take her to Atlantic City. I also have Petie with me." He held his hand out to Olga, and there sat a canary.

As Olga relayed the words to Ruth, she apologized for the silly message. "Imagine taking your mother to *Atlantic City!*"

"But Aunt Olga, it isn't a silly message," Ruth said. "Just before

Mother died she said, 'I'm going to get well because I want to go to Atlantic City to walk the boardwalk and shop.' Not only that, but about an hour after Mother's passing, our canary called Petie dropped dead!"

XVII

THE PROS: OLD AND NEW

THERE ARE SO many remarkable accounts from the really great mediums of past and present that it is difficult to select certain instances as more outstanding than others. Unfortunately, most of the best of them are old standbys and have been restated many times, but they bear repeating in the context in which we are using them. So here are some stories which have been told before, and before that . . . and they will be told again, as long as men look to mediums for evidence of survival. And here are also a few brand new stories that have never before been published.

Because she was so magnificent, not only as a sensitive but as a human being as well, we will start with Gladys Osborne Leonard, a woman investigated for over fifty years by the S.P.R. without ever one word of condemnation or one hint of fraud. In her book *My Life in Two Worlds* she tells of a test case which brought evidence of a high sort. In 1916 Mrs. Kelway-Bamber came to her because her son Claude, an airman, had been killed in France. She obtained a great deal of personal evidence which convinced her that it was undoubtedly her son who was communicating.

One day during a sitting he said to her, "Mother, I know that you often wish I could give you a test that would be absolutely watertight . . . something that no one on earth knows anything about."

His mother replied, "Yes, I wish you could do that; it would help so many people to believe in the afterlife if I could tell them something that excluded the theory of telepathy."

"Well," he replied, "do you remember a boy who was a particular friend of mine at school whom we always called 'Little Willie'?"

"Of course I remember him," said his mother. "But we haven't heard of him for some time."

Claude proceeded, "Willie has just passed over. He was killed in France, shot down in an aeroplane. His body is in a spot where it is not likely to be found for some time. I have been helping his soul to get away from the body and the conditions of war, because it will be a great shock to him when he awakens and finds out what has happened. No one knows that he is killed—not a living soul on earth at this moment, because they are not expecting him back at base yet. He has only just been killed, and I'm so glad to have this sitting with you now, so that I can tell you about it before anyone else knows."

Mrs. Kelway-Bamber went immediately to the War Office and made inquiries, but was told that as far as they knew the officer in question was safe and sound. In a few days he was reported "missing," but it was not until a year later that it was proved he had been killed. It was then found that he had been shot down that very day just before the sitting.

All the anecdotal material in the world is not as convincing to some researchers as statistics. Yet it is a rare sitter who is aware of the value of keeping accurate records of everything said by a medium and then totaling the number of hits and the number of misses. It would be so helpful to psychical research if more of this were done. A few persons have, however, kept detailed records. Apparently both Dr. John Thomas and his deceased wife Ethel were aware of the need for this, and so, working from both sides "of the veil," they amassed quantities of data. So now, for a change of pace, let us review some statistics. Not many, for they are not as entertaining to read, but a sizeable number of figures can add up to a lot of evidence for survival. As Dr. Gardner Murphy says in "An Outline of Survival Evidence," it should be kept in mind "that one topic taken out of context is scarcely likely to carry much weight; it is the sweep of the material *as a whole* which carries conviction."

Dr. John F. Thomas, Assistant Superintendent of Schools for the city of Detroit, lost his wife Ethel in April, 1926, and this naturally turned his thoughts to psychic matters, but he wanted it understood that he had always been peripherally interested in the subject. He says in *Case Studies Bearing Upon Survival:* "A point that I want to emphasize here is that these investigations were undertaken because previous interest was deepened by special circumstances, and that they do not represent a disturbance of emotional balance with consequent grasping at anything that might serve to steady one in an emergency." A friend at that time recommended Boston's Mrs. Minnie Minerva Soule (the medium who had been known as Mrs. Chenoweth in Dr. Hyslop's reports of his sessions with her). Thomas began a series of investigations with Mrs. Soule that were to continue with a number of other mediums here and in England for fourteen years. The rigid lines of conduct that he planned to follow would endeavor to avoid weaknesses which, he felt, he had found in other investigations. They were:

1. To hold all sittings in places distant from his home.
2. To select sensitives who had never known the communicators.
3. To hold a series with his identity unknown to the psychic.
4. To make arrangements for this series through recognized societies.
5. To vary the sitter.
6. To conduct "proxy" inquiries, by means of a secretary-stenographer who had also never known the communicators.
7. To have a medium do automatic writing with no one else present.
8. To use extreme care not to give information to mediums and secretaries, and, on the other hand, to give casual facts at times, intentionally, to see whether they would reappear in trance states.
9. To conduct carefully, to record accurately, and to analyze critically all sittings.
10. To have the records studied by critics of scientific training.

11. To study the records at a university as a problem in abnormal psychology.

12. To set up experimental tests, ultimately, for awareness, for evidential memories, for facts unknown to himself, and for instances of continuing purposes.

Ethel's continuing purpose was revealed at a sitting on September 3, 1925, with Mrs. Soule in Boston, when she said: "I am the most alive dead one you ever saw, and I have plans and hopes for cooperative work, which will keep us busy and happy and give us a new life together."

At a later date she stated: ". . . and I repeat what I said at another sitting, 'you can't lose me,' and while it may seem strange to write it in this way after the seeming tragedy of the first separation, I know you will understand me, dear, and know that death did not kill my sense of humor."

Dr. Thomas replied, "Yes, that is one of the first things that I have found out here."

Ethel said, "It would be a tragedy indeed if death so changed us that all the gay and happy badinage of life were lost. I am glad that it does just the reverse of that."

No final tally of Thomas successes was published, for he died before he completed his extensive campaign. But his totals for the combined sittings up to 1932 are as follows:

Total points made	1,908.0
Unverifiable	99.0
Inconclusive	89.0
Verifiable	1,720.0
Points Correct	1,587.0
Percentage correct of total points	83.2
Percentage correct of total verifiable	92.3

An example of the kind of evidence Ethel gave to bring out the fact that her memories were still intact comes from a proxy sitting in November, 1929, with Mrs. Osborne Leonard. Feda, Gladys' spirit control, described Mrs. Thomas as dressed in rather primitive, unconventional costume, walking about with a stick and making a noise with it that sounded like, "Pump! Pump!" She had a short stick and a much longer stick. She said, "I used to have to be very careful about the oil." There were eleven correct points mentioned in this sitting. The house which was obviously here referred to had an oil heating system. Mrs. Thomas after retiring sometimes rose and, wearing her nightgown, went into the basement with a long stick and a short stick to measure the amount of oil in the tanks. The *Pump, Pump* sound was made by the stick striking the bottom of the tank.

It will be noticed in the following that Dr. Thomas does not always recall his wife's references and has to verify some of them: Mrs. Soule, Sept. 16, 1927. Mrs. Thomas communicating: "I want to refer to a ride which we used to take near Orchard Lake. Yes, and a little bridge we rode over that gave us a view of the lake as we approached it. And the stream flowed from the lake. And as I recall our life together, we nearly always had some water in our view, our picture of life." This was true.

Dr. Thomas first doubted the story about the bridge, because on examination of the terrain he found a road culvert at the outlet to the lake. However, an old resident of Orchard Lake informed him that at the time that the Thomas cottage was built there, there had been a small bridge at the place, but Thomas did not remember it.

It is interesting that the spirit communicant seemed to know of Dr. Thomas' imminent death some long time before it occurred in an automobile accident on November 21, 1940, at the age of sixty-six. From a proxy sitting with Mrs. Leonard May 19, 1939:

> FEDA: But please tell Mr. Buddy [her name for Dr. Thomas] that she is getting very much nearer to him. And will you please say to him, "Yes, he will be with me; he will be with me at once, when the time comes. Now and again, lately he has thought about his passing more than he used to. Tell him, please, this is not evidence," she says, "but I want to tell him. It will be evidence in a way because it will answer the thoughts he has been thinking, but he wouldn't ask you to ask. There will be no difficulty, no confusion, just an emerging from a shell that he no longer needs, and joining me in—will you say the outer world, please, the outer larger world. . . ."

The last proxy sitting held before Dr. Thomas' death was on August 26, 1940.

> FEDA FOR ETHEL: "My position to him is altered. I am nearer to him. I am nearer to him than I have ever been before, but I am trying to make him understand. This is not something that I am doing, or I have done myself only. It is because of certain things happening to him that I am nearer to him. I want to make that clear, certain changes in him and about him. . . ."

So she was able to help him to prepare a little bit for the transition that was soon to come so suddenly.

Mrs. Leonore Piper was the first important American medium to be investigated by science. She was discovered by William James and studied carefully by him, Dr. Richard Hodgson, Dr. James Hyslop and many others in this country and England. Much of a highly evidential nature was recorded, two which are perhaps among the best being children's cases. As an illustration of the way evidence for true identity comes through a medium, they are interesting.

Margaret and Ruthie, the twin children of Dr. A. B. Thaw had both died in babyhood, Margaret at the age of six months and Ruthie at the age of fifteen months. Ruthie had begun to say a few words before she died. When Mrs. Piper's control, Phinuit, first saw her—in her spirit form—he thought she was a boy, for her hair was short. This is important, for if all the information had been drawn by the medium from the subconscious minds of the parents, this mistake could not have occurred.

At the first sitting the Thaws had with Mrs. Piper, Phinuit mentioned trouble with teeth. (Margaret had been teething when she died.) He said one of the children wanted "baby's beads." (Margaret used to play with an older sister's bead necklace.) Phinuit said Margaret had some flowers in her hand, that she liked them and took them with her. (Mrs. Thaw had placed three little flowers in Margaret's hand after her death.)

Because Ruthie could talk, Phinuit got much more from her.

Among the first things he mentioned was that she wanted to see the stars. For two or three months before her death Ruthie had pointed at the stars through the window. The medium put her hand on Dr. Thaw's head and wanted to pat his face, actions characteristic of the living Ruthie toward her father. Similarly she wanted to hear the *tick tick* in connection with her Uncle Alec, and it was he who chiefly used to hold his watch for her to hear. References were made to her picture. (Mrs. Thaw was painting a picture of Ruthie when she was taken ill.) The first time Mrs. Thaw wore fur at a sitting, the medium's hand stroked it, and Phinuit whispered "pussy" as Ruthie used to do.

Two or three times there seemed to be a direct control of the voice by Ruthie as if she were taking the place of Phinuit in the medium and speaking herself. She whispered *pt-tee* and *pussee* (pretty and pussy). The second time that Ruthie seemed to speak for herself was when Mrs. Piper had been asked to visit the Thaws at their country home up the Hudson River in New York. Dr. Hodgson, participating in the séance held there the first day, and taking notes of what was said, observed the medium's hand raised, turned somewhat diagonally with the forefinger pointing toward a picture on the far side of the room. At the same time she was saying in Ruthie's inflections, *pt-tee, pt-tee.* The parents exclaimed over this because, as Dr. Thaw noted later: "During the last month of Ruthie's life it was a regular morning custom to bring her to the room in which this sitting was held, and she would always point, as Mrs. Piper's hand had done, with *one* finger (unusual for a baby) and say *pt-tee, pt-tee,* just as in the sitting." This little habit had not been consciously in either the father's or mother's mind since the baby's death six months before. Mrs. Piper had never been in the room until the actual time of the sitting. There were many other pictures in the room, but she pointed only to the one the baby had particularly loved.

Another Piper baby case that is fantastic in the amount of material produced is the following:

The Reverend and Mrs. S. W. Sutton, who had lost their little daughter Katherine (Kakie) some six weeks previously, held their first sitting with Mrs. Piper on December 8, 1893. A friend of

Richard Hodgson's who was a very rapid writer took notes of everything that was said, and Mrs. Sutton made remarks about their accuracy for the original published report.

Shortly after the medium became entranced Phinuit said, "A little child is coming to you." The medium's hand was reached out as to a child and Phinuit said coaxingly, "Come here, dear. Don't be afraid. Come darling, here is your mother." He describes the child and her lovely curls. The transcript goes on:

> Where is Papa? Want Papa. [He takes from the table a silver medal.] I want this—want to bite it. [She used to bite it.] [Reaches for a string of buttons.] Quick! I want to put them in my mouth. [The buttons also. To bite the buttons was forbidden. He exactly imitated her arch manner.] I will get her to talk to you in a minute. . . . A lady is here who passed out of the body with a tumor in the bowels. [My friend Mrs. C., died of an ovarian tumor.] She has the child—she is bringing it to me. Who is Dodo? [Kakie's name for her brother George.] . . . Tell Dodo I am happy. Cry for me no more. [Puts hands to throat.] No sore throat any more. [She had pain and distress of the throat and tongue.] Papa, speak to me. Can't you see me? I am not dead, I am living. I am happy with Grandma. [My mother had been dead many years.] Phinuit says: Here are two more. One, two, three here—one older and one younger than Kakie. [Correct.] That is a boy, the one that came first. [Both were boys.]
>
> Was this little one's tongue very dry? She keeps showing me her tongue. [Her tongue was paralyzed and she suffered much with it to the end.] Her name is Katherine. [Correct.] She calls herself Kakie. She passed out last. [Correct.] Tell Dodo Kakie is in a spiritual body. Where is horsey? [I gave him a little horse.] Big horsey, not this little one. [Probably refers to a toy cart-horse she used to like.] Dear Papa, take me wide. [To ride.] Do you miss your Kakie? Do you see Kakie? The pretty white flowers you put on me I have here. I took their little souls out and kept them with me. [Phinuit describes lilies of the valley, which were the flowers we placed in her casket.]
>
> Papa, want to go wide horsey. [She pleaded this all through her illness.] Every day I go to see horsey. I like that horsey. I go

to ride. I am with you every day. . . . [I asked if she remembered anything after she was brought downstairs.] I was so hot, my head was so hot. [Correct.] [I asked if she knew who was caring for her, if it was any comfort to have us with her.] Oh, yes—oh, yes. [I asked if she suffered in dying.] I saw the light and followed it to this pretty lady. You will love me always? You will let me come to you at home. I will come to you every day, and I will put my hand on you, when you go to sleep. Do not cry for me, that makes me sad. Eleanor. I want Eleanor. [Her little sister. She called for her much during her last illness.] I want my buttons.

Row, row, my song, sing it now. [They all sang together the words of a song Kakie had loved. Phinuit then hushed the parents and Kakie finished alone.]

Where is Dinah? I want Dinah. [Dinah was an old black rag doll, not with us.] I want Bagie. [Her name for her sister Margaret.] I want Bagie to bring me my Dinah. I want to go to Bagie. . . . I see Bagie all the time. Tell Dodo when you see him that I love him. Dear Dodo. He used to march with me, he put me way up. [Correct.] Dodo did sing to me. That was a horrid body. I have a pretty body now. . . .

In order to shorten this, I have left out an occasional item. But imagine any medium being able to bring all these facts and significant names at one sitting!

Professor James H. Hyslop was one of those great unsung heroes of psychical research—a man who laid his professional integrity on the line by coming out in complete favor of the "spirit hypothesis." Professor of philosophy and psychology at several colleges, then professor of logic and ethics at Columbia University from 1895 to 1902, Hyslop was one of the first American psychologists, like his fellow William James, to relate psychology to psychic research. In 1904 Dr. Hyslop organized the American Institute for Scientific Research, one section of which eventually became the American Society for Psychical Research. He was secretary-treasurer and director of the organization from 1907 to 1920.

Of mediumship, Dr. Hyslop wrote in "The Mental State of the Dead":

> . . . in spite of all the influence of fraud, of chance coincidence, of suggestion as it is known in hypnotic phenomena, of the extravagances about telepathy, of subconscious mental action and secondary personality or double consciousness, as it is called, there is a mass of well-authenticated facts which baffle all explanation unless we at least provisionally suppose they attest the possibility that there is a soul and that personal consciousness survives death. . . . What is necessary is undoubted evidence that the facts claiming a spiritualistic source shall be the result of supernormal knowledge, that is, acquired by some process not producible by any normal action of the mind or body of the "medium." When that is secured it must be measured against every possible and conceivable source of information before the spiritistic hypothesis can be accepted even tentatively. The kind of facts which will prove this supernormal must be . . . beyond explanation by chance or fraud, and of that specific character which would prove intelligence or causal nexus, one or the other, or both. In support of the spiritistic theory we must have that kind of facts or incidents which would prove a man's personal identity. . . . This personal identity means that the evidence must at least show that the facts refer unmistakably to a given person as facts in his experience, no matter how we explain them. Mere personal identity is independent of a spiritistic explanation. This last view of the phenomena may be adopted after excluding all other hypotheses.
>
> Now, after we have eliminated fraud, it is very easy to establish personal identity, whether in telegraphy or supernormal phenomena. This evidence need be only a few facts known only in the experience of the "communicator" and the receiver of the messages. But it is not so easy to establish the spiritistic theory, since we have, in addition to excluding fraud, chance and suggestion, to exclude also an explanation by telepathy or some similar supernormal process, if there be such. . . .

Some of the material in this chapter from Mrs. Leonard and Mrs. Piper might almost seem to accomplish these aims.

Mediums today seldom train as long and as carefully as their great predecessors did, and they seem to go in more for specialization. Healing and "past life readings" are "in" today and materializations are "out." There are thus very few going in for trying to develop the ability to achieve physical phenomena of any kind. Oh, yes, there are some who *profess* to be producing physical phenomena . . . but they perform in the dark without any controls, so who can say?

It almost seems as if the good old days are gone when mediums had as their goals the proof of life after death. Most whom I know in this country give a certain amount of personal information at a reading, but it can frequently have been acquired by telepathy or clairvoyance. Yet occasionally the report of a séance pops up in which fantastic evidence of supernormality has been received.

Such an instance involved the late Eileen J. Garrett. She had been born in Ireland with natural psychical gifts from her earliest childhood, and her powerful mediumship was developed in London under the tutelage of J. Hewat McKenzie, founder of the British College of Psychic Science. In her later years she was the president of the Parapsychology Foundation in New York City. Her most famous case involved the airship R 101.

Early in the morning of Sunday, October 5, 1930, the largest airship in the world crashed on a hill near Beauvais, France. Forty-six of those on board were incinerated in the worst tragedy of its kind in British air history.

Two days later at a séance being held at the National Laboratory of Psychical Research in South Kensington, an intruder dropped in and found scant welcome because Sir Arthur Conan Doyle was expected in his stead. Ian Coster, a journalist commissioned to acquire articles for *Nash's* magazine, had conceived the idea of trying to get in touch with the spirit of the recently deceased Conan Doyle for an interview. He contacted researcher Harry Price, who arranged a sitting with Mrs. Garrett. Besides Coster, Price and Garrett, the only other person present was Eileen Beenham, Price's secretary.

Shortly after the meeting began, Uvani, Mrs. Garrett's Arab control, said, "I see for the moment I-R-V-I-N-G or I-R-W-I-N. He says he must do something about it. He is not coming to you—does not belong to anyone—apologizes for coming, for interfering. . . . He says, 'Never mind about me, but do, for heaven's sake, give this to them. . . . The whole bulk of the dirigible was entirely and absolutely too much for her engine capacity. . . .'"

Coster was inclined to resent the intrusion of a stranger, because the whole object of the séance was to get in touch with Doyle. Fortunately Harry Price realized immediately the drama of the communication. He allowed the proceedings to go on as Uvani had apparently scheduled them.

At this point, Flight Lieutenant H. C. Irwin, captain of the ill-fated R 101, controlled the medium. Speaking rapidly in staccato sentences, he gave as many facts about his experience as he could. "Engines too heavy," he said. "It was this that made me on five occasions have to scuttle back to safety. Useful lift too small. Gross lift computed badly—inform control panel. And this idea of new elevators totally mad. Elevator jammed. Oil pipe plugged. . . ."

As the flow of page after page of technical details continued, Miss Beenham had difficulty in getting it all down. Eventually Irwin's messages ceased, and then Conan Doyle appeared and gave an excellent interview. The article, including the Irwin material, duly appeared in *Nash's* magazine under Harry Price's byline, and it came to the attention of W. Charlton, who had been an officer at the Royal Airship Works in Bedford during the construction of the R 101. He was so impressed that he wrote to Price asking for a copy of the Irwin statement.

The document, which to Charlton and his colleagues was "astounding," contained more than forty references to highly technical and confidential details, and furnished impressive information about what occurred on the last ill-fated flight. Charlton said, "It appeared very evident to us in Cardington that for anyone present at the séance to have obtained information beforehand was grotesquely absurd." The only explanation that he, a technical expert, could give was that "Irwin did actually communicate with those present at the séance after his physical death."

Mrs. Garrett had no technical knowledge of airship construction and engines. Indeed, she had never even owned or driven an automobile, knew nothing about aeronautics or engineering. The conversation of Irwin was packed with terms that few men could use fluently. And yet every one used was relevant. She rattled off such terms as "disposable lift," "starboard strakes," "cruising altitude," "tension on the fabric," "fuel injection," "bore capacity" as if she had been a member of the crew.

It is important to note that the transmitted comments on the fate of the R 101 preceded any official detailed report as to what had caused the accident to occur. So there was no possibility that Mrs. Garrett could have read such things and memorized the terms.

"Same with S.L. 8—tell Eckener," was one of the comments by Irwin. After Charlton had been through complete records of German airships he found that S.L. stood for Schutte Lanz, involved in another air disaster. Eckener was the constructor of the German Graf Zeppelin.

"This exorbitant mixture of carbon and hydrogen is entirely wrong," was another comment. Charlton revealed that at the time of the R 101 flight highly important technical experiments were contemplated at Cardington, with the idea of burning a mixture of hydrogen and oil fuel.

Describing the tragic flight, Irwin said: "Fabric all waterlogged and ship's nose is down. Impossible to rise. Cannot trim . . . two hours tried to rise, but elevator jammed. Almost scraped the roofs at Achy."

Now Achy, a small village between Amiens and Beauvais, is not marked on ordinary maps, but it was marked on the large-scale flying map which Irwin had before him on the trip. At the inquiry a French air official stated that at Poix airdrome, sixteen miles north of Achy, the R 101 was only three hundred feet from the ground and struggling hard against the wind.

Flight Lieutenant William H. Wood, another expert, told Coster, "My particular interest in the séance was due to the fact that I was an airship pilot in the First World War and I knew Irwin personally. We had been brother officers at various airship stations and we were both flying airships in the Eastern Mediterranean."

Wood was especially impressed by Price's statement that Irwin spoke very quickly and disjointedly and was extremely difficult to follow.

"In life," he said, "Irwin was always rather difficult to understand owing to his peculiar manner of speech; his quick and jerky delivery was very marked, and I consider this evidence very important in establishing his identity."

Charlton and Wood compared notes several times, and both were convinced that no one but an airship pilot could possibly have given the information regarding the causes leading to the disaster —and then only if he had been in the airship at the time. Wood was so impressed with the evidence that he wrote: "If this séance does not prove survival, then nothing ever will. I consider the R 101 case to be cast-iron."

If Arthur Ford is as busy after his death as the many reports of his activities would indicate, he isn't having time for much else in the spirit world except communication back to earth. Almost any medium will report either seeing him or hearing from him since his passing on January 4, 1971. There is one instance of a message purporting to come from Ford, however, that has the ring of authenticity to it, for it brought evidence of information unknown to the medium, and not uncharacteristically, it showed that he still cares for his friends.

Dorothy Moore of Arlington, Virginia, is a registered nurse reared a Quaker in western Pennsylvania. She has been strongly psychic all her life, and her mediumship was encouraged by her friend Arthur when he introduced her to an audience in 1946 for the first time as a professional medium. Later he said of her, "I have been happy to watch her develop into a spiritual medium. I highly recommend her to all of my friends."

"There is little doubt," says the *Psychic Observer* (September, 1972), "that it was this direct and personal relationship which triggered the events which took place on that otherwise uneventful Sunday morning, January 10, 1971." This was just five days and nineteen hours after Ford had died in Miami, Florida.

Miss Moore says, "Suddenly, at 10 A.M. I became aware of a presence and knew I was being visited by a spirit." She did not see him right away, but heard a voice saying, "I'm sorry," and, "Please call. Please call, call, call. . . ."

Then she saw him . . . and it was Arthur Ford! He mentioned a few names, and then said quite clearly, "Call Clem at Bud's. Susan is having a heart seizure."

It was exactly 10:30 when Dorothy picked up the phone and called the home of Mr. and Mrs. Harry (Bud) Hayes in Miami. Pat, Bud's wife, is the daughter of Susan Graham, who has for many years been a close friend of Arthur's. Clem is Clem Tamburrino, one of Ford's students, well known today as a healer. Reaching the Hayes home, Mrs. Moore said, "Bud, may I speak to Clem, please."

"Certainly," replied Bud, and in a moment the healer was on the line.

"Clem," she asked, "is Susan Graham having a heart problem?"

"How did you know?" he reacted excitedly. "Pat is just going out the driveway with Mrs. Graham in the car now to take her to the hospital."

"I've just had a beautiful communication from Arthur," she explained.

Clem was still astonished. "How did you know I was here?" he asked. He had been in Florida for Ford's funeral and had just happened to call on the Hayes at that time.

"Arthur told me," said Dorothy Moore.

The Reverend Theodore N. Tiemeyer, pastor of Miami's beautiful Christ Congregational Church since 1960, was the minister who performed Arthur Ford's burial service. He has been interested in the psychic ever since his days in seminary, when he had a few experiences which aroused his curiosity about the supernormal. He studied at the University of Cincinnati and received his AB in social sciences at Elmhurst College in Illinois and his BD at Eden Theological Seminary. He has studied further at Yale and the Chicago Theological Seminary. And he has bravely continued to pursue his interest in psi through many bouts with traditional orthodoxy.

Long ago my friend Ted Tiemeyer gave me the following account of an experience with Arthur Ford. I have been saving it for just the right spot where it might be used as evidence, and this seems like a good one. It, among other cases used in this book, might help to defend Arthur's reputation as a medium whom his friends knew frequently gave information which had never appeared in newspapers or in any other way been available to him by normal means.

This incident also helped to clear Tiemeyer's Uncle George, who had, in 1916–17, been mayor of Cincinnati, of charges of dishonesty in office. George Puchta, Ted's mother's uncle, had been part of an administration that became famous for its corruption.

In Miami in 1962 the entranced Arthur Ford brought Ted greetings from his Uncle George. Since he had two Uncle Georges, he inquired cautiously which one it was and learned: "This Uncle George is one who held a public office in the city where you were born and raised. He is here with your mother and seems to have been a judge or lawyer in your city in the early part of this century."

Ted blurted out, "Oh, that Uncle George! He was the mayor."

"Yes, *that* Uncle George," Ford went on. "He was a mayor. He often has been close to you and finds interest in your work. In the light of your moral teachings he has been reviewing his political life and ideas. He says, 'I was mixed up with an unsavory group. There was August Herrmann who ran the middle part of the city and George Cox who controlled the slums and suburbs. There was also a Polish accountant named Rudy Hiesike [or something that sounded like that]. These three really ran the city when I was mayor.' "

Uncle George continued to try to explain that he had not been a conspirator in the corruption of these men. He resented his family's willingness to impugn his integrity, insisting that he was sincere in his dedication to his office but that the other three men had taken advantage of his naïveté.

Reverend Tiemeyer could only verify this by checking Cincinnati records to learn if the names he had been given by the entranced medium were correct. After all, he had been a small child during his uncle's regime, and had no personal memory of the episode. In several archives he discovered that the names were accurate. George B. Cox had been the political boss at the time; August Herrmann had been on the city council; and the city comptroller had been named Rudolph K. Hynicka.

To any Cincinnatians living today who remember the bad old days, the name of George Puchta may still be besmirched. But to surviving members of his family, because of Arthur Ford, his honor has been vindicated.

On August 10, 1960, Raymond Hamilton, of Baltimore, Maryland, had an anonymous reading from Arthur Ford while at a Spiritualist camp. Mr. Hamilton has written me about the stranger who spoke to him at that time, bringing information neither he nor Ford would appear to have had any normal way of knowing. About halfway through the reading, Fletcher said, "A man is here who says he heard you sing and wanted to engage you to sing in his church choir, but before he could do so his organist went over his head and committed the church position to someone else. Robert Hubbs, he says, was rector of Christ Episcopal Church in your town, had many friends, some of whom had told him about you. 'Glad of the opportunity to make contact with you and chat,' he says. 'Look me up when you get back.'"

"Looking up" someone requires a different technique when that someone is no longer among the living. But Mr. Hamilton had never heard of any Reverend Hubbs, so he thought it would be interesting to track him down. He told me, "On my return to Baltimore, I phoned Christ Episcopal Church and asked if the church had ever had a minister by that name. He explained to the clergyman to whom he spoke that he'd had a message from Reverend Hubbs from spirit and wanted to verify what had been given. The undoubtedly surprised minister replied, "I have heard of such things, but this is my first experience with anything of the sort." He then confirmed that Robert Hubbs had been the rector of that church for about three years at one time. "He died several years ago," he said.

Here is another story about the clergy, this one involving one of Britain's top present day mediums, Helen Hughes, and retired Congregational minister, George Sharp of Chesterfield, Derbys, England. At a sitting with Mrs. Hughes his grandfather communicated, followed by an entity who said he had been the Bishop of Auckland and had met Sharp's grandfather in New Zealand.

"My grandfather never visited that country," was Sharp's sharp retort. But the bishop insisted they had met there.

"I gave him a Bible," he added. "On the fly-leaf I wrote, 'To Robert, my friend, from the Bishop of Auckland.'"

The communicant was so insistent, that Reverend Sharp began a quest to check his statement. Three close relatives he queried denied that Robert had ever been there. Finally he questioned his ninety-four-year-old grandmother, Robert's widow. "Who told you?" she asked quickly.

Without disclosing the reason, Sharp pressed the question, and his grandmother then admitted that early in their marriage her husband went into exile in New Zealand after an unfortunate episode. "He would never have come back to me," she said, "had it not been for a man of your cloth." Then she told Sharp to fetch a parcel from an old chest in her bedroom. He opened it to find that it was a Bible. On the fly-leaf was the exact inscription he had received through the medium.

One of the foremost mediums of this century is British Ena Twigg, who has become almost as well known in the United States as in her own country. As a child she used to see "misty people" who seemed as real to her as her parents or anyone else. When she was fourteen, the misty people told her that her father would join their world in a week. A week later her father slipped on the stairs and suffered a fatal injury. So she has been aware of evidence in her mediumship from its earliest beginnings.

Ena's fame spread when Bishop James Pike said he had received communication through her that convinced him it was his son, and later when Pike's widow appealed to her for help in locating his body. A recent book entitled *Ena Twigg: Medium*, written with Ruth Hagy Brod, gives several instances in which information of a supernormal nature was received through Ena's mediumship. One case is as follows:

Mrs. Allen S. Topping, in April, 1962, was on a tour of the Holy Land. Her husband, the president of the American Wholesale Hardware Company, was in England, but he planned to pick up a car in Milan on April 19 and meet his wife in Rome on the twenty-third. On April 16, however, he had a heart attack in London. Mrs. Topping flew to his bedside at the Savoy Hotel, where he died on April 18 at 8 P.M.

Knowing Ena Twigg from a previous visit to her home, Gladys Topping got in touch with her immediately, asking for an appointment. While they were talking on the phone a message from her husband began to bombard Mrs. Twigg. She stopped and listened, and learned that he wanted his wife to look at the bottom of his billfold for a document concerning a matter requiring immediate attention. When she did this, she found a receipt for a thousand dollar deposit on a car that Mr. Topping was to have taken delivery of on the following day in Milan. Mrs. Topping notified the agency of her husband's death and the deposit was refunded to her.

Another delightful Ena Twigg story involves Mrs. Serafina Clark, founder-manager of the swinging London restaurant Nick's Diner, who was very depressed at the time because of the death of her fiance. A close friend sent her to Ena Twigg for comfort, but instead of her sweetheart, her grandmother came through, giving a message for Serafina's mother.

"Tell your mother she didn't fool me one bit," the grandmother said. "There is nothing wrong with the tombstone, but I'm not there. Nobody is."

Since her fiance began communicating immediately after, Serafina almost forgot about this message, but later she became curious about it and asked her mother what it meant. Then, Serafina said:

My mother confessed that Granny was right and that she was not in the grave under the tombstone marked with her name and date of birth and death. What had happened was that Granny died during the war, and Mother had her cremated. When the war was over, Mother's brother who had been living in Africa decided to come home for a visit and said he wanted to see "Mama's grave." Well, my mother was in a panic because she had never told him that his mother had been cremated, so she rushed down to the village where their father was buried, got a stonecutter, and added her mother's name and all the rest to the tombstone. It was really very funny that we found out about this through Mrs. Twigg. I had never known a thing about it before.

XVIII

BOOK TESTS

A TECHNIQUE KNOWN as book tests is said to have been originated by Gladys Osborne Leonard's communicators in an effort, once again, to squelch that old bugaboo "telepathy from the sitter." To provide some kind of information investigators could not claim to be inspired by living minds, certain books available to the sitter but from a library the medium had never seen were used to produce messages which might help establish the communicator's identity. Deceased friends or relatives of Mrs. Leonard's regular sitters would come to each session prepared with the location of a book, the page, and the line of a message which would have special significance involving them. The clues were unintelligible until after they were followed up and the message decoded.

An excellent example of a simple Leonard book test is described in *The Earthen Vessel* by Pamela Glenconner. Edward Wyndham Tennant, known as "Bim," a son of Lord and Lady Glenconner who fell in the Battle of the Somme, is the purporting communicator. At a Leonard sitting on December 17, 1917, Bim's brother, David Tennant, and his father were the sitters.

In the years before the war, Lord Glenconner's chief interest was forestry. Often in the course of family walks through the woods, he would gloomily say that the trees were being ruined by the beetle. Young Bim sometimes whispered to his mother at the start of a family walk, "See if we can get through the wood without hearing about the beetle."

Feda, Mrs. Leonard's control, gave a book test which she said was from Bim. "*This book is particularly for his father,*" she said. "Underline that, he says. It is the ninth book on the third shelf counting from left to right in the bookcase to the right of the door in the drawing room. Take the title, and turn to page thirty-seven."

When father and son returned home and went to their bookshelf, they found that the ninth book on the third shelf was *Trees* by T. H. Kelman. On page thirty-six it read, quite at the bottom and running over to page thirty-seven: "Sometimes you will see curious marks in the wood; these are caused by a tunneling beetle, very injurious to the trees."

Needless to say, Mrs. Leonard had never been in the Glenconner drawing room.

Nora Sidgwick, widow of the first president of the S.P.R., evaluated 532 items from Feda's book tests, with the aim of finding out how many hit the mark. She discovered that 92 could be classed as successful; 100 approximately successful; 204 complete failures; 40 nearly complete failures; 96 dubious. Taking the first two classes together, she concluded that 36 per cent of the tests were approximately successful.

Mrs. Sidgwick also made a study of the element of chance in book tests: Was it possible that the apt phrases Feda and the communicators directed sitters to could be found by chance in any book? She chose at random page numbers and lines and then looked up these references in randomly selected books, seeking messages which might be considered applicable to her. She found that very few seemed suitable in any sense. I have found the same thing to be true. It is actually difficult to find any randomly selected phrase or sentence in a book that will make any sense at all in its application to you personally. Nora Sidgwick's experiments were too limited to base definite conclusions on, but as far as they went, they tended to show that chance is not a likely explanation of success in even simple book messages.

Taking Mrs. Sidgwick's pioneer work as a model, the Society for

Psychical Research conducted a group of similar tests on a larger scale. Under controlled conditions a number of people were asked to turn to specified locations in given books and to try to find messages which might apply to them personally. The results of the tests were then analyzed by Colonel C. E. Baddeley, whose report was published by the S.P.R. Out of 1,800 items, complete success was found in 34; partial or slight success in 85; complete, partial, and slight success in 138. All the rest were negative. The percentage of complete and partial success was 4.7.

Thus Mrs. Sidgwick's analysis of the 532 items in the book tests conducted by Feda showed a percentage of complete or partial success very much greater than that obtained by the S.P.R. random experiments—36 percent compared with 4.7 percent.

In her paper in which the above was reported, Mrs. Sidgwick gave an account of a sitting by Mrs. Hugh Talbot with one of the earliest book tests of which we have a record. It was received on March 19, 1917, and recorded on December 29 of the same year.

Mrs. Talbot said, "Mrs. Leonard at this time knew neither my name nor address, nor had I ever been to her or any other medium, before, in my life." After a few general messages, some of which were intelligible and some not, she writes:

Feda gave a very correct description of my husband's personal appearance, and from then on he alone seemed to speak (through her of course) and a most extraordinary conversation followed. Evidently he was trying by every means in his power to prove to me his identity and to show me it really was himself, and as time went on I was forced to believe this was indeed so.

All he said, or rather Feda for him, was clear and lucid. Incidents of the past, known only to him and to me were spoken of, belongings trivial in themselves but possessing for him a particular personal interest of which I was aware, were minutely and correctly described, and I was asked if I still had them. . . . All this was very interesting to me, and very strange, more strange because it all seemed so natural.

Suddenly Feda began a tiresome description of a book, she said it was leather and dark, and tried to show me the size. Mrs.

Leonard showed a length of eight to ten inches long with her hands, and four or five wide. She [Feda] said, "It is not exactly a *book*, it is not printed, Feda wouldn't call it a book, it has writing in." It was long before I could connect this description with anything at all, but at last I remembered a red leather notebook of my husband's. . . . I then said, "Is it a red book?" On this point there was hesitation, they thought possibly it was, though he thought it was darker. The answer was undecided, and Feda began a wearisome description all over again, adding that I was to look on page twelve, for something written . . . there, that it would be so interesting after this conversation. Then she said, "He is not sure it is page twelve, it might be thirteen, it is so long, but he does want you to look and to try and find it. It would interest him to know if this extract is there." I was rather half-hearted in responding to all this, there was so much of it, and it sounded purposeless and also I remembered the book so well, having often looked through it wondering if it was any good keeping it, although besides things to do with ships and my husband's work there were, I remembered, a few notes and verses in it. But the chief reason I was anxious to get off the subject was that I felt sure the book would not be forthcoming; either I had thrown it away, or it had gone with a lot of other things to a luggage room . . . where it would hardly be possible to get at it. However, I did not quite like to say this, and not attaching any importance to it, replied rather indefinitely that I would see if I could find it. But this did not satisfy Feda. She started all over again becoming more and more insistent and went on to say, "He is not sure of the color. . . . There are two books, you will know the one he means by a diagram of languages in the front . . . Indo-European, Aryan, Semitic languages" . . . and she said, "There are lines, but not straight, going like this"—drawing with her finger lines going out sideways from one center. Then again the words, "A table of Arabian languages, Semitic languages."

This all sounded like rubbish to Mrs. Talbot, and she went home remembering primarily the interesting things said in the beginning of her sitting and thinking very little of this last part. She mentioned it to her sister and niece, and the latter begged her to look for the book at once. Knowing that it was all nonsense, Mrs. Talbot wanted to wait until the next day, but was finally persuaded. She says:

> In the end I went to the bookshelf, and after some time, right at the back of the top shelf I found one or two old notebooks belonging to my husband, which I had never felt I cared to open. One, a shabby black leather, corresponded in size to the description given, and I absentmindedly opened it, wondering in my mind whether the one I was looking for had been destroyed or only sent away. To my utter astonishment, my eyes fell on the words, "Table of Semitic or Syro-Arabian Languages," and pulling out the leaf, which was a long folded piece of paper pasted in, I saw on the other side, "General table of the Aryan and Indo-European languages." It was the diagram of which Feda had spoken. I was so taken aback I forgot for some minutes to look for the extract. When I did I found it on page thirteen. I have copied it out exactly.

Page thirteen of the notebook contained an extract from *Post Mortem*. Author anonymous. Blackwood & Sons, 1881. It read:

> I discovered by certain whispers which it was supposed I was unable to hear and from certain glances of curiosity or commiseration which it was supposed I was unable to see, that I was near death. . . .
> Presently my mind began to dwell not only on happiness which was to come, but upon happiness that I was actually enjoying. I saw long-forgotten forms, playmates, school-fellows, companions of my youth and of my old age, who, one and all, smiled upon me. They did not smile with any compassion, that I no longer felt that I needed, but with that sort of kindness which is exchanged by people who are equally happy. I saw my mother, father, and sisters, all of whom I had survived. They did not speak, yet they communicated to me their unaltered and unalterable affection. At about the time when they appeared, I made an effort to realize my bodily situation . . . that is, I endeavored to connect my soul with the body which lay on the bed in my house . . . the endeavor failed. I was dead. . . .

Some of Feda's book tests were quite complicated, involving a number of different items. One such was received on September 29, 1917, by Mrs. S. E. Beadon. The communicator was her deceased husband, Colonel Beadon. Feda started off by announcing that in a square room there was a row of books running between the window and to the corner.

"Counting from right to left, remove the fifth book," she said. "On page seventy-one, second paragraph on about the middle of the page, will be found a message from him to you, not as beautiful as he would like to make it, but you will understand he wants to make the test as good as he can."

Feda said that the message would bring out the following points for Mrs. Beadon:

1. It refers to a past condition.
2. It also has an application to the present.
3. It is an answer to a thought which was much in mind at one time but is not now—especially since you have known Feda.
4. On the opposite page is a reference to fire.
5. On the opposite page is a reference to light.
6. On the opposite page is a reference to olden times.
7. On the same page or opposite page or perhaps over the leaf is a very important word beginning with S.

"These last four," said Feda, "have nothing to do with the message but are just tests that you have the right page."

The room referred to proved to be the dining room of Mrs. Beadon's mother's house where she was then staying. Mrs. Leonard had never been inside that house. The fifth book from the right was a volume of poems by Oliver Wendell Holmes, whose poetry Mrs. Beadon had never read. The second paragraph on page seventy-one was "The Pilgrim's Vision." It is about early settlers in America—the "past condition" of Item 1. It also had an application to the present, as suggested by Item 2, for it applied to the communicator's own situation. The poem read as follows:

The weary pilgrim slumbers,
His resting place unknown,
His hands were crossed, his lids were closed,

The dust was o'er him strown.
The drifting soil, the mouldering leaf
Along the sod were blown,
His mound has melted into Earth
His memory lives alone.

Mrs. Beadon's husband had been killed in action in Mesopotamia and was buried by the chaplain and officers the same night near where he fell. He received reverent burial; his resting place was unknown. The officer in charge wrote to Mrs. Beadon that all traces of the grave had been carefully obliterated to avoid desecration by the Arabs. After she heard the news, Mrs. Beadon was quite worried for a time because her husband was in an unmarked grave. She wondered constantly whether it would be possible later to identify the spot with the help of the officers who had been present at his burial, so that when the war was over his grave could be marked with a cross. This was obviously a reference to Item 3. Since she began to receive communication from her husband through Gladys Osborne Leonard, however, she had thought about that idea very little and had not felt as concerned as she did at first that his grave was unmarked and unknown.

On the opposite page were Items 4, 5, and 6, the references to fire, light, and olden times, in the following verse:

Still shall the fiery pillar's ray
    Along the pathway shine,
To light the chosen tribe that sought
    This Western Palestine.

On the following page there was the title of a poem, "The Steamboat," fulfilling Item 7: an important word beginning with S.

When Feda had given the page as 71 she had at first been hesitant that it might be 17 instead. After repeating both numbers several times she said she was sure it was page 71. Oddly enough, page 17 also contained mention of an unmarked grave, and on the opposite page appeared the words fire and sunset glow. When, as a test, Mrs. Beadon checked other pages of the book, however, she could not find any page which fulfilled the conditions of the message at all.

It almost seemed from all this that someone, somewhere was definitely trying to tell Mrs. Beadon something.

American violinist Florizel von Reuter became interested in psychical research when in his thirties, but he did not attempt to communicate with spirits until he discovered an object called an "additor," which was somewhat like a Ouija board but with the addition of a hollow box with a protruding pointer used to designate the letters. Messages of a most complicated character were said to be forthcoming from it because the little box was supposed to be the collector of some mysterious force in the human body called "Od."

Florizel and his mother Grace began experimenting with this unusual contraption, but for a long time nothing happened. Then the activity began one evening when Florizel was playing a sonata and his mother had her fingers on the box. Her eyes were tightly closed. Then, though she was barely touching it, she became conscious of a "peculiar impelling force causing the box's pointer to glide about."

Von Reuter put aside his violin and began jotting down the letters pointed to, but they made no sense. Then he recalled reading that spirit writings were sometimes inverted. When he transcribed the eighty letters backwards a complete sentence in German emerged, giving a message from a communicating guide.

Florizel said, "I do not believe even the most confirmed skeptic would credit my mother with the skill to respond consciously in inverted German without the slightest hesitation, at a lightning speed, to chance questions put by a second person, her eyes tightly closed and her natural language being English."

At a subsequent sitting a book test was arranged. Florizel and his wife had lost touch with a close friend, Jean, and he asked the additor for news of her. The reply was that she was well and they would soon hear from her.

Florizel then suggested a test. "If you can refer to a book in my library of over five hundred, indicating a page where the name Jean appears, I will consider that excellent proof."

The pointer spelled: "Pick out a gray book from the lowest shelf of the bookcase on the left side of the next room. Find the place where a chapter ends on the left page and another beings on the right."

Following the directions, Florizel found a gray-bound volume, *The Song of Bernadette* by Franz Werfel.

"Though I knew this book was in my collection, I had not the slightest idea where it was," he comments.

Carefully examining the first and last words of each chapter, he eventually found toward the end of the book, as indicated, the name Jean on the right-hand page of a new chapter.

That afternoon Jean phoned confirming that she was in good health.

Laura Archera Huxley gives a good book test in *This Timeless Moment*. It occurred in 1965, two years after her famous husband Aldous had died, at a time when Keith Milton Rhinehart of Seattle had called at her home to show some movies of famous people he had taken on his recent round-the-world tour.

Keith gave Laura a private reading first, and then they went downstairs from the study and started preparations to show the filmed interviews. K.M.R. was trying to solve the threading of the film when, without diverting his attention, he said to her, "Please give me a pencil and paper. Aldous is saying I must write this down." He wrote:

> 17th page
> 6th book from left
> 3rd shelf
> or
> 6th shelf
> 3rd book from left
> 23rd line

Laura went up to the room which had been Aldous' and began to search for the books on the small wall, next to the door, which had six shelves about four feet in length. Soon she called the assembled guests up there, for what she had discovered had been quite exciting to her. She writes:

> I counted to the third shelf from the floor, counted to the sixth book from the left, and took it out. . . . It was a soft-

cover book inside a cardboard container, in Spanish. It looked and felt as if it had never been opened before. The title *Coloquio de Buenos Aires*, 1962, published by the P.E.N. Club of Argentina, in Buenos Aires; the printing was finished August 20, 1963. I opened the book to page 17. Before I even counted to line 23, the name Aldous Huxley, from the paragraph in the center of the page, leaped to my eyes. [This is the translation of the paragraph containing line 23:]

Aldous Huxley does not surprise us in this admirable communication in which paradox and erudition in the poetic sense and the sense of humor are interlaced in such an efficacious form. Perhaps the majority of the listeners to this conversation will not have a complete idea of the spiritual richness of this communication through the summary which the faithful translator, and learned scholar in scientific disciplines, who is Alicia Jurado, has just made for us.

This book had arrived either shortly before Aldous' death or just after. Laura's sister from Italy had since reorganized the library, and Laura herself had never seen the book before. It was the report of a literary meeting held in Buenos Aires in October, 1962, where Aldous was to give an address on "Literature and Science," but did not go. The paragraph quoted referred to Aldous' last book, *Literature and Science*.

To test the rest of the message, they took the bottom shelf to be the sixth shelf, counting down from the top. The third book from the left was a small, black hardcover, *Proceedings of the Two Conferences on Parapsychology and Pharmacology*. On page 17 the paragraph containing line 23 read as follows:

Parapsychology is still struggling in the first stage. These phenomena are not generally accepted by science although many workers are firmly convinced of their existence. For this reason the major effort of parapsychological research has been to demonstrate and to prove that they are working with real phenomena.

One more book was found that met the requirements of location and page. It was *My Life in Court* by Louis Nizer. The paragraph on page 17, line 23 describes a man bearing no resemblance to Aldous, *except* for his exceptional height of six feet five. Aldous was six feet four.

The group was stunned. Then someone suggested that perhaps in any book in that library on page 17, line 23, one could find something that could relate to Aldous. They gave this possibility a full trial; none of the books they picked at random had, on page 17, line 23, meanings which could be specifically or even remotely related to Aldous or to what was happening that evening.

Naturally people who were told about this suggested the possibility that the medium had browsed among the shelves. But he had never been in that room alone at any time. And anyway, as Christopher Isherwood suggested, even if he had been, it would have taken thousands of hours of reading to find three books which, at specified locations, would have had three paragraphs so directly related to Aldous and to the experiment of that evening.

And now for a couple of book tests that were originated in less orthodox ways. Information for one was provided to the Phoenix medium Sarah Evanston in February, 1972, two days after her uncle, a West Virginia dentist, had died. Sarah told me: "While I was asleep, I heard my name called. As I opened my eyes there was a very short man in a long white jacket. Now my uncle had been a very short man, but I didn't know whether or not he ever wore long jackets."

Being very critical to evaluate evidence properly, even when awakened in the middle of the night, Sarah did not tell herself this actually was her uncle appearing to her, for she was unable to see his face. However, when he began to talk to her, she was convinced because he spoke of personal family matters. She says, "He instructed me to go to the Phoenix library and get two law books. He gave me the names of the books and the pages on which I was to look." Then he told her to have those pages photostated because her husband Bob would have to make a trip to West Virginia in connection with his estate. This did not sound very likely to Sarah, but she had the photostating done anyway; and twenty-four hours later her mother called and asked Bob to come east to help them. While he was on the plane he read the pages Sarah's uncle had caused her to have reproduced for him. On them, it turned out, was exactly the information needed for the protection of the family property.

Sarah later checked for evidence with her mother, who told her that her uncle had invariably worn long white medical jackets rather than the shorter ones more usual among dentists.

Both Sarah's mother, Mrs. Verna Brown, and her husband, Robert Evanston, have independently confirmed this account to me.

In March 1957 while Reverend Paul Lambourne Higgins was meditating quietly in the front room of his home in Chicago, he felt the presence of his old friend, Dr. Walter B. Hill, who had died in California several years before. Higgins said: "Dr. Hill, I know you are here. Please make an effort to prove it to me. Can you give me, do you think, some message from this book on the desk?" The book was *Man Being Revealed*, and he had not yet read it.

Immediately he began receiving impressions, the first being "turn to page 67," and then "and to line 6." Then, Dr. Higgins told me: "I turned to page 67, line 6 and there read these words: 'Death has lost its sting, and the grave its victory.' It was a clear word of assurance from Dr. Hill."

On another occasion, as Mr. Higgins recorded the incident in his book *Encountering the Unseen*, he asked for a book test again . . . and this time in the Bible. He writes:

> One evening my wife and I, while sitting with two young couples of our parish, were using the Ouija board. It seemed clear to us that my mother, deceased for some years, was in touch with us. After asking several test questions, for which we received correct answers, we proceeded with an experiment. I asked the communicator if she could see the New Testament in my hand. The answer was immediate and affirmative. Then, without looking at the pages, I put my finger inside the book, and asked if she could tell me where my finger pointed. One of the young men present then took the book from me, putting his finger where mine was, but still without looking at the pages. Not one of us knew the page or the book of the New Testament where his finger rested. Upon asking the communicator, she immediately replied through the Ouija board, saying the finger pointed to the word "nevertheless," and that it was in II Corin-

thians, chapter 3, verse 16. We excitedly opened the New Testament, and discovered that she was correct in every detail.

There is a gifted psychic in Chicago named Irene Hughes, who gave Reverend Higgins a series of messages which he felt to be in some respects highly evidential. One was a book test. Higgins writes: ". . . Mrs. Hughes had never been in our home, and knew nothing of my library. She said she felt the presence of William Yeats, and that he wanted me to read a poem he had written about a priest which he felt fitted me. I would find it on page 87 of a little red-covered book in my library. I jotted down this date, but was unimpressed, knowing I did not have a book of Yeats's poems. Upon returning home, however, I went through my shelves of poetry, suddenly coming upon a little red anthology in which there were three poems by Yeats. I found the one referring to the priest, only it was on page 187, instead of 87."

Oh, well, let us allow the famous poet the poetic license to be just that small amount inaccurate.

XIX

DIRECT VOICE

With some especially gifted mediums a phenomenon known as direct voice sometimes occurs. Direct voice and trumpet mediumship are two different things, yet each seems to involve a similar technique of communication. Occasionally a spirit who has been talking through a trumpet or through the control of the entranced medium will find himself able momentarily to somehow project his voice out in space so that it can be heard by the sitter. Although startling and exciting, the evidence it brings is still the criterion by which we must judge the genuineness of such manifestations.

Phoney trumpet mediums abound, but the real thing is quite rare. If a medium insists that the room must be absolutely dark for a trumpet service, you can take it for granted that whatever comes will be fraudulent. This is not to say that genuine phenomena cannot occur in the dark and do not on occasion. But with the consistent low caliber of most physical mediumship, in this country especially, they seldom do occur.

I have been to several trumpet séances that were so obviously fraudulent as to be humorous, if it were not that money is being taken under false pretenses. Although I know that the pitch dark room is not likely to produce anything of value, I will always go along with the medium's wishes and maintain the darkness. I don't doubt the stories at all that a sudden light might damage an entranced medium. I know how withdrawn from reality one gets at such times, and being abruptly startled by light or by loud sound can be traumatic.

Once, however, someone did provide a light at a trumpet séance I attended, and it revealed just what I had suspected. On this occasion I was accompanied to a sitting with a St. Louis, Missouri, trumpet medium by a very nervous man. I didn't know he had a "thing" about the dark until the medium gave us her initial spiel and then turned out the light. He at once became panicky and struck a match, which revealed the medium's hand picking up the trumpet ready to begin talking through it. (Of course, in a genuine trumpet session, the medium would have no physical contact at all with the trumpet.)

Yet there have been fantastic mediums in the past who have produced voices even in the light, either with or without trumpet, and under controlled conditions. It is easy for us to suggest that just because a sitter was a clergyman or a buinessman, he was not as critical as a professional psychical researcher might have been, and so was easily hoodwinked, and that thus we need not take his reports seriously. Yet you will find in the accounts of many of these oldtimers that they were just as critical and just as careful to record every word spoken as any modern parapsychologist would have been. And they were not taken in by pious platitudes even if they were supposed to emit from the mouth of a trumpet. They demanded evidence.

Listen to the careful account of the procedure and safeguards given by the Reverend V. G. Duncan in *Proof*. Duncan's mediums were two little Glasgow ladies, the Misses Moore, in whom he had absolute trust as persons. Yet he still always took precautions. The séances were held in his own study, a small room on the ground floor with one door and one window. While a sitting was in progress, the shutters of the window were closed and fastened so the room was in darkness. Two aluminum trumpets were used, one belonging to the mediums, the other to the Church-of-England clergyman. Both were generally in operation, but frequently the communicating voice spoke independently of them.

"It should also be observed," Duncan says, "that the greatest care was taken to avoid any disclosure of information to the mediums.

The sitters came from all parts of the city and occasionally from outside it. Their names were never mentioned and they did not meet the mediums until the moment they entered the séance room."

The first of the series of sittings he is here relating is especially interesting because it is linked up by cross correspondence with a medium over 400 miles away, and again to another séance held some two years later in England. It took place at 3 P.M. on May 23, 1927. The only sitter apart from the mediums, the pastor and his wife, was Mrs. Mary L. Cadell, of Murrayfield, Edinburgh, who permitted the use of her right name and also gave Reverend Duncan all her notes on the other sittings involved in the cross correspondence. Mrs. Cadell was a member of the Society for Psychical Research. For a number of years she had studied both practically and theoretically the various phases of psychic phenomena and had contributed to the *Journal* of the S.P.R., as well as to other similar publications. She was by no means unversed in either the procedure of the séance room or the canons of evidence. The preacher sat at a writing table and took down, after much practice writing in the dark, everything that was said and done. "These notes," he says, "I deciphered after each sitting, when I wrote a full account of the proceedings while it was fresh in my mind."

The meeting was opened with a prayer, the 23rd Psalm, and then a hymn was played on the gramophone. Soon a trumpet whizzed up to the high ceiling and moved about overhead. Then it touched Mrs. Cadell so gently that it seemed to be caressing her. Next Andrew, the control, described a tall young officer standing behind her, very upright and boyish looking. This was a good description of her son, Dick Cadell. Shortly after this she heard a low, immensely moving voice say, "Mother, Mother, I love you. I am always with you. There is no death. I long for you. I am 'Cadell'." The name "Cadell" came quite clearly and distinctly. She could not make out very well the rest of what he said except these sentences. The Misses Moore, incidentally, did not know her name. The voice she heard was a set voice with a sweet tone, which Richard Cadell's was, but, she says, "I should not have recognized it as my son's."

Whenever the voices ceased, the gramophone was started, to help the vibrations. As the hymn, "Hark, hark, my soul, angelic songs are swelling" was played, all participated in the singing, and then, she says, "Quite suddenly we heard a new voice join in. It was a very deep, very sweet man's voice singing through the trumpet. *It was unmistakedly my son's voice*. It went on and off, leaving the high tones to the gramophone and then joining in again as the lower notes came. It sang right on throughout the hymn. It was a heavenly experience. After the hymn came to an end the trumpet fell down near my feet and the sitting was over."

Now to the cross correspondences. On March 12 and 13, 1928, Mrs. Cadell attended two private séances with Gladys Osborne Leonard. She deliberately refrained from mentioning anything about having had any previous sittings with other mediums. In the Leonard sitting on March 12, Feda said: "His voice (R's) comes like in the trumpet sitting." On March 13, Feda said: "He can sing and pretty well too. Something only a little while ago reminded you of it. He's tried to make you hear him sing. He sang something that had words in it with a promise." This is true, of course, of the hymn "Hark, hark, my soul."

Now, when Mrs. Cadell was not present, her son came to a sitting Reverend Duncan held at his Hampshire rectory with the Misses Moore on October 3, 1929. He gave his name. "I'm Dick," he said. At the time Reverend Duncan couldn't place him, and said so. "Oh," the spirit answered, "I've met you before in Edinburgh." When asked his full name he said, "Richard Cadell." Then he answered some questions, explaining that he had been a professional soldier conscripted in 1916. He had been to school in England at a place which sounded like "Charterhouse." He ended up by saying that he was interested in these notes of the sitting which the pastor was making and that he would certainly help him to put them into book form.

Now Reverend Duncan knew nothing about the young man except his name, so he wrote the mother to see if the facts given at the séance were true. They were. But there was more to come. On October 10, 1929, at a sitting with Mrs. Osborne Leonard, Feda said: "R. went to a trumpet sitting because he hoped to get a message through. He said it was with people you had a link with—a *parson*. . . . He was the one we knew in Edinburgh. He and his wife make nice psychic conditions. Can you write to the parson and ask him to keep a lookout for me? I am particularly anxious. He's going to have some more sittings. *I'm going to try to get the voice without a medium. I know I have done* [direct voice words are italicized] *something already. He was a trumpet medium. I tried to get through. . . . Will you tell him I'm working with Rachel? He'll know who I mean and there are others. We are going to work all together. You may be invited down there. I've got an ulterior motive."*

On Saturday, October 26, 1929, a direct voice sitting was held in the study at the Hampshire rectory, and a pleasing feminine voice manifested giving the name "Rachel." She was recognized by two of the sitters, the Reverend Lionel Corbett and his wife, as their daughter who had died some years before. From Mr. Corbett's report comes the following:

> My daughter Rachel came and spoke to us in the direct voice —being clearly heard by all—while later in the evening I heard a spirit voice who gave his name as Dick Cadell conversing freely with Mr. and Mrs. Duncan.
>
> I should like in passing to pay a humble tribute to the mediumship of these two Scotch ladies. Since March 1925, I have had the privilege of sitting with them a number of times, and I can testify to their remarkable powers, while to all who know them their integrity and honesty of purpose is beyond question.
>
> When conditions are good and harmony prevails, truly wonderful results are obtained, the "voices" coming clear and distinct and generally carrying evidence of identity. Such mediumship is indeed rare and valuable. . . .

At another session on the evening of this same day Richard Cadell manifested again and spoke without using the trumpet. He said that his mother would be taking a trip south later on. She would not be traveling by train but by road. She would make an effort to see Mr. Duncan, but he did not think this would be successful. The business part of the program would prevent it.

This communication was not very clear to the parson. He could not understand when Dick said that his mother would combine "a

business and pleasure trip South." It seemed to him there must have
been some confusion and he did not pass this news on to Mrs. Cadell.

On March 10, however, he received a letter from Mrs. Cadell saying
she might visit him sometime between March 22 and 30, because
she and her husband were planning a motor tour with another son
which would combine pleasure and the son's study of architecture.
At the last moment, however, the trip was shortened and they did
not get to Hampshire.

This case is especially interesting because of the many kinds of
manifestations, including trumpet, direct voice, cross correspondence, and precognition. As Reverend Duncan says: "These instances
moreover, contain items of information of which it was impossible
for the mediums to have any knowledge. It is information of this
kind and which is found afterwards to be true, which provides some
of the best evidence for psychical research."

Another noted trumpet medium, also a Scot, was John Campbell
Sloan, who was immortalized by Arthur Findlay in several books.
Findlay, for many years a prominent stockbroker in Glasgow, Scotland, eventually saw so much that was evidential in Sloan's mediumship that he was completely convinced of the genuineness of the
phenomena and of communication with the spirit world.

In *On the Edge of the Etheric* he tells of an experience involving
his brother whom he took with him to a séance shortly after he was
demobilized from the army in 1919. The brother knew no one present and was not introduced. No one, except Arthur, knew that he
had been in the army, or where he had been stationed. His health
had not permitted him to go abroad, and so he spent part of the time
near Lowestoft at a small fishing village called Kessingland, and
part of the time at Lowestoft training gunners.

After various voices had come for others, the trumpet tapped
Arthur's brother on the right knee, and a voice directly in front of
him said, "Eric Saunders." The brother didn't recall anyone of that
name and said so. Since the voice was not very strong, someone suggested that the company should sing to build up the psychic power
in the room. While this was going on, the trumpet kept tapping the
brother on his knee, arm and shoulder. It was so insistent that he

said, "I think we had better stop singing, as some person evidently is most anxious to speak to me."

He again asked who it was, and the voice, by now much stronger, replied, "Eric Saunders." The brother asked where he had met him and he said, "In the army." A number of places were mentioned, such as Aldershot, Bisley, France, and Palestine, to see if the communicant would take the bait, but Lowestoft was carefully not mentioned. The voice was not deceived. It replied, "No, none of these places. I knew you when you were near Lowestoft."

"Why do you say *near* Lowestoft?"

"You were not in Lowestoft then, but at Kessingland."

"What company were you attached to?" But it not being possible to ascertain whether the reply was "B" or "C," the brother asked if he could remember the name of the company commander. The reply, "MacNamara" was correct for "B" Company.

As a test, the brother now pretended that he remembered the man and said, "Oh, yes, you were one of my Lewis gunners, weren't you?" The reply was: "No, you had not the Lewis guns then. It was the Hotchkiss." This was correct. After several other correct answers to questions, the voice of Saunders said: "We had great times there, sir; do you remember the general's inspection?"

The brother laughed and said they had been continually being inspected by generals, to which one did he refer? The voice replied, "The day the general made us all race about with the guns." This was an incident which had caused a good deal of amusement to the men at the time. Then Saunders said he had been killed in France in the Big Draft in August, 1917. As there had been only one especially big draft, it had been something well remembered by both of them.

Findlay writes: "He then thanked my brother for the gunnery training he had given him, and said it had been most useful to him in France. My brother asked him why he had come through to speak to him, and he said: 'Because I have never forgotten that you once did me a good turn.' My brother has a hazy recollection of obtaining leave for one of the gunners, owing to some special circumstances, but whether or not his name was 'Saunders' he could not remember." Since hundreds of men passed through his training, it had been difficult for the brother to know them individually, but all of them would have known him.

About six months after the séance the brother was in London, and met, by appointment, the corporal who had been his assistant with the light guns in his battalion. He asked him if he remembered "Eric Saunders." He did not, but he had his old pocket diary with him. In it he had been in the habit of keeping a full list of men under training, including the dates they were sent overseas. They looked at it for Company "B" during 1917 and sure enough, there was "Eric Saunders, f.q., August '17." F.q. meant fully qualified and the red ink line meant that Saunders went out in August, 1917.

Findlay says: "Unfortunately my brother did not ask Saunders the name of his regiment, and consequently I could not trace his death, the War Office, without this information, being unable to supply me with any details beyond the fact that over 4,000 men of the name of Saunders fell in the War. Men came to Lowestoft from all over the country for training, so my brother had no record of Saunders' regiment."

But Findlay felt that even allowing for this it is a remarkable case, fraud-proof, telepathy-proof, and clairvoyance-proof. It contains fourteen separate facts, each one correct, and each one "up to my 'A1' standard," says Findlay.

In 1922 British newspaper correspondent Robert Blatchford became interested in psychical research in the course of his own investigation for a series of articles on the subject. In 1923 he wrote in the *Illustrated Sunday Herald* of his first experiences after his wife's death as follows:

"My first step was to ask a South African gentleman, who had written to me, if he and his private circle would try to get news of my wife. The circle responded cordially, and I very soon heard that 'the little lady' had appeared, having been introduced by a soldier killed in France, and that she had been accompanied by a taller woman, who was, she said, a relative of hers named Margaret.

"This was discouraging. I was quite confident that my wife had no relative or friend named Margaret. I concluded that the soldier had made a mistake."

Nearly a year later J. Hewat McKenzie made arrangements for Blatchford to visit Gladys Osborne Leonard, telling him she was one of the best mediums in the world. On September 23, 1923, he went to her, anonymously so that he would not later be able to suggest that the medium had used any kind of fraud to get the material she gave him. He admitted himself to be watchful, not hostile, but rather skeptical.

One of the first things Feda, Mrs. Leonard's trance control, told him was that a lady was there who wanted to speak with him, and then she gave a number of personal things involving his wife. But he knew them, so he was not impressed.

"Very good, Mr. Skeptic," was his reaction. "The clever Mrs. Tranquil [a pseudonym he used for Mrs. Leonard in his *Herald* piece] had read all that in my mind, by telepathy." But then she began to bring out points he did not know, revealing her continued interest in things going on about the house . . . even things of which he was not aware. She mentioned where a box of handkerchiefs was that she wanted her daughters to have. She even referred to little family jokes. Then she hit into a double play, confirming by a cross correspondence the information given a year before in South Africa.

She said that one of the first to meet and help her on the other side was a relative of hers named Margaret who had died in childhood. "You would not know Margaret," said Feda, "but inquire and you will hear about her."

Toward the close of the sitting Mrs. Blatchford said through Feda, "George is here." Afterward he puzzled over the name George with his daughters, and none of them could guess who he was. But the next day, as he sat wondering, he suddenly got the idea that George was the name of the soldier who introduced his wife and Margaret at the Johannesburg circle. He looked up his South African report and found that George was indeed the name given.

Here comes the best part. Blatchford did not know that the regular communicators through Mrs. Leonard occasionally were able to produce direct voice, aloud in the air, away from the medium, and away from the sitter. And so he received the surprise of his life when he suddenly heard his wife's voice. He was able to identify her own eager, anxious tone as she spoke the words, "Barb, I am here. I am with you, Barb." It was her pronunciation of his name that was especially exciting to Blatchford, because his wife had been a Yorkshire woman who said "Bob" as if it rhymed not with *nob* but with *garb*. He wrote in the book he published in 1925 titled *More Things in Heaven and Earth* that to have her speak his name twice in her own special way was highly evidential to him.

His summary of the entire sitting in the newspaper article went as follows:

> I am satisfied that Mrs. Tranquil is a genuine medium and an honest woman. I believe that my wife is alive and that it was she who spoke to me. I am convinced that she visits our home, and that she was with me in London on the twenty-third, and that she twice appeared to the circle in Johannesburg.
>
> He added that when he had heard the direct voice, ". . . I was too much astonished to speak to my wife directly. But I knew her voice, and I knew that no one else ever pronounced the word Bob as she pronounced it. . . .

We have met Sir William Barrett as a careful researcher and as a writer who analyzed others' experiences. Now let us meet him in a much more improbable role, that of a communicator after his death. Lady Barrett had many sittings with Mrs. Leonard which she published in a book called *Personality Survives Death*. In it she mentions several instances of direct voice.

Sir William was giving his message through Feda one day, but occasionally interjecting words of his own to emphasize something Feda said. At such times it sounded as if he was standing just in front of the medium and at the sitter's left shoulder. He started out by interrupting Feda to say, "Will's here," very clearly in direct voice. Then he sent word through Feda, "I like taking bits myself in between."

"I want you to," replied his wife.

"But I can't," he said via Feda.

"Yes, but later on can't we try?" asked Lady Barrett.

"I've tried at night when you're going to sleep," said Feda for him. Then in direct voice came, "You may hear my whistle."

At the moment his wife could not think what he meant by that. "Did you say, 'My whistle'?" she asked.

"Yes, I did," he replied through Feda. "Don't you remember my own little brand of whistle?" Then it all came back to her, though she hadn't thought of it since he died. When he was very happy and content he used to make a clear little whistle in breathing. She would say, laughing, "You are like a pussycat purring when you're happy, only you whistle instead."

XX

VOICE PHENOMENA

THE NEWEST, AND to me the most challenging, thing going on in psychical research today is the upsurge of interest in what appear to be voices captured on tape recorders when no human present is speaking. These voices purport, of course, to come from spirits. They are very faint, at a rapid speed, and quite difficult to hear in most cases, but they are definitely human voices from somewhere. Naturally there is a great deal of controversy about where they come from, and it will undoubtedly go on for a long, long time. Quite a few people here and abroad are working on the project, for anyone who owns a tape recorder can get into the research. So it is to be hoped that very soon something will be received of such a substantial nature that it can be said to be proof of the personality and identity of specific deceased entities.

Apparently the first person who wrote about making such attempts to capture voices on tape was George Hunt Williamson, who said in 1952 that supernormal voice contact had been made over a variety of radio appliances. But he thought that alien intelligences were behind them, according to accounts I have read.

Next came a Baltic painter and producer of documentary films named Friedrich Jürgenson, who lives near Nysund, Sweden. Harald

Bergestam of Stockholm wrote a letter to *Fate* (March, 1973), telling how Jürgenson got started. He says:

> In September, 1971, I visited Mr. Jürgenson. As we sat near the open windows in his villa looking out over the sea, Jürgenson told me how his experiments began. He said, "About fourteen years ago I placed my microphone in the open window in order to tape the birdsongs in the garden. When playing back the tape I heard among the singing of the birds my father's voice."
>
> Later this same afternoon he turned on the tape recorder and we heard many voices calling my first name: "Harald, Harald." Then in German: *"Wir kommen"* (We are coming). My wife, who died nearly four years ago, was Hungarian. I heard her speaking in Hungarian: "Harald, are you there? I am here. Welcome, darling."

Certainly Mr. Bergestam was luckier than almost anyone else I've heard about, for very seldom is it possible to get actual sentences that seem to bring evidence of identity. Jürgenson claimed to have some, however. After experimenting painstakingly for four years, consulting with trained acoustical engineers about the problems of reception, he wrote a book called *Voices from Space*.

Jürgenson's best known disciple so far is a man of Latvian birth named Konstantin Raudive, a psychologist and philosopher and the author of six books. All his life he had been preoccupied, he says, with problems concerning death and life after death. After he read Jürgenson's book carefully several times, he decided that the author was a highly sensitive and susceptible man with a vivid imagination, who was nonetheless utterly sincere. He was so interested in Jürgenson's voice research that he contacted him and was permitted to attend recording sessions. The phenomena so gripped his attention and awakened all his explorer's instincts that, in June, 1965, he started his own independent experiments. Over four hundred persons have participated with him in tests he has undertaken constantly since then. His collaborators include physicists, psychologists and electronics experts, as well as doctors and teachers. They all say quite simply, "Here are voices which identify themselves, call our names, tell us things which make sense (or sometimes puzzle us); these voices do not originate acoustically, and the names they give belong to people we know to have left this earth." The physicists cannot explain the phenomenon. Neither can the psychologists. Scientific tests (even in the Faraday cage) have shown that these voices originate outside the experimenter and are not subject to autosuggestion or telepathy, according to Raudive. Philologists and linguists have examined the phenomenon and testify to the fact that, although audible and understandable, the voices are not formed by acoustic means; they are twice the speed of human speech and of peculiar rhythm which is identical in all the 72,000 examples Raudive says he has so far examined.

Dr. Raudive published *Breakthrough* in 1971 and it has become somewhat of a sensation. What does it all mean? As I said in a review of the book in *Parapsychology Review:*

"*Breakthrough* by Konstantin Raudive, purporting as it does to prove that the voices of spirits of the dead have been captured on tape recordings, presents a concept so overpowering that it could revolutionize the philosophy of the world if it is true."

Certainly we are tempted to embrace the idea wholeheartedly, and yet as in all past psychical reasearch, we know that initial enthusiasm can be quickly subdued when others attempt to reproduce the same phenomena. Also, unfortunately, the content of most of the messages reportedly received by Raudive and his associates is so unintelligible as to be difficult to comprehend. Spoken phrases picked at random from the book produce such startling information as the following: "Here is a shirt." "It is good here, Irene." "Yes, Kostja, act very carefully." "Gossip! Never friend!" and "I would like to take the light of the moon with me."

Our immediate reaction is that this cannot be! Surely those who communicate from the spirit world would have more of value to say. And yet if the dead really could be attempting to get their messages through to our dimension, the effort must be tremendous and the difficulties almost insurmountable. Perhaps we should be patient with them and not make snap judgments. We should take into consideration the difficulties of transmission as we have recognized them involving mediumship of various kinds. Even in direct voice séances with the most competent mediums, only an occasional word or phrase may be heard of what were obviously intended to be coherent sentences. So let us wait to see what the future will bring in the way of more research and better results.

The record that accompanied review copies of Raudive's book (but not those for sale in the stores) definitely has voices on it, even though most of them are quite indistinct and in foreign languages. I listened to this recording first in the company of two firm materialists who scoffed all the way through it. With the difficulty we had hearing the faint voices because of the background noise and static on the record—owing to the fact that the recorder had to be turned to its highest volume in order to capture them—my friends' levity was quite understandable. Still, one weird little voice calling the author's name, "Raudive," faintly as if from way off in outer space, sent chills up and down my spine.

"There may very well be nothing to this," I told my doubting companions. "And yet again . . . some day you may look back on this moment as being just as significant as the one when you first TV-watched a man set foot on the moon."

Raudive's methods of recording are via microphone, radio, frequency-transmitter and diode. He discusses each in detail, explaining his techniques for achieving results.

It has been suggested, of course, that the tape picked up a scatter of radio signals. This is discounted, since in the thousands of recordings not once was music heard. Messages received are spoken in either male or female voices in a curious mixture of tongues, often including words in two or three different languages in the same sentence. Dr. Raudive's native Latvian predominates, but there are also many German, Swedish and Russian words, as well as Spanish, French and English. In my opinion, this mixture of languages has been done deliberately in order to counteract the radio signals argument.

The voices differ from ordinary human voices in pitch and sound volume. There is unusual rhythm, pitch, intensity and a strange mode of expression. "After a time of diligent practice," Raudive says, "when the ear has become attuned, we can find in these very deviations from the accustomed the clues to help us determine the structure of voices. Voices may vary in sound volume from whispering to fortissimo, their timbre is usually well defined." He adds:

> I would like to repeat here that the decisive factor in studying the voice-phenomenon is not the theoretical interpretation, not the philosophizing, but the empirical result, arrived at through experiment, that can be verified under test conditions. The fact that the voices are audible to our ears and we can understand that speech, confirms that they exist physically and independently from us, and the experiments prove that the voices can be heard by anybody with a fair sense of hearing, regardless of his or her personal views, sympathy or antipathy. The voices are objective entities that can be verified and examined under psycho-acoustic, physical conditions. This concurrence of psycho-acoustic and paranormal data can hardly be brushed aside as mere coincidence; the voices must therefore be deemed to stem from a different plane of existence than our own.

The voices attempt to identify themselves. The investigators are addressed by their own names, the tone and inflection often being recognized as coming from people they once knew. Among the many thousands of examples listed in the book are those which indicate this point strongly. In Latvian the words may come in a female voice: "Kostulit, this is your mother." Or they may claim to be Raudive's sister Tekle, his cousin Mona, his aunt or many others. They come for other experimenters in a similar manner. Raudive says that 25,000 of the voices have been identified. Yet even more often the words come in brief phrases which do not designate the speaker. Usually when they claim to be a famous person no evidence of any kind is offered.

"Here is Nietzsche," a voice will say, or "Here are the Tolstoys. Kosti is praised here. . . ." And then no more is given to verify who the speaker really is.

On the record I heard a voice purporting to be Winston Churchill and sounding remarkably like him. But it merely says something a bit like, "Mark you, make believe, my dear, yes." All of which makes one question the reality of this phenomenon. One tends to query, as British psychical researcher Rosalind Heywood did when interviewed on the BBC *Late Night Line-up* program, which discussed the Raudive voices, how they can make such ineffectual statements, which are frequently banal and at times almost menacing. Mrs. Heywood shuddered to contemplate, she said, an afterlife inhabited by entities of the seeming mental stature of the owners of most of the taped voices.

Besides the difficulties of any kind of alleged spirit communication, we might also consider the possibility of "intruders" to explain these problems. When speakers on Dr. Raudive's tapes claim to be Jung, Maxim Gorki, Sir Oliver Lodge, or, yes, even Mussolini, Stalin and Hitler—many say they are his followers and are still "Heil Hitlering" in their afterlife—perhaps it is a matter of role-playing by intruding "earthbound" spirits.

Certainly those of us who have experimented with Ouija boards or automatic writing are aware that much that is dull, commonplace and even foolish appears, purporting to come from famous people, but possibly originating from other, less enlightened, entities. At least these overt Raudive voices give support to the argument that such communications do not come from the subconscious mind of the automatist.

Supporting the spirit hypothesis is the late Dr. Gebhard Frei of the Mission Society of Bethlehem and president of the International Society of Catholic Parapsychologists, who is quoted in *Breakthrough*'s Appendix as writing:

> When I now consider that the voices speak in five or six different languages, often several in a single sentence, that the experimenter or his collaborators are often addressed by name, that the voices repeatedly mention their own names and allude to situations in their past earthly lives which are quite unknown to those present, when I think how the voices change in a flash and consider the fact that in your absence too, and even when the room is empty, voices can be heard on the tape when the tape recorder is switched on—then one must ask oneself if a psychologist exists who could produce sufficient scientific data to explain the phenomenon aetiologically as arising from your

or any other living person's subconscious mind. If someone points to the mass of electro-magnetic waves used in radio and television, then the fact that your voices answer specific questions and comment on conversations that have just taken place, still remains unexplained. All that I have read and heard forces me to assume that the only hypothesis able to explain the whole range of the phenomenon is that the voices come from transcendental, individual entities.

Many of those who believe in the possibility of spirit communication like to think that only wise spirits make the effort and that everything that comes through mediums or automatists must be factual. Yet there is more evidence to lead us to believe that in the afterworld there is an entirely different dimension that provides us with all too many of our communicants. It would seem that those who were misguided, dull or ignorant in life continue for some time after death to be the same, in a condition known as "earthbound." These types are said to be the ones who rush to answer the call of any effort to communicate. They then wield the pencil or push the pointer on the Ouija board, and what they say is frequently platitudinous or incoherent. They will respond to any name requested, or purport to be any famous person they might think might be welcome.

Long considered completely unworthy of serious attention by parapsychologists, such alleged spirit communication must once again be discussed if we are to try to explain the inconsistencies of the Raudive voices. Dr. Theo Locher, president of the Society for Parapsychology in Switzerland, is quoted on this subject in *Breakthrough*:

> The thesis of "elementals" or mischievous spirits is supported in many instances by messages received through trance or automatic-writing-mediums. In these cases such entities seem at times able to masquerade as deceased persons and often imitate voices and mannerisms. They are particularly fond of impersonating famous people such as Goethe, Churchill, Napoleon, etc. and this certainly seems to be the case with some of the "voices." It strikes one as odd when well-known men or women express themselves in words of a language they did not

know in life. The language used most frequently is Latvian, the experimenter's mother-tongue. Imitation of a dead person's voice could be achieved through telepathic tapping, as human memory also contains the memory of sound; it may even be possible for elements to tap psychic remnants (so-called "memory complexes") of the deceased. . . .

Perhaps because of the interest shown by prominent churchmen in Raudive's work, there are rumors that the Vatican is now doing research of its own in voice phenomena. Whether this is true or not, plenty of others are. In the summer of 1972, Walter Uphoff, who teaches at the University of Colorado and, with his wife Mary Jo, writes a column called "Beyond the Five Senses" for the Madison, Wisconsin, *Capitol Times*, visited a number of people in Europe who were doing voice research. He and his wife talked to Father Leo Schmid in Oeschgen, Switzerland, who, working independently, has obtained hundreds of voices which he has methodically classified according to one or more of thirty-four characteristics—male-female, personal-impersonal, well-known-unknown, etc. He told the Uphoffs that the content of the messages is so specific that he no longer has doubts about their transcendental origin.

They also visited Frau Hanna Buschbeck of Stettin-Horb, Germany, who, having obtained voices, is now serving as coordinator for persons experimenting with the phenomena. She had just completed tallying forty-one questionnaires and had sample tapes sent by others who were attracted by the work of Jürgenson and Raudive.

Peter Bander, the translater of the English edition of *Breakthrough*, had initially advised against publishing the book because it seemed too fantastic to be comprehensible. Then he had a personal experience which reversed his decision. His publisher, Colin Smythe, had purchased a fresh tape and let the recorder run according to the procedure described by Raudive. He obtained an indistinct voice he could not understand, but Bander recognized it as a soft, but to him distinct, voice saying: "Mach die Tur mal auf!" (Why don't you open the door?) And it was the voice of his mother, who had died the previous year. The message shook him, for he had been more withdrawn than usual the previous week and his colleagues had chided him for keeping the door to his office closed at all times.

I prefer instead to interpret it that he, by his translation and advocacy of Raudive's book was "opening the door" of the world to this phenomenon. The communicating spirits always seem to have the wider view.

Peter Bander has since written a book *Carry on Talking* about his experiences. He says that he has a Great Dane named Rufus who hears the taped voices. When Bander first became involved with attempting to receive them, he had to put the dog out in the garden, for he showed great restlessness during the playback of the tapes when complete silence was needed. The dog's odd behavior was noticed one day when Bander was playing tapes recorded by friends. He had a great difficulty hearing the supernormal voices, but he observed that Rufus seemed to show signs of anger at certain spots. His actions were similar to the way he acted when a stranger walked toward the house or somebody talked outside the front garden. His bristles stood up, the coloring on his back became deep red, he gave a growling bark which denoted "intruders."

Intrigued by the animal's behavior, Bander took out another recorded tape. He noticed that each time a supernormal voice came through, Rufus reacted, although the Great Dane normally took little or no notice of voices coming over the television or radio. In other experiments, tapes were played first to Rufus for him to give some indication where voices would be heard on it, and he never once failed to indicate the proper spot.

Bander told a recent audience in England that "Rufus is selling more books than all our travelers and representatives together." Recently, he said, he visited Harrods and looked for copies of *Carry on Talking*. He found them on a shelf for pet books, next to another book entitled *Get to Know Your Great Dane*.

Richard K. Sheargold is an electronics expert who is a radio "ham," and also a psychical researcher, being chairman of the Survival Joint Research Committee. He wrote in *Psychic News*, September 2, 1972, that he was receiving voices almost daily. He said:

"Strictly as the result of my experiments I am in no doubt whatever that the existence of the voices is a scientific reality. To doubt this now would be to question my sanity. Further, these voices do make remarks and answer simple questions somewhat after the style of the Ouija board." He has received voices of both sexes and many whispers. They are rhythmic in character and very quick in utterance—probably "sharp" would be more descriptive, he says. "Anyone who thinks it is easy to hear these voices is in for a disappointment. At the same time anyone with average hearing can achieve success if he also possesses the necessary patience and perseverance. Listening is an art; to listen superficially is normal; to listen intently we must train."

All Mr. Sheargold's voices come in very weak. He describes the techniques he uses:

> At present I have employed only what is known as the "microphone method"—which is merely using the tape recorder with a microphone in the usual manner—and the "diode" method. The diode is a very simple electronic device. It is merely a "crystal set" using a modern diode instead of a crystal and a radio frequency choke in place of the usual tuned circuit. Its aerial is a piece of stiff wire 10 cms. in length. The output is fed into the tape recorder. In my experience the voices received using the diode are not so loud, but are far more natural in character. The phrases received tend to be longer. . . . When making a preliminary announcement the recording level should be kept rather low. When actually attempting to record, the sound volume must be set at maximum.

This, of course, is what makes it so difficult to listen for the voices. The recorder volume has been set so high that there is a terrific roar when the tape is played back. Anyone who invents a technique so that this will not be necessary will do researchers a great favor.

There is a good bit of research being done in the United States today, the most curious of which, I believe, comes from the state of Washington. In the summer of 1972, Michael Lamoreaux of Kittitas read Raudive's book and started experimenting, but for the first two months he got nothing paranormal. Then he visited his family in White Salmon and interested his brother Joe, who had worked as a radio signal interceptor for the Air Force. Since then these men, who have been described to me as honest, intelligent, and committed to exploring a phenomenon that they believe may turn out to be important, have spent many hours recording, listening and transcribing. What they are receiving is incredible.

Most of the voices were very soft, elusive, almost entirely inaudible. Mike wrote me, "It was these voices that we concentrated on and learned to hear. I can remember in October, 1972, putting in eight to ten hours a day transcribing ten or fifteen minutes of tape and playing each response as many as 150 to 200 times. My brother was the first to recognize that the voices were speaking continuously, using every second of recorded tape with no pauses and many overlaps. We became determined to try to decipher not just the infrequent loud voices, but all the words uttered in the recorded section."

Walter Uphoff has also heard the Lamoreaux tapes, and he says there definitely are voices speaking that can be deciphered. The language is English, but the names of the places and people described as the inhabitants of the spirit world who are communicating are more likely from old Indo-European roots. According to the taped information, the first place one goes after he dies is Deenah. If he cannot function there he may be sent to Ree, or even Nilow, which is a conditioning center. The higher and more advanced stages of existence are designated as Montayloo, Piloncentric, Metanah and Ulta Reenah. The people on Deenah, who comprise most of those talking on the tapes, call themselves the Moozlah.

Michael has sent me transcriptions of the material that has come from these Moozlah and it sounds like the prattle of children. It is difficult to take it seriously, but when you realize that this is received on tape in rooms where no human being is speaking, it has to be considered supernormal and highly interesting. Yet what in the world can it be? Walter Uphoff says about such things: "I am willing to live with uncertainty, letting the evidence and raw data accumulate until it becomes so preponderant that conclusions become quite clear."

My own personal experience has been most productive when I have worked with Attila (Art) von Szalay of Van Nuys, California. In Los Angeles during the summer of 1972 we held a number of sessions which were fairly fruitful, usually achieving our best results only in the wee small hours when everyone present was exhausted. Fortunately our results were on tape, which can then be listened to again and again when senses are clearer and one is telling himself, "I couldn't possibly have heard what I thought I heard."

One 3 A.M., for instance, our co-researcher Clarissa Plantamura called out to her deceased husband Ed to come through to us if possible. Shortly after that we got a faint, high pitched, hurried statement which can be translated as either "Ed is here" or "Eddie's here." As the tape runs on you can hear Art ask Clarissa what Ed did for a living and her reply that he was the musical librarian for M.G.M. Studios. Just then comes the tiny voice again, saying, "Symphony."

Art von Szalay is a very psychic person, and our mutual friend Raymond Bayless, who has been experimenting in voice phenomena with him since 1956, is convinced that it is his strong mediumship which causes his successful results. Sheargold and Raudive do not think the presence of a medium is necessary; however, they themselves may have the psi factor strongly enough to help with the production of their voices without being aware of it. Everyone agrees that it is wise not to have any ardent disbelievers in the group making the attempt to receive voices. Natural skepticism is all right, but actual antagonism to the effort seems somehow to set up "bad vibrations" which cause negative results.

Art uses a standard tape recorder, and frequently Ray monitors it by using his own recorder as well. On occasion, the same voice sounds are received on both tapes.

Ray describes their process: "The usual experimental technique is extremely simple. We merely turn on a tape recorder at full amplification, frequently in normal light, and ask questions. The recording intervals last from a few minutes to over forty-five minutes. Many types of sitting arrangements have been used. At times we have sat within three feet of the recorders and the microphones have been closer than that. During other tests we have sat separated from the microphone by a distance of twelve feet and a plywood partition. At times I have been holding the microphone in my own hand when my name was called on the tape."

The argument that the voices may be picked up from some radio interference is eliminated by the fact that the voices Ray and Art receive occasionally answer questions, frequently call one or the other by name, sometimes give appropriate remarks to personal matters. Further, the pattern of the voices is not in the least characteristic of radio reception.

Ray says emphatically, "In my opinion, the voices received during our experiments fall easily within the pattern of spiritistic phenomena." It is no wonder Art and Ray believe that, when you realize that a voice has frequently called out "Edson," which is the name of Art's brother and also his son, both dead for many years. And once Ray asked if a communication might be received from his grandmother and the correct name "Emma" was loudly given. They have received many other bits and pieces of conversation and sentences among which were, "You're kidding," "Ed, put this around you," "Then why do you remember?" and "God bless you."

Art von Szalay spends hours at his tape recorder when he is at home alone, as well as the time he gives to Bayless and to me. On September 30, 1971, he made a record in his notebook which he later read to Bayless. The underlined words were blurred, but the others came through so clearly that the intent was obvious, "Bayless *is* (?) virtually *become* (?) *a* (?) recluse."

The interesting thing about this is that at home that very day Ray, who admits to being somewhat antisocial, had spoken with unusual vehemence to his wife, saying that he wished he could cut himself off from the world and have nothing to do with most people. Marjorie remarked in turn that they both knew a man who had accomplished just that and had become an actual recluse, and his personality had consequently suffered. They had had a similar conversation two or three days previously. Ray was impressed because of the fact that he had spoken *extremely vehemently*. Did Art's subconscious mind pick it up telepathically over the miles and then translate it into a voice on tape? *Some* mind seems to have been in operation.

Whoever or whatever it is that is putting weird, quick, difficult, but definitely human voices on tapes these days is presenting us with a challenge that many people are eagerly accepting. We don't know yet what to make of them, but we will keep working with them under as many controlled conditions as possible until we do learn what is going on.

Sheargold summed it up very well: "There is no longer room for doubt that the science of psychics has at last achieved its first real breakthrough since serious research began nearly one hundred years ago. An enormous field of research is thereby opened up. I for one am excited and elated at the prospect, as well as being deeply grateful that it has come during my active life."

XXI

TOWARD THE FUTURE

"LEARN TO DIE and thou shalt learn to live," says *The Tibetan Book of the Dead*. It goes on in most timely fashion: "The exploration of man's inward life is incomparably more important than the exploration of space. To stand on the moon adds only knowledge of things transitory. But man's ultimate goal is transcendence over the transitory. . . ."

In recent centuries we have attempted to forget the fact that we would eventually have to die. We ignore the subject as much as possible, refusing to let ourselves think of it because we are so afraid of it, or because we have convinced ourselves there is nothing afterward.

Yet in earlier days it was not considered bad taste to discuss death, or to try to learn how to die properly so that we might learn to live properly. Primitive peoples are invariably at home with their beloved dead, whose presence they continue to accept. A belief in life after death goes back as far as history, and includes all great religions.

Socrates said: "Then beyond question the soul is immortal and imperishable and will truly exist in another world." And Plato said: "Our soul is immortal and never at all perisheth."

As I mentioned in the first chapter, many people are not going to believe in a life after death just because it seems logical and fair. We want facts, demonstration, evidence. If anything is going to help us to believe, it would have to be the kind of material we have seen in this book. Perhaps to realize that there are vast amounts more of a similar nature would be helpful. I could go on and on. There is much, much more of the well-documented material from the early part of this century and the latter part of the last century, for the S.P.R. members in those days took a census that brought them in a great amount of information.

There are many other categories I could have used, had I the space, which cover areas of information convincing to some people. The cloudy form that some have seen escaping physical bodies at the time of death could have been discussed, or the materializations produced by certain apparently genuine physical mediums, which have looked like the spirit persons they purported to be and have brought information known only to them and to the sitter. There are many cases of what is called evidence for reincarnation, which have influenced some people to believe they have lived before on earth. There has just not been room to cover a vast amount of information that is highly interesting. Certainly there should be enough in this book, however, to give an answer to the Omar Khayyáms who say "No one has returned to tell us."

We should not accept the belief in a life after death wholeheartedly without being aware of the possible dangers accruing. Says James Hyslop in *Science and the Future Life*, "I am well aware of the follies which might easily be aroused by the reinstatement of a belief in a future life, if that belief should become as badly abused as it has been in the past. But the dangers of abuse are no reason for trying to suppress facts. We cannot shy at the truth because some unwise people lose their heads about it. On the contrary, our supreme duty is to appropriate that truth and to prevent its abuse."

Many of those who purport to communicate from the "other side" are not so concerned with proving their identity as with bringing a philosophy which will help us adjust to the revolutionary ideas they present. Also they give us descriptions of their transition and the places they find themselves after death. Geraldine Cummins in *They Survive* tells us that Miss E. B. Gibbes's sister-in-law, Hilda, died in

1941 and soon afterward began to communicate through automatic writing. Filled with the wonder and joy of her new life, she said:

> Well, when I died, I found that the most foolish mistake in my life was my long, long terror of death. . . . At the moment of death there was no pain. . . . I wasn't unhappy or frightened or lonely, for I saw my father, my sisters, my brother, whom I had thought of as dead—asleep till Judgment Day. But they weren't asleep, they were quite close to me. . . . So my message to the world is that, for me, one of the happiest moments of my earth-life was the moment of death. Of course, it was much longer than a moment, but the wonderful freedom from pain, the feeling of peace and security when I saw my loved dead alive, smiling, waiting for me, drove away loneliness, fear and, for a while, all the grief of separation from my two boys [still on earth]. . . . I do want people to know that whatever they are afraid of, they needn't be afraid of death.

Apparently death makes no break in the continuity of mental consciousness. You may sleep for a while, but when you awaken you are still yourself, just as you always were. At first there is difficulty in realizing that death has taken place, because of the vivid sense of continued identity with earth. The environment is not even different at first, for you find yourself in the same place you always were. It is good to realize that, as famous British journalist W. T. Stead's spirit communicant Julia told him, ". . . the period of growth and probation is no more complete at death than it is on leaving school, finishing an apprenticeship, or retiring from business. . . . The principle of growth, of evolution, of endless progress towards ideal perfection continues to be the law of life."

The wise human being should prepare himself as much as possible while on earth and thus be ready for a quick transition to the spiritual heights after death. For as good a picture of what the conditions and purposes and duties and pleasures are in this afterworld, I can do no better than to suggest that you keep your eyes open for *The Book of James*, a Putman book (due in 1974), giving the inspiring philosophy of my alleged communicant James.

Sherwood Eddy says in *You Will Survive After Death*, "We lose all fear of death as soon as we become convinced of the fact of immediate conscious and active survival. . . . Proof of survival is the beginning and not the end of the road."

It is hoped that what has been written here may have somewhat suggested the possibility of that proof.

Don't forget, "While there is death, there's hope."

BIBLIOGRAPHY

ADAMS, FRANK D., A *Scientific Search for the Face of Jesus*. Tucson, Arizona, Psychical Aid Foundation, 1970.

ANDRESKI, STANISLAV, *Social Sciences as Sorcery*. London, Andre Deutsch, n.d.

ASHBY, WILMA S., "My Personal Miracle," *Fate*, June, 1972.

BANDER, PETER, *Carry on Talking*. Gerrard's Cross, Eng., Colin Smythe Ltd., 1973.

BARRETT, LADY, *Personality Survives Death*. London, Longmans, 1937.

BARRETT, SIR WILLIAM F., *Death-Bed Visions*. London, Psychic Book Club, 1926.

———, *On the Threshold of the Unseen*. New York, E. P. Dutton, 1918.

BELFRAGE, BRUCE, *One Man in His Time*. London, Hodder & Stoughton, 1941.

BENNETT, J. G., "Existence Beyond Death," *Tomorrow*, Spring, 1958.

BLATCHFORD, ROBERT, *Illustrated Sunday Herald*. London, September 30, 1923.

———, *More Things in Heaven and Earth*. London, Methuen & Co., 1925.

BOND, F. BLIGH, *The Company of Avalon*. Oxford, Basil Blackwell, 1924.

———, *The Gate of Remembrance*. Oxford, B. H. Blackwell, 1920.

BROWN, ROSEMARY, *Unfinished Symphonies*. New York, Wm. Morrow & Co., 1971.

CAMERON, MARGARET, *The Seven Purposes*. New York, Harper & Bros., 1918.

CASS, RAYMOND, "Supernormal Voices on Tape Emanate from Surviving Humans," *Psychic News*. London, September 16, 1972.

Coronet, April, 1949.

CUMMINS, GERALDINE, *Mind in Life and Death*. London, Aquarian Press, 1956.

———, *They Survive*. London, Rider & Co., 1946.

DUCASSE, C. J., "Realities of Perception," *Tomorrow*, Winter, 1954.

249

DUNCAN, V. G., *Proof*. London, Rider, n.d.

EDDY, SHERWOOD, *You Will Survive After Death*. New York, Rhinehart & Co., 1950.

EVERETT, KENNY, *Destiny*. London, September, 1972.

Fate, April, 1953; March, 1961; May, 1961; March, 1962; April, 1972; June, 1972; July, 1972; May, 1942.

FINDLAY, ARTHUR, *On the Edge of the Etheric*. London, Psychic Press Ltd., 1931.

FITZGERALD, EDWARD (Trans.), *The Rubáiyát of Omar Khayyám*. New York, Dodge Pub. Co., 1905.

FORD, ARTHUR, in collaboration with Margueritte Harmon Bro, *Nothing So Strange*. New York, Harper & Bros., 1958.

——, as told to Jerome Ellison, *The Life Beyond Death*. New York, Berkley Medallion Book, 1971.

GADDIS, VINCENT, "Jesse Shepard the Musical Medium," *Fate*, June, 1972.

GAULD, ALAN, "A Series of 'Drop In Communicators,' " *Proceedings* S.P.R., July, 1971.

——, *The Founders of Psychical Research*. London, Routledge and Kegan Paul, 1968.

GIBSON, EDMOND P., "The Alice Grimbold Case," *Tomorrow*, Winter, 1954.

——, "The Possession of Maria Talarico," *Fate*, April, 1953.

GLENCONNER, PAMELA, *The Earthen Vessel*. New York, John Lane Co., 1921.

Guideposts, June, 1963.

GUMPERT, GUSTAV, "Did I Speak with Angels?" *Fate*, April, 1961.

HARE, ROBERT, *Experimental Investigation of the Spirit Manifestations*. New York, 1855.

HIGGINS, PAUL LAMBOURNE, *Encountering the Unseen*. Highland Park, Ill., Clark Publishing Co., 1966.

HOCKING, WILLIAM ERNEST, *The Meaning of Immortality*. New York, Harper & Bros., 1957.

HODGSON, RICHARD, *Religio-Philosophical Journal*, December 20, 1890.

HUXLEY, LAURA ARCHERA, *This Timeless Moment*. New York, Ballantine Books, 1968.

HYSLOP, JAMES H., "The Mental State of the Dead," *The World Today*, January, 1905.

——, *Psychical Research and the Resurrection*. Boston, Small, Maynard & Co., 1908.

——, *Science and a Future Life*. Boston, Herbert B. Turner & Co., 1905.

Journal, of the American Society for Psychical Research. Vol. 12, 1921; Vol. 64, January, 1970.

Journal, of the Society for Psychical Research, November, 1906; September, 1972.

JÜRGENSON, FRIEDRICH, *Voices from Space*. (Published in Sweden. No information.)

KENAWELL, WILLIAM, "Frederick Bligh Bond's Psychic Search," *Tomorrow*, Summer, 1962.

KENNER, JIM, "Chopin Guides Her Hands," *Fate*, March, 1973.

LEONARD, GLADYS OSBORNE, *My Life in Two Worlds*. London, Cassell & Co., Ltd., 1931.

Light, London, April 7, 1888.

MACKENZIE, ANDREW, *Frontiers of the Unknown*. London, Arthur Barker, Ltd., 1968.

MILLER, R. DeWITT, *You Do Take It with You*. New York, The Citadel Press, 1955.

MOSES, W. STAINTON, *Human Nature*. 1875. (No further information.)

MULDOON, SYLVAN J. and HEREWARD CARRINGTON, *The Projection of the Astral Body*. London, Rider, 1929.

MURPHY, GARDNER, "An Outline of Survival Evidence," *Three Papers on the Survival Problem. Journal* of the A.S.P.R., January, 1945.

MYERS, F.W.H., *Human Personality and Its Survival of Bodily Death*, edited by Susy Smith. New Hyde Park, N.Y., University Books, 1961.

———, "The Subliminal Consciousness," S.P.R., 1894.

The National Enquirer, March 4, 1973.

NEECH, W. F., *No Living Person Could Have Known*. London, Spiritualist Press, 1955.

NICOL, FRASER, "The Founders of the S.P.R." *Proceedings*, S.P.R., March, 1972.

OSIS, KARLIS, *Deathbed Observations by Physicians and Nurses*. Parapsychology Foundation Monograph No. 3, 1961.

OWEN, ROBERT DALE, *Footfalls on the Boundary of Another World*. Philadelphia, J. B. Lippincott, 1860.

PALMSTIERNA, BARON ERIK, *Horizons of Immortality*. London, Constable & Co., Ltd., 1937.

Parapsychology Review, September–October, 1971.

PRINCE, WALTER FRANKLIN, *Human Experiences*. Boston, Boston Society for Psychical Research, n.d.

Proceedings, Society for Psychical Research, Vols. IV, VI, VIII, IX, XI, XX.

Psychic, February, 1973.

Psychic News, November 13, 1971; January 15, 1972; May 20, 1972; July 19, 1972; August 5, 1972; September 23, 1972.

Psychic Observer, September, 1972.

RAUDIVE, KONSTANTIN, *Breakthrough*. New York, Taplinger Publishing Co., 1971.

ROGO, D. SCOTT, "Deathbed Visions and Survival," *Fate*, June, 1972.

ROSHER, GRACE, *Beyond the Horizon*. London, James Clarke & Co., 1961.

SALTMARSH, H. F., *Evidence of Personal Survival from Cross Correspondences*. London, G. Bell & Sons, 1938.

SHEARGOLD, RICHARD K., "Existence of Paranormal Voices is a Scientific Reality," *Psychic News*, September 2, 1972.

SHERMAN, HAROLD, *How to Make ESP Work for You*. Greenwich, Conn., Fawcett, 1964.

——, *Your Power to Heal*. New York, Harper & Row, 1972.

SIDGWICK, MRS. HENRY, "An Examination of Book Tests Obtained in Sittings with Mrs. Leonard," *Proceedings* S.P.R., Vol. XXXI.

——, "On the Evidence for Clairvoyance," *Proceedings* S.P.R., Vol. VII.

SMITH, ELEANOR TOUHEY, *Psychic People*. New York, Bantam, 1969.

SMITH, SUSY, *Confessions of a Psychic*. New York, Macmillan, 1971.

——, *The Enigma of Out-of-Body Travel*. New York, Garrett Publications, 1965.

——, *The Mediumship of Mrs. Leonard*. New Hyde Park, N.Y., University Books, 1964.

STEAD, W. T., *After Death*. New York, George H. Doran Co., n.d.

STEVENS, E. W., "The Watseka Wonder," Religio-Philosophical Publishing House, Chicago, 1887.

STEVENS, WILLIAM OLIVER, *The Mystery of Dreams*. London, George Allen & Unwin Ltd., 1950.

——, *Psychics and Common Sense*. New York, E. P. Dutton & Co., 1953.

STEVENSON, IAN, *Twenty Cases Suggestive of Reincarnation*. Proceedings A.S.P.R., Vol. 26, 1966.

TABORI, CORNELIUS, "The Case of Iris Farczady: An Unsolved Mystery," *My Occult Diary*. New York, Living Books, 1966.

TAYLOR, DAVIDSON, *Modern Music*, January, 1938.

TERHUNE, ANICE, *Across the Line*. New York, The Dryden Press, 1945.

THOMAS, JOHN F., *Beyond Normal Cognition*. Boston, Boston Society for Psychical Research, 1939.

——, *Case Studies Bearing Upon Survival*. Boston, Boston S.P.R., 1929.

THOULESS, R. H., *Journal* S.P.R., Vol. 46, No. 753, September, 1972.

TWEEDALE, CHARLES L., *Man's Survival After Death*. London, Spiritualist Press, 1909.

——, *News from the Next World*. London, T. Werner Laurie Ltd., 1940.

TWIGG, ENA, with Ruth Hagy Brod, *Ena Twigg: Medium*. New York, Hawthorne Books, 1972.

BIBLIOGRAPHY

Uphoff, Walter and Mary Jo, "Beyond the Five Senses," *Capital Times*, Madison, Wis.

Veinus, Abraham, *The Concerto*. New York, Doubleday Doran, 1944.

Walters, J. Cuming, *Some Proofs of Personal Identity*. Manchester, The Worlds Publishing Co., Ltd., n.d.